CONTENTS

Chapter 1	Law Hustice and Human Rights
Chapter 2	Human Rights Introduction
Chapter 3	Human Rights ,Freedom of Expression
Chapter 4	Human Rights of Disabled Persons
Chapter 5	Human Rights implementation by government
Chapter 6	Human Rights in armed conflict
Chapter 7	Selected International case law on human rights(racial discrimination)

Chapter 1

Law, Justice and Human Rights

Law, Justice and Human Rights:

Some Implications of a
In academic life there is a widespread tendency for bodies of literature to talk past each other. This seems to be the case with much of the literature on environmental law, environmental justice, mainstream jurisprudence, and globalisation. This chapter

suggests some chasms and some connections between them, and relates to the question: "What are the implications of so-called 'globalisation' for the institutionalised discipline of law and especially for jurisprudence, conceived as the theoretical or more general part of that discipline?".1 I shall reflect on a number of themes, concepts, and distinctions that are broadly relevant to debating issues about environmental justice in today's world: including the nature of theorising about law; the discourses of globalisation; picturing law from a global perspective; normative jurisprudence, especially theories and discourses of justice and human rights.

I treat jurisprudence as the theoretical or more abstract part of law as a discipline.2 Philosophy of law is the most abstract part of jurisprudence, which is also concerned with a wide range of theoretical issues that are not primarily philosophical. Jurisprudence can be conceived of as both a heritage and an activity. Western jurisprudence has a vast heritage of texts, questions, answers, and arguments. It can also be conceived of as an activity directed to posing, reposing, reflecting on, hypothesising answers to, and arguing about these questions.

1 This paper draws on my current project on "General Jurisprudence". It also draws together some
themes that have been explored at greater length elsewhere, especially: William Twining,
Globalisation and Legal Theory (London: Butterworth, 2000) (hereafter GLT); *Law in Context:*
Enlarging a Discipline (Oxford: Oxford University Press (1997) (hereafter LIC); "General Jurisprudence" in M. Escamilla and M. Saavedra (eds.) (2005) (hereafter GJ) .and "Reviving General
Jurisprudence", in *The Great Juristic Bazaar* 335-363 (Ashgate, 2003) (hereafter *GJB*). See also
Twining 2003a, 2003b, 2005a, 2005b, 2005c, 2006, and 2007. I am grateful to Andrew Halpin, Jonas
Ebbeson, and John Tasioulas for helpful comments and suggestions.
2 LIC 110-14.

2

In the Anglo-American tradition the heritage and the activity are sometimes classified into broadly defined, but overlapping, fields: Julius Stone categorised them as analytical jurisprudence, sociological (or functional) jurisprudence, and theories of human law and justice (censorial, critical, or ethical).3 I prefer to talk rather more broadly of analytical, normative, empirical (or socio-legal), and critical jurisprudence. Such classifications serve a modest purpose provided that two points are born in mind: first, the boundaries between these activities are not precise and are often contested; and, second, most practical questions about law involve a combination of analytical, empirical, and normative elements. So any classification of these broad fields or activities should not be expected to bear much weight.4

If one stands back and surveys the vast heritage of Western legal theorising about law, one is reminded of two tendencies that are in tension. First, the Western heritage is vast. However, viewed from a global perspective that same heritage can be criticised for being insular, parochial, quite narrowly focussed, and even ethnocentric. Nearly all of it concentrates on the municipal law of sovereign states, mainly those in advanced industrial societies; it operates within and across only two of the world's major legal traditions, common law and civil law, with other major traditions marginalised or completely ignored. The "Country and Western Tradition" of legal theorising and comparative law is vulnerable to charges of parochialism and ethnocentrism.5

2 Globalisation and G-Talk

Words like "globalisation" and "global" are used very loosely. Here, it is useful to distinguish between two primary uses. First, "globalisation" is sometimes used to refer to certain recent tendencies in political economy – the domination of the world economy by a group of interrelated ideologies and practices, sometimes referred to as "The Washington Consensus". This usage is clearly illustrated by "the antiglobalisation" movement, which has rather diffuse targets, including American
hegemony, Western dominated international financial institutions, free market ideology, and capitalism in general. The issues are important, not least in respect of environmental matters, but this usage is too narrow in the present context. I shall use

3 Stone (1946) Ch. 1 (discussed Twining (2003a)).
4 Hart (1983) at 88-9..
5 GLT at 184-189..

the term "globalisation", following Anthony Giddens, in a much broader, less politically fraught sense, to refer to those processes that increase interaction and interdependence in respect of not only economy and trade, but also communications, science, technology, language, travel, migration, ecology, climate, disease, war and peace, security and so on.6

This second broader meaning can be quite useful, but it too is problematic. Terms such as global corporations, global law, global lawyers, global law firms, and global jurisprudence are indicative of a tendency to make exaggerated, misleading, meaningless, superficial, ethnocentric, or just plain false generalisations about processes and phenomena that are better discussed in less hyperbolic terms.7 In particular, it is worth emphasising three points that are particularly pertinent to law.

(i) Lawyers need to be especially sensitive to boundaries, jurisdictions, and levels of ordering. Not only are national boundaries becoming more porous, but we are all familiar with the idea of different levels of ordering – for example, the differences between general public international law (some of which is genuinely global), regional, state, sub-state and so on. We are also familiar with the elusiveness of subsidiarity and margins of appreciation. But other complexities are often overlooked. For example, there is a tendency to move back and forth between the global and the local, not only leaving out intermediate levels but also implicitly accepting a picture of levels of law as being stacked in a single neat vertical hierarchy from outer space, through global, regional, and national down to the very local. But there are important legal patterns that are geographically more complex than that: for example, the Jewish and Islamic diasporas, the former European empires, the common law world, the British Commonwealth, NATO, OPEC, and other alliances, networks, religions, cartels, spheres of influence – all of these cut across simple vertical hierarchies and greatly complicate the picture of patterns of ordering and the diffusion of legal ideas.

6 Giddens, (1990) 64. See further GLT Ch. 1, at 4-10.

7 Most global generalisations, even if true, refer to surface phenomena. In a sense it may be true that
Holiday Inns or CNN or British Airways circle the world, but these refer to surface phenomena that
may conceal more than they reveal. This theme is developed in a forthcoming paper on "Surface Law"
(Twining 2007).

4

(ii) Not all interaction between legal orders takes place at one level. Comparative law and studies of legal transplants have tended to focus on the relationship between different state legal systems and to neglect other aspects of interaction – cross-level diffusion, different forms of interlegality and, above all, legal and normative pluralism are now central concerns as the discipline of law becomes more cosmopolitan.8

(iii) Talk of "levels" of relations and of ordering involves spatial metaphors that are not always appropriate in respect of law. There is a developing sub-field of law and geography and the idea of mapping law has its uses. Gordon Woodman has forcefully argued that state law is typically defined in terms of relatively determinate territory, but many laws and legal orders are not.9 This is especially the case with personal and religious laws. Similar arguments apply to "spheres of justice".10 The point is valid. However, if we conceive of law as a form of institutionalised social practice and if we are concerned with the law in action, then we are dealing with actual behaviour, which does take place at particular times in particular places. For example, if we agree that *shar'ia* travels with every devout Muslim, a good map of Islamic diasporas can at least give a general indication of where Islamic law is likely to exist at a given time as an institutionalized social practice.11 We need to guard against overusing spatial metaphors, but there is still scope for legal geography.12

Of course, there are genuinely global phenomena and issues that are or should be of concern to all humankind, such as climate change, nuclear proliferation, war and peace, radical poverty, the exploration and exploitation of outer space. But even then there are still important questions about what are the most appropriate levels of policy and law for dealing with each issue.

8 GLT Ch. 6.
9 Woodman, (2003)..
10 Singer (1983).

11 On Islamic law in England as a form of custom that has slowly influenced English municipal law,
see Pearl and Menski (1998) especially Ch.3
12 Blomley (1994), Economides (1996), Holder and Harrison (eds.) (2003).

3 A global perspective

If one is sensitive to different levels of relations and of ordering, then a global perspective can serve as much to emphasise diversity and complexity as to simplify. Thinking globally at least sets a *context* for focussing at other levels. A quick way in is to consider the limitations of a map of law that is confined to municipal legal systems, i.e. the domestic law of nation states. There are some obvious criticisms to be made:

(i). A map confined to national legal systems leaves out other levels of supranational, sub-national and trans-national levels of legal relations: public international law, European Commmunity law, Islamic law, Maori law, and *lex mercatoria* for example. (ii) It leaves out some of the major legal traditions in which law is not conceptually or politically tied to the idea of the state. For example, it leaves out Islamic law or confines it to countries in which Islamic law is formally recognized as a source of municipal law. But it is obvious that this distorts the extent, scope, and nature of *shari'a*. (iii) However, if we decide to include major religious and customary normative orderings, and perhaps other examples of non-state law, we run into major conceptual problems. First, we have to adopt a conception of law that includes at least some examples of "non-state law". That re-opens the Pandora's box of the problem of the definition of law and all its attendant controversies.13 Second, there is the problem of individuating legal orders. What counts as one legal order or system or unit for the purposes of mapping? How does one deal with vaguely constituted agglomerations of norms, which may be more like waves or clouds than billiard balls?14 (iv) If one decouples the notion of law and state, one is confronted with another set of problems. If one moves away from the idea of one kind of institution having a legitimate claim to monopoly of authority and force, one has to accept the idea of legal and normative pluralism – i.e. the co-existence of more than one legal order in the same time-space context – and all the difficulties that entails.
13 Twining (2003b).
14 id.

4 Analytical and empirical jurisprudence: some brief comments

The topic of environmental justice prima facie falls within the province of normative jurisprudence. But because most legal discourse, scholarship, and debate involve conceptual, factual, technical, and normative (i.e. ethical and evaluative) dimensions, it is useful to make some other general points about the implications of adopting a global perspective for legal theory and the discipline of law and for sub-fields, such as environmental law.

(i) *Analytical jurisprudence*. Conceptual analysis is one important aspect of analytical jurisprudence.15 Adopting a global perspective highlights the need for adequate analytical concepts that can transcend different legal cultures and traditions. Because traditional legal scholarship was mainly confined to domestic law and most analytical jurists have focused on the concepts of legal doctrine (e.g. legal rights, ownership, causation) and its presuppositions (rules, legal system, validity), the focus has been mainly on law talk rather than talk about law. The doctrinal concepts of a legal system (such as English law) or a legal culture (such as the common law) are mainly "folk concepts" with limited transferability across legal cultures and traditions. Conceptual elucidation is just as important for socio-legal studies as it is for legal analysis and exposition. But concepts such as dispute, institution, process, function, impact, and even court have been relatively neglected. Precise well-developed analytical concepts are needed for making comparisons and generalisations about legal phenomena across legal systems, traditions, and cultures. Our stock of usable transferable concepts is limited, so is our bank of reliable comparative empirical data. So our capacity to make comparisons and generalisations across legal cultures and tradition is correspondingly limited.

(ii) *Empirical jurisprudence*. Most socio-legal and empirical studies of legal phenomena have been confined to a single society, even in regard to non-state law. Recently, comparative and transnational empirical legal studies have started to develop, but the field is still at a relatively primitive stage. From a global perspective, one of the most important topics in need of empirical research is what social scientists call the processes of diffusion – often referred to by lawyers as transplants or reception. I have argued elsewhere that legal writings about this subject have tended to be unempirical

15 This argument is developed in HCWT op cit.

7

and have been unduly influenced by "a naïve model of reception".16 This is an "ideal type", which postulates a paradigm case with the following characteristic assumptions:

"[A] *bipolar* relationship between *two countries* involving a *direct one-way* transfer of *legal rules or institutions* through the agency of *governments* involving *formal enactment or adoption* at a particular moment of time (*a reception date*) *without major change* …. [I]t is commonly assumed that the standard case involves *transfer from an advanced (parent) civil or common law system to a less developed one*, in order to bring about *technological change* ("to modernise") by *filling in gaps or replacing* prior local law."17

It is easy to show that none of these elements is necessary or even characteristic of actual processes of diffusion of law, which are much more diverse and complex than the "naïve model" suggests. This is relevant in the present context because so many environmental problems involve cross-level interactions between different state and non-state legal orders and the development of environmental law and justice involves diffusion of ideas developed at many different levels.

5 Adjusting the canon: Filleting Hart, Extending Bentham, Realizing Rawls

If one accepts the points about the importance of differentiating levels of ordering, about the significance of non-state law, and about legal pluralism, this raises some important questions about the relevance of twentieth century canonical jurists to considering law and justice from a global perspective. For example, most of the leading Western jurists of the twentieth century have focused very largely on municipal state law, have had strong conceptions of sovereignty, and have assumed that legal systems and societies can be treated as discrete, largely self-contained units. They have either articulated or assumed that jurisprudence and the discipline of law is or should be concerned with only two kinds of law: the domestic municipal law of nation states and public international law, which was widely accepted as a secondary

16 Twining 2005b and 2005c.
17 Ibid.

8

form of law, mainly concerned with relations between states ("The Westphalian Duo").

At first sight this suggests that many of these canonical jurists have become out-dated and irrelevant. However, a younger generation of theorists has begun to adjust the Western liberal tradition in ways that suggest that, with due modifications, some twentieth century canonical jurists are of continuing relevance.

For example, Brian Tamanaha, stayed with Hart's two basic positivist premises – the separation thesis and the social sources thesis – but pared away all Hart's criteria of identification in order to construct a broadened conception of law that would include several forms of non-state and religious law, but which differentiated it from other social rules and institutions, such as those involved in the governance of hospitals, schools, and sports leagues.18

Thomas Pogge, a pupil of Rawls, has argued that Rawls' two principles of justice (somewhat modified) can be transferred directly to the international sphere, largely by challenging the idea of a society as a self-enclosed unit.19 Pogge has been sharply critical of Rawls' attempts to limit his principles of justice to the domestic sphere.20 Pogge has transformed what had increasingly come to be seen as a rather complacent and conservative theory of domestic justice into a quite radical theory as the basis for a sharp critique of the existing international order and its institutions. I shall return to Pogge in due course.

In a somewhat different way, Peter Singer has applied Benthamite utilitarianism to contemporary issues in international ethics, including environmental ethics.21 Jeremy Bentham prided himself in being "a citizen of the world", he coined the term "international law", but has generally been interpreted as a theorist of strong sovereignty.22 Bentham posed the question whether the sovereign's duty is to maximise the interests of his own people or of humankind as a whole?23 Bentham did not really answer this question, but Peter Singer, who is widely considered to be the leading contemporary proponent of classical utilitarianism, has come out firmly in

18 Tamanaha (2001), discussed Twining (2003b).
19 Pogge (1989), (2002), discussed below.
20 John Rawls (1971) 378-82, developed in *The Law of Peoples* (1999). Pogge's original criticism was
directed to the treatment of transnational ethics in *A Theory of Justice*, but later he developed and

extended his critique (especially, Pogge (2001) and (2002).
21 Especially Peter Singer, *Animal Liberation* (1975/1990) cf. Singer (1972) (1993);and (2004)
22 See generally, Dinwiddy (2004). On Bentham's subtle analysis of sovereignty see Hart (1982) Ch. IX.
23 J. Bentham, *Principles of International Law* (1806-9) discussed GJB at 237-42.

9

favour of the idea that national leaders owe a duty to humankind, even though this presents problems when democracy is largely confined to some nation states.24
Thus, already there are jurists who are re-working our heritage of legal thought to adjust to the changing global scene. In rather different ways, Patrick Glenn could be interpreted as reviving an earlier tradition of world history applied to law25 and Boaventura de Sousa Santos could be viewed as a post-modern successor to Weber and Marx.26

6 Normative Jurisprudence

Normative jurisprudence encompasses general questions about values and law. It deals with the relations between law, politics and morality, including debates between and among positivists and others about the relationship between law and morals, whether law is at its core a moral enterprise, and about political obligation and civil disobedience. It includes questions about the existence, scope and status of natural, moral and non-legal rights; the relationship between needs, rights, interests, and entitlements; theories of justice; constitutionalism and democracy; and standards for guiding and evaluating legal institutions, rules, practices and decisions. Normative jurisprudence now occupies a central place on the agenda of Anglo-American jurisprudence.

If one steps back and considers the Western heritage of normative jurisprudence from a global perspective, one can identify a number of tendencies that are relevant to discussing issues of environmental justice.

(i) The collective ignorance of other traditions

As with other branches of jurisprudence, Western normative jurisprudence has been quite insular. Western Jurisprudence has a long tradition of universalism in ethics. Natural law, classical utilitarianism, Kantianism and modern theories of human rights

24 "This book argues that as the nations of the world move closer together to tackle global issues like
trade, climate change, justice, and poverty, our national leaders need to take a larger perspective than
that of national self-interest." Peter Singer, *One World* (2004) (Preface to second edition). While a
utilitarian, such as Singer, would argue for harmonising national and global interests, the scope of a
locally elected leader's duty to humankind needs further development.
25 Glenn. (2004), discussed in symposium in Foster (ed.) (2006).
26 Santos (2002). The first edition (Santos (1995) is discussed in GLT Ch.8.

have all been universalist in tendency.27 But nearly all such theories have been developed and debated with at most only tangential reference to and in almost complete ignorance of the religious and moral beliefs and traditions of the rest of humankind. When differing cultural values are discussed, even the agenda of issues has a stereotypically Western bias. How can one seriously claim to be an informed universalist if one is ethnocentrically unaware of the ideas and values of other belief systems and traditions?

As the discipline of law becomes more cosmopolitan it needs to be backed by a genuinely cosmopolitan general jurisprudence. To this end we need to adjust the conventional canon of juristic texts to include significant writings and salient ideas and controversies from other traditions or which represent other viewpoints. Until now this has been considered the province of specialists. The task is daunting, but not impossible. Despite criticisms of "orientalism", there has been some excellent work by Western scholars on Islamic, Hindu, Bhuddist and Chinese legal thought.28 To a lesser extent, there are accessible writings by contemporary "Southern" writers. As a modest first step I have considered the general approaches to human rights of four "Southern jurists": Francis Deng, Abdullahi An Na'im, Yash Ghai and Upendra Baxi.29 All four deserve to be better known, but this is a limited exercise as these particular ones were all trained in the common law, write in English, and belong to the immediate post-Independence generation. There are many others, including not least Southern feminists, and prominent jurists whose work has not been translated into English.

(ii) Secularism and a world-wide religious revival

During the twentieth century Western Normative jurisprudence has been dominated by three main types of ethical theory: utilitarianism, deontology (including Natural Law and Kantian theories of justice and human rights), and virtue ethics.30 These have, of course, been subjected to persistent challenges from various forms of scepticism, relativism, subjectivism, post-modernism and, lately, in a different way, communitarianism. Eco-centric theories of environmental ethics could also be

27 "Universalism" is a highly ambiguous concept. Here it will suffice to use it to refer to claims that a

given moral principle applies to all humans at all times and in all places.
28There are useful select bibliographies in Glenn (2004), Huxley (2002).
29 Twining (2006).
30 Griffin (1996) Ch. VII.

interpreted to fall outside the mainstream.31 Apart from Natural Law, nearly all of our stock of normative theories are explicitly or implicitly secular. Classical utilitarianism and consequentialism, Rawlsian justice, and most variants on these have their roots in post-Enlightenment rationalism. Human rights is sometimes presented as a form of secular liberation theology32 or as an ethical theory for a Godless Age.33

That we live in a secular age may be true of, say, most of the United Kingdom and of most, but not all of Europe; but the rising visibility of religious minorities may soon change that perception here. It is not true of the United States. The reverse is true of the rest of the world, which is more appropriately characterized as going through a period of religious revival, some but not all of which is characterized by some quite aggressive and evangelical kinds of fundamentalism. This refers not only to the headline-catching spread of fundamentalism in Islam, but also to Christianity, as Philip Jenkins' important book *The Next Christendom* vividly portrays.34 From this perspective, secular liberalism appears to be on the decline and is beginning to look "distinctly dated".35

From a global perspective, a central challenge to human rights is to provide a vision that is attractive not only to non-believers, but also to believers, be they Christians, Muslim, Hindus, or others. It needs to be shown to be compatible with their core religious beliefs, as Abdullahi an Na'im, and other committed Muslims, are trying to do.36

(iii) *Belief Pluralism*

A third tendency in Western normative jurisprudence has been that leading liberal thinkers have beaten a partial retreat into an odd kind of particularism.37 Ronald Dworkin states that "interpretive theories are by their nature addressed to a particular legal culture, generally the culture to which their authors belong."38 Similarly, John Rawls has stated "The aims of political philosophy depend on the society it

31 See below.
32 Baxi (2006).
33 E.g. Gearty (2006) and Klug (20000).
34 Jenkins, (2002). Cf. Miztal and Sharpe (eds.) (1992).
35 Jenkins (2002) at 9.
36 E.g. An Na'im (1990), Lindblom and Vogt (1993).
37 MacIntyre (1985), Hampshire(1989).
38 Dworkin (1986) at p. 102.

addresses"39 and went quite close to acknowledging that his project was to develop a criterion of justice that would appeal to reflective Americans.40 Whereas in *A Theory of Justice* there is a consensus among its members about the appropriate moral basis for a well-ordered democratic society, *Political Liberalism* confronts the problem of belief pluralism.

In response to this new concern, Rawls insisted that "justice as fairness is political, not metaphysical".41 It is a practical theory aimed at providing a moral foundation for political, social and economic institutions in a modern constitutional democracy in which the members have diverse, incompatible views. It is not a metaphysical or epistemological theory dealing with universal moral conceptions; nor does it apply to all societies.42 It is a limited secular theory that can provide a basis for co-existence and co-operation in a diverse society independently of religious beliefs and ideologies. A key idea is that of an overlapping consensus: this does not refer to those doctrines that are common to the different belief systems in a given society, but rather to what free and equal citizens would accept as a freestanding political view of society as a fair system of cooperation.43

This aspect of political liberalism is clearly relevant when we think about the institutions and practices needed for co-existence and co-operation in a world characterized by a diversity of belief systems, traditions, and cultures. On most interpretations of "globalisation", which emphasise interdependence, the decline of sovereignty, and the permeability of borders, only one such society exists: the world. A well-constructed and coherent political theory which provides a coherent moral basis for the design of structures and institutions that can ensure stable, orderly and

[39] As Rawls' writings are discussed extensively, the particular works will be referred to by
abbreviations as follows: John Rawls, *A Theory of Justice* (1971) (hereafter TJ); *Political Liberalism*
(1993) (hereafter PL); *The Law of Peoples* (1999) (hereafter LP); *Collected Papers* (ed. S. Freeman)
(1999) (hereafter *Papers*). Especially important in the present context are three papers: "Kantian
Constructivism in Moral Theory" (1980) (reprinted in *Papers* Ch.16) (hereafter KCMT) (see now PL
Lecture III); "Justice as Fairness: Political, not Metaphysical" (1985) (hereafter JFPM) (reprinted in
Papers, Ch. 18)(see also PL Lecture I "Fundamental Ideas") and "The Idea of an Overlapping
Consensus" (1987) (hereafter IOC) (reprinted in *Papers*, Ch 20).
[40] KCMT pp. 518-19.
[41] JF p. 226. cf. Joseph Raz on Rawls' "epistemic abstinence" in Raz (1994) at 62.
[42] JFPM. Justice as fairness is mainly concerned with individual liberty and distribution. Rawls deals
only briefly with procedural justice, expletive justice (under the Rule of Law), and institutionally
dependent concepts, such as "access to justice". So far as I know, he did not use the terms
"environmental justice" or "transitional justice". He treated questions about our duties to animals,
endangered species, trees, and the environment as falling outside the scope of his theory of justice as
fairness. See further below n.<>
[43] PL 40.

fair arrangements for co-existence and co-operation between its diverse members is badly needed. In light of the critical issues of radical poverty, environmental crises, and increasing inequalities, a theory that claims to deal with global justice is especially welcome.

(iv) *Moving beyond domestic justice*

In recent times liberal democratic political and legal theories have tended either to be geographically indeterminate or to place some limits on their geographical claims. A great deal of recent Anglo-American normative jurisprudence has been relatively local in respect of provenance, audience and even focus.44 For example, most writings about the new communitarianism, critical race theory, and republicanism have been explicitly or implicitly or unselfconsciously American or at least Americaninfluenced.45 Feminist jurisprudence has only recently begun to be genuinely transnational.46

For many commentators Rawls' *A Theory of Justice* has been the almost inevitable stating-point for any contemporary theory of justice. It was natural in the nineteen-sixties and nineteen-seventies to think of justice in terms of domestic justice within societies, conceived as clearly bounded units. As awareness of "globalisation" developed and interest in "international ethics" increased it was hoped that Rawls would rethink the extension of his basic ideas to the international/transnational sphere and would develop a robust theory of global justice. Unfortunately, Rawls did not fulfil such hopes. His later works mark a retreat into a position that, from a global perspective, is a huge disappointment.47

44 GLT 128-9. There are some important exceptions to the trend towards greater geographical
particularity. The field of international ethics, exemplified by Peter Singer, Brian Barry, Onora O'Neill,
Martha Nussbaum, Amartya Sen, and Thomas Pogge, addresses transnational issues from a global
perspective. There have been lively debates about human rights and cultural relativism, and about
universalism versus contextualism. The most politically influential ideas are probably still the
ideological assumptions underlying the "Washington Consensus" which links free market economics to
the seductive catch-phrase "human rights, good governance, and democracy". However, see now the
Millennium Development Goals, which have been influenced by somewhat different other strands of
thought including the ideas of Amartya Sen (see Sen (1999)..
45 GLT 58-60. Critical legal scholars have quite recently turned their attention to comparative law,
international law, and Latin America ("Lat-Crits") and issues of globalization, but it is too early to
assess the significance of these developments.
46 E.g. Nussbaum, (2000).
47 A sample of critical reviews includes Buchanan (2000) (This is part of a generally critical
symposium on *The Law of Peoples*); Kuper (2000); Tasioulas (2002b); and Singer (2004) at 176-80.
For a partial defence see Tasioulas (2005).

From a global perspective, it is bizarre to find a purportedly liberal theory of justice that rejects any principle of distribution, treats an out-dated conception of public international law as satisfactorily representing principles of justice in the global arena, and says almost nothing about radical poverty, the environment, increasing inequalities, American hegemony (and how it might be exercised), let alone about transitional justice or reparations or other issues that are now high on the global agenda. What had promised to be a progressive critical theory ended up with a position that one of his pupils, Thomas Pogge, concluded amounted to "arbitrary discrimination in favour of affluent societies and against the global poor".48 Fortunately, Pogge, has ably defended and refined Rawls' original theory and has substituted his own quite radical theory of international justice and human rights. Mainly by changing one of Rawls' key conceptions – the postulate that justice as fairness is only concerned with the internal ordering of societies conceived as selfcontained
units –, he has shown how much of Rawls' scheme can be converted from a parochial and quite conservative theory into one that could be of real value in providing a moral basis for a substantial critique and re-design of supra-national and international institutions. Rawls' core ideas for a practical theory aimed at providing a criterion of justice for basic institutions can be applied to the global system with a few adjustments along the following lines: We live in an interdependent world, in which all are involved and from which "we cannot just drop out". There are no selfcontained national societies in the modern world, nor are there likely to be. The only closed social system is humanity at large.49 A theory of justice for any other kind of association, including the nation state, is dependent on background principles or "ground rules' formulated at the global level.50 This is a world of widespread deprivations and disadvantages, many of which have been promoted by existing transnational institutions. One test of basic institutions is the benefits and burdens

48 Pogge (2002) 108.
49 Pogge talks of "the global system" (about which I have reservations), not much would be changed by
substituting some looser term, such as humankind. He envisages an extension of the Rawlsian model
of a hierarchy of associations acting as systems within systems, whereas the picture that I have
suggested is a much more complex one of overlapping and cross-cutting semi-autonomous social
spheres operating in a complex global context. However, we agree on the point that any theory of
justice has to be set in a broad context which prescribes background rules and constraints for more
localised spheres of justice.
50 Rawls follows Kant (1795)) in rejecting a centralised regime of world government on the grounds

that it would either be a global despotism or else an unstable and fragile empire torn by civil strife. (PL
at pp. 54-5). This is a quite different point from the argument that the justice of any domestic political
order needs to be set in a wider, transnational or global context, especially as societies become
increasingly interdependent. (cf Pogge (1989) at 255-6)

15

they engender. The position of the least advantaged is one important measure of just institutions. It is highly probable that improved global institutions would help to alleviate at least some of the existing deprivations and disadvantages of the worst off. Rawls' two principles (modified and extended to give more weight to social and economic needs) and some of his basic ideas, such as the the veil of ignorance, search for an overlapping consensus, the individual as the ultimate unit of justice,51 and the basic structure are more coherently applicable to "the global system" than to artificially bounded societies or states, not least because "all institutional matters, including the ideal extent of national sovereignty, are now systematically addressed within a single framework."52 On the basis of this neo-Rawlsian approach, Pogge concludes that "our current global institutional scheme is unjust, and as advantaged participants in this order we share a collective responsibility for its injustice."53

For present purposes it is sufficient to make three points about the significance of Pogge's contribution: First, as a disciple of Rawls he has modified and refined the ideas in ways that many may agree represent an improvement on *A Theory of Justice*. Second, as an increasingly sharp critic of Rawls he has substituted a theory of international justice that is radically different from Rawls' own late effort, but which is nevertheless Rawlsian in spirit. Third, by confronting in detail the facts of global poverty and some of the political practicalities it involves he has engaged with one of the major issues of our age from the point of view of a philosopher, who believes that abstract ideas are important in addressing practical problems. Whether or not one agrees with all of his arguments, the message is clear: If you are concerned about justice in relation to world poverty, read *World Poverty and Human Rights* rather than *The Law of Peoples*. In the present context, however, Pogge's approach has two limitations. First, it is highly focused on only one aspect of global justice, radical poverty, and he touches only incidentally on environmental issues. Pogge adopts a thin interpretation of human rights for the specific purpose of arguing that present

51 Pogge (1989) Ch.2, defends Rawls against charges of atomism __ that is of treating individuals as if
they are socially and politically isolated and self-sufficient; but Rawls does treat the individual human
being as the ultimate moral unit.
52 id. 258.
53 id. 277. cf. id. at p.36: "It is not easy to convince oneself that our global order, assessed from a

Rawlsian perspective, is moderately just despite the widespread and extreme deprivations and

disadvantages it engenders. Even if we limit our vision to our advanced Western society, it is hardly

obvious that the basic institutions we participate in are just or nearly just. In any case, a somewhat

unobvious but massive threat to the moral quality of our lives is the danger that we will have lived as

advantaged participants in unjust institutions, collaborating in their perpetuation and benefiting from

their injustice."
16
institutional arrangements contribute to poverty. Second, Pogge is constructing an argument that is intended to have a broad appeal that transcends a range of positions. He does not rely on arguments that we owe a positive duty to help the worst off, as Singer does, but restricts his argument to a negative duty not to maintain institutions that maintain or contribute to radical poverty.54

(v) The Salience of Human Rights Discourse: The only show in town?
Some commentators claim that the language of human rights has become the dominant mode of moral discourse of the last fifty years, edging out moral tropes such as distributive justice, the common good, and solidarity. 55 Such claims to dominance and universality seem to me to be overstated. It is true that after "the collapse of communism", symbolised by the fall of the Berlin Wall, some former Marxist and socialist intellectuals adopted the discourse of human rights. It is also the case that enormous advances have been made in the development of an international regime of human rights law and that domestic bills of rights have also proliferated in the past twenty-five years.56 Partly as a result, many other interested parties have jumped on the bandwagon. Indeed one of Baxi's central themes is that human rights discourse has become commodified, professionalized by technocrats, and sometimes hijacked by powerful groups, so that it is in grave danger of losing touch with the experiences of suffering and the needs of those who should be the main beneficiaries – the poor and the oppressed.57 More pragmatically, Yash Ghai has argued on the basis of his extensive experience of constitution-making in multi-ethnic societies, that human rights discourse provides a workable framework for negotiating claims between different interest groups, provided that the substance of the claims are not taken too literally.58 In other words, human rights is best conceived as a language for expressing claims and arguments rather than as an abstract set of universal standards. Whether

54 As Singer has modified his pure utilitarianism in order to broaden the appeal of his argument, Pogge

appears to be have trimmed his philosophical views in order to persuade a broader political

constituency. In reading contemporary writers like Pogge and Singer, it is often difficult to distinguish

clearly between their philosophical positions and their more activist concern to persuade broader
audiences about their conclusions. From a global perspective, if one accepts belief pluralism as a fact, I
suggest that it is important to distinguish between constructing cogent philosophical arguments and
advancing persuasive arguments that have a broad appeal and may contribute to workable political
agreements among people with different ideologies and potentially conflicting interests. Both are
worthy enterprises, but they should be recognized as separate.

55 Baxi, (2006) 1 and Ch.4. Cf. similar claims made by Conor Gearty (2006);. Henkin (1990).
56 Gearty (2006), at 63-64.
57 Baxi (2006). discussed in HRSV op. cit., n.2.
58 e.g. Ghai (2000), discussed Twining (2006).

17

rights-based approaches to foreign assistance, development, and ecology are more than passing fashions is an open question. But claims that secular human rights can become a universal moral language are over-stated and need to be treated with great caution. Let me give just two reasons:

First, belief pluralism is a fact and human rights discourse just does not fit
easily with the languages and ways of viewing things of the major religions and many other belief systems. For example, Abdullahi An Na'im in his invaluable attempts to reconcile the values of liberal Islam and of the Universal Declaration of Human Rights, acknowledges that while some, but not all, of the basic values are compatible, to be persuasive the discourse has to be translated into terms that fit the beliefs and ways of thinking of most Muslims.59 Broadly speaking the language of Islam is not the language of rights. There are also other belief systems that are more comfortable with the language of responsibility, or community, or civic virtue. Critics of the claim that human rights are Western values being imposed on Asian countries and cultures have rightly pointed out that the *origin* of human rights does not negate its *validity*, that there is no monolithic Asian culture, that there are many Asian supporters of human rights and civil liberties, and that the Asian Values debate was largely stimulated by dictatorial leaders responding to outside criticism of repressive practices and in the process invoking the right to self-determination.60 Such criticisms are no doubt justified, but the fact remains that the language of Confucianism and many other traditional cultures is different from the language of individual human rights.61 A second warning about the expansionist tendencies of human rights talk
relates to the scope of human rights. One of the unresolved questions of human rights theory concerns the criteria for distinguishing between appropriate and inappropriate usages of human rights discourse.62 In the present context it is especially important to clarify the relationship between the discourses of justice, human rights and utility. It is worth remembering that Rawls developed his theory of justice as fairness to limit the

scope of utilitarianism, not to reject all consequentialist arguments. Rawls also explicitly limited the scope of justice as fairness, allowing for other social values

59 E.g. An Na'im, (1990; An Na'im and Deng (1990) (1992). An Na'im's approach is discussed at
length in Twining (2006). See also Lindblom andi Vogt , (1993).
60 Amartya Sen (1997) at 40; Ghai (1993); (1995) (1998b); Castellino and Redondo (2006)..
61 This is acknowledged by Yash Ghai in Ghai (1998a).
62 Griffin (2001), criticised in Tasioulas (2002a)

(such as efficiency, and economic development)63 and repeatedly disclaiming that his theory of justice was a comprehensive theory of human flourishing or the good life.64 Furthermore, while acknowledging that humans owe some duties "to animals and to the rest of nature", he explicitly excluded these from the province of his theory of justice.65 It is also important to bear in mind the distinction between using consequentialist arguments instrumentally to work out the details of a deontological approach (as, for example, Aquinas and Finnis have done clearly) and using rights- or justice- based arguments to trump consequentialist ones.66

In pluralist ethical theories the spheres of human rights, justice, and consequentialism are not co-extensive. To put the matter simply: climate change threatens to have catastrophic consequences for all humankind. The fact that most poorer individuals and communities are less well-equipped to deal with the consequences means that the impact will be distributed unjustly. That is an exacerbating, but secondary factor. Similarly, considering environmental issues exclusively from a human rights perspective can have a distorting effect. For human rights discourse tends to be binary: either one has a human right or one does not. Moreover, many human rights set minimum standards in an all-or-nothing way, often not allowing for differences of degree. In the same vein, I suggest that one of the key issues should be to what extent a theory of environmental justice leaves scope for other values and to what extent the language of justice is the most appropriate way of expressing all major concerns about the environment.

(vi) *Universalism and cultural relativism*

Accompanying the recognition of belief pluralism and the rise of evangelical human rights, there has been a resurgence of debates about relativism and universalism. There is a long tradition, especially in regard to human rights, to talk of a divide between universalism and cultural or other relativism.67 But there is also a widespread tendency to treat such talk as involving a false dichotomy. Aristotle, and modern Aristotelians such as Gordley and Nussbaum, quite explicitly allow for differences between cultures; they merely insist on the universality of underlying principles.

63 e.g. Rawls, *TJ* at 9.
64 E.g. Rawls, *PL* at 11-15
65 E.g. TJ at 17, 505ff, 512; *PL*, 245.(quote here or below)
66 Pressure of space precludes doing justice here to the complex issues concerning claims for the

relative merits of the language of rights, justice, and utility as rhetorical discourses.
67 See generally, Wilson (1997)

Another universalist, Alan Gewirth argues that universalism can justify certain kinds of ethical particularism, in the sense that "one ought to give preferential considersation to the interests of some persons against others, including not only oneself but also other persons with whom one has special relationships."[68] Similarly, Joseph Raz, a committed universalist, sees "the universal and the particular to be complementary rather than antagonistic", and argues that "At the heart of multiculturalism lies the recognition that universal values are realised in a variety of different ways in different cultures and that they are all worthy of respect."[69] Indeed, among serious thinkers there seem to be very few strong universalists or extreme cultural relativists. And, of course, "relativism" is a highly ambiguous concept.[70] There is a widespread view that polarising the debate merely serves to obscure a complex variety of issues that need to be differentiated.

(vii) Anthropocentric and ecocentric views in normative jurisprudence

A topic not much discussed in the mainstream jurisprudential literature, but prominent in the environmental literature is the distinction between anthropocentric and ecocentric perspectives. For the sake of brevity, one can borrow a quite stark definition of these terms:

"An anthropocentric action is taken to be one in which the reason to act is the provision of a benefit to human beings.

An ecocentric action is taken to be one in which the reason to act is the provision of a benefit to the environment"[71]

It is striking to which extent the canonical jurists seem to be anthropocentric. Utilitarianism focuses on the pains and pleasures of human beings, but Bentham

68 Gewirth, (1988). "The ethical particularism with which I am concerned here, then, is confined to
preferences for or partiality towards various *groups*, ranging from one's family and personal friends to
larger pluralities of one's community, nation, and so forth." (at 286). On utilitarianism and loyalty see
GLT 66-7 and 131; on loyalty see Fletcher (1993)..
69 Raz (1998) at 204 (citing earlier writings). Raz acknowledges that morality can change, but not
radically, but only against an unchanging background of continuing moral principles that explain the
change. "Since... radical moral change is impossible, it follows that social relativism is untenable."
(1999) at 180. An even stronger universalist might argue that it is not fundamental moral principles that
change, but our understandings of them
70 Haack (1998) Ch. 9.

71 Donnelly and Bishop (forthcoming, 2006) arguing that "new" Natural Law, as exemplified by
Finnis and George is necessarily anthropocentric, because it does not purport to derive natural law
principles from human nature, thereby avoiding criticism concerning the naturalistic fallacy. On the
other hand, "traditional Natural Law" can provide support for ecocentrism in that it can be based on
the idea of human nature being but one part of the general natural environment.

20

famously extended the application of utility to all sentient beings.72 Peter Singer followed him.73 So utilitarianism seems to be committed to protect non-sentient nature only insofar as it bears on the pleasures and pains of sentient beings. Human rights discourse is anthropocentric on its face; ascribing rights to trees or plants or artefacts is generally acknowledged to be an extension, which many feel is analytically dubious. Rawls' justice as fairness is a virtue of social institutions, meaning human institutions. Dworkin's basic notion of "equal concern and respect" relates to human beings only;74 Similarly, concern for the interests of future generations is generally taken to mean future human beings.

However, on closer examination these jurists, while focusing on human rights and interests, do not necessarily exclude all ecocentric reasons. Rawls, for example, acknowledges that we have moral duties in respect of animals and nature, but he treats these as falling outside his theory of justice as fairness as a political conception, which only applies to those who have a moral personality.75 Similarly, Peter Singer may have given a different impression in *Animal Liberation*, but when he was accused of "speciesism" in limiting his argument to sentient beings, he hotly denied the charge.76 Singer argues that to restrict "rights" to human rights and to restrict utility to sentient beings are not arbitrary boundaries, but such restrictions do not rule out the possibility of extending the circle of our moral concern to other aspects of nature on the basis of other moral principles. Singer has difficulty with the philosophical basis of a non-speciesist ethic, such as Rolston's "respect for life". Singer does not put forward an alternative basis. Instead, he extends the range of anthropocentric reasons for preserving the environment, by emphasising aesthetic, scientific, and recreational values of preserving natural ecosystems and argues that the environment should be preserved for future generations, not least to allow them to choose how to deal with

72 "The question is not: can they *reason*? Nor, can they *talk*? but can they *feel*? Bentham (1789/1970)
283n).
73 Singer, *Animal Liberation* (1975/1990).
74 See, however, the discussion of the Snail Darter case in Dworkin (1986) at 20-23.
75 TJ 504-12, esp. 512. PL 20, 244ff. "[T]he status of the natural world and our proper relation to it is
not a constitutional essential or a basic question of justice, as these questions have been specified [in

Rawls' theory]. It is a matter in regard to which citizens can vote their non-political values and try to
convince other citizens accordingly. The limits of public reason do not apply." (PL 246). Rawls also
enumerates a number of examples in which, because the treatment of animals and other aspects of
nature bear on human interests, political values are involved." (id. p.245).
76 Rolston (1999); Singer's response in the same volume is at 327-32. His position on environmental
ethics is set out art greater length in Singer(1993) Ch. 10.

it.77 As I read him, Singer cares passionately about the environment; the main reasons he advances for valuing the environment are ultimately anthropocentric, but he leaves the door open for the evolution of a philosophically coherent econcentric ethos, which in his view has yet to be achieved.

To sum up: it is undoubtedly the case that nearly all of the thinkers that I have discussed have an anthropocentric *focus*. However, it would be a mistake to infer from this that they are indifferent to environmental concerns or that they treat ecocentric reasons as invalid. Most do, however, seem to take the position that ecocentric reasons fall outside the scope of the mainstream discourses of utility, human rights, and justice as fairness.78

7 Conclusion

The French philosopher, Jacques Maritain, who played a significant role in the preparation of the Universal Declaration of Human Rights, relates a story of someone expressing amazement that proponents of opposed ideologies had reached agreement on a list of rights: "Yes, they replied. We agree on these rights, *providing we are not asked why*."79 Maritain drew a sharp distinction between "practical conclusion" and "rational justification".80 He had a well-developed Thomist conception of dignity as part of his theory of Natural Law. But, to use a later distinction, he supported the use of the concept in the draft Declaration, but argued strongly for leaving the conception undefined.81

When Jacques Maritain drew a quite sharp distinction between philosophical arguments and pragmatic approaches to human rights, he was not saying that philosophy was unimportant. Rather, like Rawls and many twentieth century philosophers, he emphasised that belief pluralism is a social fact that has implications for both philosophy and for the practical politics of co-existence and co-operation. Maritain's strategy in respect of rights suggests that we need coherent philosophies, ecumenical arguments, *and* a willingness to negotiate working agreements patiently, in detail, in a pragmatic fashion accepting the need to compromise.82 Concepts like

77 See above n.<65>.
78 In earlier versions of this paper, there were sections on ecumenical arguments and *ius humanitatis*,
but these have been cut for reasons of space.
79 Maritain (1954) 70.

80 Id. Ch. IV.
81 On dignity as a "placeholder concept" see McCrudden (2006).
82 On ecumenical arguments, see above n.<XXX>

justice, utility, and rights all have a role to play in constructing such arguments and negotiations.

In concluding, six themes should be re-emphasised:

1. When using G-words it is best to remember that nearly all processes of socalled "globalisation" operate primarily at sub-global levels.
2. From a global perspective, if one adopts a reasonably broad conception of law, it is almost inevitable that the picture is one of great variety and complexity, involving multiple levels, non-state law, legal pluralism, cross-level diffusion, complex kinds of interlegality, and largely surface homogenisation and convergence. With due respect to Thomas Friedman, so far as law is concerned, the world is not yet flat.83
3. At first sight many of the canonical jurists may seem out of place in a post-Westphalian world. However, a younger generation of jurists is developing new kinds of general jurisprudence, which builds on their predecessors as well as stabbing them in the back: Tamanaha fillets Hart; Pogge transfers Rawlsian justice to the world stage more convinvingly than Rawls; Singer modernises Bentham; and Santos post-modernises Weber and Marx.
4. Most post-Enlightenment moral theories in the West are avowedly secular. Human rights is sometimes conceived of as a critical secular theology or a theory of values for a Godless Age. But from a global perspective, most of the world is going through a period of religious revival. Believers and nonbelievers alike need to be persuaded about global policies.
5. Most Western jurists have an anthropocentric *focus*. It does not follow that they are indifferent to environmental concerns nor that they treat ecocentric reasons as invalid. Most do, however, seem to take the position that ecocentric reasons fall outside the scope of the mainstream discourses of utility, human rights, and justice as fairness.
6. One of the challenges in approaching environmental issues is to what extent a theory of environmental justice leaves scope for other values and to what extent the language of justice is the most appropriate way of expressing all major concerns about the environment.

83 Friedman (2006).

Human Rights in Global perspective

Human rights have pervaded much of the political discourse since the Second World War. While the struggle for freedom from oppression and misery is probably as old as humanity itself, it was the massive affront to human dignity perpetrated during that War, and the need felt to prevent such horror in the future, which put the human being back at the centre and led to the codification at the international level of human rights and fundamental freedoms. Article 1 of the Charter of the United Nations declares "promoting and encouraging respect for human rights and for fundamental freedoms for all without distinction as to race, sex, language, or religion" as one of the purposes of the Organization.

The Universal Declaration of Human Rights, adopted by the United Nations General Assembly in 1948, was the first step towards achieving this objective. It is seen as the authoritative interpretation of the term "human rights" in the Charter of the United Nations. The Universal Declaration together with the International Covenant on Civil and Political Rights and the International Covenant on Economic, Social and Cultural Rights, both adopted in 1966, constitute what has become known as the International Bill of Human Rights. Since 1948, human rights and fundamental freedoms have indeed been codified in hundreds of universal and regional, binding and non-binding instruments, touching almost every aspect of human life and covering a broad range of civil, political, economic, social and cultural rights. Thus, the codification of human rights has largely been completed. As the Secretary-General of the United Nations, Mr. Kofi Annan, has recently pointed out, today's main challenge is to implement the adopted standards.

In previous years, attention has increasingly turned towards the parliament as the State institution through which people exercise their right, enshrined in article 21 of the Universal Declaration, to participate in the conduct of the public affairs of the country. Indeed, if human rights are to become a reality for everyone, parliaments must fully play their role and exercise to this effect the specific powers they have, namely legislating, adopting the budget and overseeing the Government.

As an organization that shares the United Nations concern for human rights, the Inter-Parliamentary Union (IPU) seeks to strengthen the role of parliaments as guardians of human rights. The activities it has undertaken over the years to this end have shown that all too often parliamentarians know little about the international legal human rights framework, the obligations their countries have entered into by signing human rights treaties, and the various international and regional human rights bodies and mechanisms that exist to monitor their implementation. Indeed, parliamentarians could do a lot more in favour of human rights. Hence, the suggestion that IPU and the Office of the United Nations High Commissioner for Human Rights (OHCHR), the United Nations body specifically mandated to promote and protect the effective enjoyment by all of all civil, cultural, economic, political and social rights, should publish a handbook with basic information about human rights and the international and regional systems designed to promote and protect them.

The task of drawing up the *Handbook* was entrusted to a renowned human rights expert, Mr. Manfred Nowak, currently the United Nations Special Rapporteur on Torture. In carrying out this task he drew on the input and guidance of the IPU Committee on the Human Rights of Parliamentarians and officials of both OHCHR and IPU.

It is not difficult to see that, in spite of the human rights norms, standards and principles that have been established by the international community, we are far from living in a world "free from fear and want" to which the founders of the United Nations had aspired. It is therefore the hope of both organizations that the *Handbook* will become a major tool for parliamentarians all over the world to gauge their legislative, oversight and representative activities against the human rights obligations their countries have entered into, and will assist them in playing the important role they have for the promotion and protection of human rights at home, and worldwide.

Louise Arbour
United Nations
High Commissioner for Human Rights

Anders B. Johnsson
Secretary General
Inter-Parliamentary Union

WHAT DOES THE HANDBOOK CONTAIN?
• Part I provides an overview of the general principles governing human rights law and the obligations States have entered into under international human rights law. It presents the international and regional legal framework in the fi eld of human rights and explains the functioning of the diff erent international and regional human rights bodies, including those that monitor the implementation of the major international human rights treaties.
• In Part II, Chapter 11 is devoted to parliamentary action to promote and protect human rights. It gives concrete examples of what parliaments and their members can do in this area. "What you can do" boxes provide a checklist for such action.
• Chapters 12 and 13 aim to describe the core content of each right guaranteed in the Universal Declaration of Human Rights and answer questions such as "What does the right to fair trial mean?" or "What is the right to an adequate standard of living?" Th e chapters deal only with the fundamental rights that were further elaborated in the International Covenant on Economic, Social and Cultural Rights and the International Covenant on Civil and Political Rights, and do not include the right to property.

HUMAN RIGHTS:
A HANDBOOK FOR PARLIAMENTARIANS
TABLE OF CONTENTS
Foreword iii
PART I
Chapter 1: What are human rights ? 1
Defi nition 1
Basic human rights principles 4
Human rights and State sovereignty 8
Democracy, human rights and parliaments 8
Chapter 2: What State obligations arise from human rights? 11
Chapter 3: International human rights instruments 17
Th e emergence of international human rights law 17

The International Bill of Human Rights 17
Core human rights treaties 18
Other human rights instruments of the United Nations 19

Chapter 4: May Governments restrict human rights? 21
Limitation clauses 21
Derogation in a state of emergency 23
Reservations to international or regional human rights treaties 23
Counter-terrorism measures and human rights 24

Chapter 5: United Nations human rights treaty-monitoring bodies 27
Membership and functioning 27
Reporting procedure 28
Individual complaints procedure 29
Inter-State complaints procedure 30
Inquiry procedures under CAT and the Optional Protocol to CEDAW .. 32
The system of regular visits to detention centres established under the Optional Protocol to CAT 33

Chapter 6: Charter-based system of human rights protection under the United Nations Commission on Human Rights 35
The confidential "1503 procedure" 35
The special procedures 36
The Sub-Commission on the Promotion and Protection of Human Rights 38

Chapter 7: The Office of the United Nations High Commissioner for Human Rights 39

Chapter 8: Integrating human rights into the work of the United Nations ... 43
Human rights in the General Assembly and its permanent programmes 44

Human rights and the Security Council 44
Human rights and the "United Nations family" 45

Chapter 9: Regional human rights treaties and monitoring 49

Africa 49
Th e Americas 51
Arab region 51
Asia and the Pacifi c 52
Europe 52

Chapter 10: Combating impunity: the International Criminal Court (ICC) 55

Th e International Criminal Tribunal for the former Yugoslavia
(ICTY) and the International Criminal Tribunal for
Rwanda (ICTR) 56
Th e International Criminal Court (ICC) 56
Th e Set of Principles for the protection and promotion of
human rights through action to combat impunity 59

ix

PART II

Chapter 11: The role of parliamentarians in the protection and promotion of human rights 63

Basic principles 63
Parliamentary action to promote and protect human rights 66

Chapter 12: What parliamentarians should know about the civil and political rights contained in the Universal Declaration of Human Rights . . . 81

Th e right to life 81
Prohibition of torture and cruel, inhuman or degrading treatment
or punishment: the right to personal integrity and dignity 90
Th e right to personal liberty 94
Administration of justice: the right to a fair trial 97
Th e right to privacy and the protection of family life 100

Freedom of movement...................105
Freedom of thought, conscience and religion....................108
Freedom of opinion and expression....................110
Freedom of peaceful assembly and association....................117
Th e right to participate in government....................120
Chapter 13: What parliamentarians should know about the economic, social and cultural rights contained in the Universal Declaration of Human Rights....................125
Social and economic trends and developments....................125
Th e right to social security....................130
Th e right to work and rights at work....................132
Th e right to an adequate standard of living....................134
Th e right to education....................146
Concluding remark....................150
List of abbreviations....................151
Annex 1 Universal Declaration of Human Rights....................153
Annex 2 International Covenant on Civil and Political Rights....................158
Annex 3 International Covenant on Economic, Social and Cultural Rights.....175
Annex 4 International instruments on the Internet....................185

x
1

CHAPTER 1:
WHAT ARE HUMAN RIGHTS?
Definition
HUMAN RIGHTS ARE RIGHTS THAT EVERY HUMAN BEING HAS BY VIRTUE OF HIS OR HER HUMAN DIGNITY

Human rights are the most fundamental rights of human beings. They define relationships between individuals and power structures, especially the State. Human rights delimit State power and, at the same time, require States to take positive measures ensuring an environment that enables all people to enjoy their human rights. History in the last 250 years has been shaped by the struggle to create such an environment. Starting with the French and American revolutions in the late eighteenth century, the idea of human rights has driven many a revolutionary movement for empowerment and for control over the wielders of power, Governments in particular.

HUMAN RIGHTS ARE THE SUM OF INDIVIDUAL AND COLLECTIVE RIGHTS LAID DOWN IN STATE CONSTITUTIONS AND INTERNATIONAL LAW

Governments and other duty bearers are under an obligation to respect, protect and fulfil human rights, which form the basis for legal entitlements and remedies in case of non-fulfilment (see Chapter 2). In fact, the possibility to press claims and demand redress differentiates human rights from the precepts of ethical or religious value systems. From a legal standpoint, human rights can be defined as the sum of individual and collective rights recognized by sovereign States and enshrined in their constitutions and in international law. Since the Second World War, the United Nations has played a leading role in defining and advancing human rights, which until then had developed mainly within the nation State. As a result, human rights have been codified in various international and regional treaties and instruments that have been ratified by most countries, and represent today the only universally recognized value system.

Box 1
Examples of human rights:
freedoms, rights and prohibitions related to human rights
In the area of civil and political rights
- Right to life
- Freedom from torture and cruel, inhuman or degrading treatment or punishment
- Freedom from slavery, servitude and forced labour
- Right to liberty and security of person
- Right of detained persons to be treated with humanity
- Freedom of movement
- Right to a fair trial

- Prohibition of retroactive criminal laws
- Right to recognition as a person before the law
- Right to privacy
- Freedom of thought, conscience and religion
- Freedom of opinion and expression
- Prohibition of propaganda for war and of incitement to national, racial or religious hatred
- Freedom of assembly
- Freedom of association
- Right to marry and found a family
- Right to take part in the conduct of public affairs, vote, be elected and have access to public office
- Right to equality before the law and non-discrimination

In the area of economic, social and cultural rights
- Right to work
- Right to just and favourable conditions of work
- Right to form and join trade unions
- Right to social security
- Protection of the family
- Right to an adequate standard of living, including adequate food, clothing and housing
- Right to health
- Right to education

In the area of collective rights
- Right of peoples to:
- Self-determination
- Development
- Free use of their wealth and natural resources
- Peace
- A healthy environment
- Other collective rights:
- Rights of national, ethnic, religious and linguistic minorities
- Rights of indigenous peoples

HUMAN RIGHTS ARE MANIFOLD

Human rights cover all aspects of life. Their exercise enables women and men to shape and
determine their own lives in liberty, equality and respect for human dignity. Human rights
comprise civil and political rights, social, economic and cultural rights and the collective rights of peoples to self-determination, equality, development, peace and a clean environment.

Although it has been — and sometimes still is — argued that civil and political rights, also known as "first generation rights", are based on the concept of non-interference

of the State in private affairs, whereas social, economic and cultural — or "second generation"
— rights require the State to take positive action, it is today widely acknowledged that, for human rights to become a reality, States and the international community must take steps to create the conditions and legal frameworks necessary for the exercise of human
rights as a whole. The "generation" terminology harks back to language used during the cold war; nowadays, the emphasis is placed on the principles of universality, indivisibility
and interdependence of all human rights.

The right to development

The right to development places the human person at the centre of the development process
and recognizes that the human being should be the main participant and beneficiary of development.
The 1986 UN Declaration on the Right to Development states that:
1. "... every human person and all peoples are entitled to participate in, contribute to, and
enjoy economic, social, cultural and political development, in which all human rights and fundamental freedoms can be fully realized", [and]
2. "The human right to development also implies the full realization of the right of peoples to
self-determination, which includes, subject to the relevant provisions of both International
Covenants on Human Rights, the exercise of their inalienable right to full sovereignty over all their natural wealth and resources."
The right to development is based on the principle of the indivisibility and interdependence of
all human rights and fundamental freedoms. Equal attention and urgent consideration should
be given to the implementation, promotion and protection of civil, political, economic, social
and cultural rights.
The Millennium Development Goals of September 2000 define the eradication of poverty as the
overarching objective of the development process. United Nations Member States have pledged
to meet, inter alia, the following goals, most of them by the year 2015: reduce by half the proportion
of people living on less than a dollar a day and who suffer from hunger; achieve universal
primary education for all boys and girls; reduce child mortality by two thirds; reduce the maternal
mortality rate by three quarters; combat HIV/AIDS, malaria and other major diseases;

ensure environmental sustainability and develop a global partnership for development (for a
complete list of the Goals, see Box 76).

Box 2

4

1 *Le Droit d'être un homme*, anthology of texts prepared under the direction of Jeanne Hersch, UNESCO and Robert Laffont, 1968.

Basic human rights principles

HUMAN RIGHTS ARE UNIVERSAL

"Human rights are foreign to no culture and native to all nations; they are universal."

Kofi A. Annan, Secretary-General of the United Nations,
Address at the University of Tehran on Human Rights Day, 10 December 1997.

Human rights are universal because they are based on every human being's dignity, irrespective
of race, colour, sex, ethnic or social origin, religion, language, nationality, age, sexual orientation, disability or any other distinguishing characteristic. Since they are accepted
by all States and peoples, they apply equally and indiscriminately to every person and are the same for everyone everywhere.

HUMAN RIGHTS ARE INALIENABLE

Human rights are inalienable insofar as no person may be divested of his or her human rights, save under clearly defined legal circumstances. For instance, a person's right to liberty
may be restricted if he or she is found guilty of a crime by a court of law.

HUMAN RIGHTS ARE INDIVISIBLE AND INTERDEPENDENT

Human rights are indivisible and interdependent. Because each human right entails and depends on other human rights, violating one such right affects the exercise of other human
rights. For example, the right to life presupposes respect for the right to food and to an adequate standard of living. The right to be elected to public office implies access to basic education. The defence of economic and social rights presupposes freedom of expres-

Human rights: a Western concept?

The universality of human rights has sometimes been challenged on the grounds that they
are a Western notion, part of a neocolonial attitude that is propagated worldwide. A study
published by the United Nations Educational, Scientific and Cultural Organization (UNESCO)
in 1968 1 clearly showed that the profound aspirations underlying human rights correspond
to concepts — the concepts of justice, an individual's integrity and dignity, freedom from

oppression and persecution, and individual participation in collective endeavours — that are encountered in all civilizations and periods. Today, the universality of human rights is
borne out by the fact that the majority of nations, covering the full spectrum of cultural, religious and political traditions, have adopted and ratified the main international human
rights instruments.

Box 3

sion, of assembly and of association. Accordingly, civil and political rights and economic, social and cultural rights are complementary and equally essential to the dignity and integrity
of every person. Respect for all rights is a prerequisite to sustainable peace and development.

The international community affirmed the holistic concept of human rights at the World
Conference on Human Rights, held in Vienna in 1993.

"All human rights are universal, indivisible and interdependent and interrelated. The international community must treat human rights globally in a fair and equal manner, on the same footing, and with the same emphasis. While the significance of national and regional particularities and various historical, cultural and religious backgrounds must be borne in mind, it is the duty of States, regardless of their political, economic and cultural systems, to promote and protect all human rights and fundamental freedoms."

World Conference on Human Rights, Vienna 1993,
Vienna Declaration and Programme of Action, paragraph 5.

THE PRINCIPLE OF NON-DISCRIMINATION

Some of the worst human rights violations have resulted from discrimination against specific groups. The right to equality and the principle of non-discrimination, explicitly set out in international and regional human rights treaties, are therefore central to human
rights. The right to equality obliges States to ensure observance of human rights without discrimination on any grounds, including sex, race, colour, language, religion, political or other opinion, national, ethnic or social origin, membership of a national minority, property, birth, age, disability, sexual orientation and social or other status. More often than not, the discriminatory criteria used by States and non-State actors to prevent specific groups from fully enjoying all or some human rights are based on such characteristics.

Civil and political rights and economic and social rights are indissociable

Amartya Sen, Nobel Laureate in economics, has provided empirical proof that all human rights are indivisible and interdependent. In his research on famines, for instance, he found
that among rich and poor countries alike, no functioning democracy has ever suffered a major

famine, because in such States it is inter alia likely that the media will call attention to the risk
of famine and that political parties and the public will respond. Democracy makes parliaments,
Governments and other policymakers aware of the dangers of ignoring such risks.2

Box 4

2 Amartya Sen, *Poverty and Famines: An Essay on Entitlements and Deprivation*, Clarendon Press, 1982.

6

Difference in fact may justify difference in law

Not every differentiation constitutes discrimination. Factual or legal distinctions based on
reasonable and objective criteria may be justifiable. The burden of proof falls on Governments:
they must show that any distinctions that are applied are actually reasonable and objective.

Some groups may enjoy special rights

The principles of equality, universality and non-discrimination do not preclude recognizing
that specific groups whose members need particular protection should enjoy special rights.
This accounts for the numerous human rights instruments specifically designed to protect
the rights of groups with special needs, such as women, aliens, stateless persons, refugees,
displaced persons, minorities, indigenous peoples, children, persons with disabilities, migrant
workers and detainees. Group-specific human rights, however, are compatible with

Justified differentiation with regard to employment

Two European Union directives on racial equality and equality in employment 3 allow Governments
to authorize differentiated treatment in certain circumstances. Differentiation is thus allowed in a small number of cases involving jobs whose performance actually requires distinction
on such grounds as racial or ethnic origin, religion or belief, disability, age or sexual orientation. Examples include acting and modelling jobs, where authenticity or realism may
require performers to be of a particular origin or age, and some positions in church or similar
organizations which involve contact with the public and (unlike other jobs in the same bodies,
such as office work or catering) should be staffed with persons of a given confession or belief.

Box 6

Prohibition of discrimination
• Non-discrimination is a pillar of human rights.
• Diff erentiation in law must be based on diff erence in facts.
• Distinctions require reasonable and objective justifi cation.
• Th e principle of proportionality must be observed.
• Characteristics that have been — and still are — used as grounds for discrimination include
sex, race, colour, language, religion, political or other opinion, national, ethnic or
social origin, membership of a national minority, property, birth, age, disability, sexual
orientation and social or other status.
Box 5
3 Council directives 2000/43/EC of 29 June 2000, implementing the principle of equal treatment between persons irrespective of
racial or ethnic origin, and 2000/78/EC of 27 November 2000, establishing a general framework for equal treatment in employment
and occupation.

7

the principle of universality only if they are justifi ed by special (objective) reasons, such as
the group's vulnerability or a history of discrimination against it. Otherwise, special rights
could amount to privileges equivalent to discrimination against other groups.

Temporary special measures
To redress the long-term eff ects of past discrimination, temporary special measures may be necessary. General recommendation No. 254 on article 4 of the Convention on the Elimination of All Forms of Discrimination against Women (CEDAW)5 defi nes such measures as "a wide variety of legislative, executive, administrative and other regulatory
instruments, policies and practices, such as outreach or support programmes; allocation and/or reallocation of resources; preferential treatment; targeted recruitment, hiring and
promotion; numerical goals connected with time frames; and quota systems".
For instance, temporary quota systems designed to give women preferential treatment regarding access to specifi c jobs, political decision-making bodies or university education

Affi rmative action: an example
In Norway, the Gender Equality Ombudsman has in recent years focused on men in the context
of gender equality. As a result, the maternity leave legislation has been amended to extend
rights to them. One change has been that four weeks of the leave period are now reserved for
the father. If he fails to use that entitlement, known as the "father's quota", the family loses its

entitlement to that part of the leave. The "father's quota" was introduced in 1993, and in the
next two years the percentage of new fathers taking paternity leave increased from 45 to 70 per
cent. The Ombudsman further proposed positive action in favour of men in a limited number of
care-related occupations in order to activate men's potential in that area and thereby counteract
strict gender segregation in that labour market segment, and to provide children with a less
stereotyped concept of gender roles.

Box 8
Special rights of persons with disabilities: an example
In the United Kingdom, the Disability Discrimination Act of 1995 obliges employers to make
"reasonable adjustments" to work organization and premises to accommodate disabled workers.
The Act contains a detailed list of the types of measures required. It includes modifying
premises and equipment, transferring disabled persons to suitable places of work, reassigning
some of their duties to other workers and providing for alternative working hours.

Box 7
4 The bodies that monitor the implementation of international human rights instruments elaborate on the various rights and corresponding
State obligations in "general recommendations" and "general comments". For further details see Chapter 5.
5 For further information on CEDAW and parliaments, see *The Convention on the Elimination of All Forms of Discrimination
against Women and its Optional Protocol: a Handbook for Parliamentarians,* IPU, Geneva 2003.

8

can be considered as affirmative action aimed at accelerating the attainment of actual gender
equality in areas where women have traditionally been underrepresented and have suffered from discrimination.
Under article 4 of CEDAW, these temporary measures are encouraged and shall, therefore,
not be considered as discrimination against men. However, as soon as the objectives of equality of opportunity and treatment have been achieved, these measures must be discontinued. Otherwise, they would constitute unjustified privileges for women and,
consequently, discrimination against men.
According to general recommendation No. 25, no proof of past discrimination is necessary

for such measures to be taken: "While the application of temporary special measures often remedies the effects of past discrimination against women, the obligation of States parties under the Convention to improve the position of women to one of de facto or substantive equality with men exists irrespective of any proof of past discrimination".

Human rights and State sovereignty

In the past, when human rights were still regarded as a country's internal affair, other States and the international community were prevented from interfering, even in the most serious cases of human rights violations, such as genocide. That approach, based on national sovereignty, was challenged in the twentieth century, especially by the actions of Nazi Germany and the atrocities committed during the Second World War. Today, human rights promotion and protection are considered a legitimate concern and responsibility of the international community. However, discrepancies between *universal legal obligations* and *State sovereignty* can be resolved only on a case-by-case basis, in accordance with the *principle of proportionality,* a principle according to which any action taken by an authority pursuant to the concept of universality must not go beyond what is necessary to achieve compliance with human rights.

"The promotion and protection of all human rights and fundamental freedoms must be considered as a priority objective of the United Nations in accordance with its purposes and principles, in particular the purpose of international cooperation. In the framework of these purposes and principles, the promotion and protection of all human rights is a legitimate concern of the international community."

World Conference on Human Rights, Vienna 1993,
Vienna Declaration and Programme of Action, paragraph 4.

Democracy, human rights and parliaments

In the past decade, the interrelationship between democracy and human rights was studied extensively. Democracy is no longer considered as a mere set of procedural rules for the constitution and exercise of political power, but also, along with human rights, as a way of preserving and promoting the dignity of the person. In 1995, the Inter-Parliamentary Union embarked on the process of drafting a Universal Declaration on Democracy to advance international standards and to contribute to ongoing democratization worldwide. In

the Declaration, adopted in 1997, democracy and human rights are so closely linked as to
be considered inseparable.

Democracy is premised on the idea that all citizens are equally entitled to have a say in decisions affecting their lives. This right to participation in the conduct of public affairs is enshrined in article 21 of the Universal Declaration of Human Rights and article 25 of the International Covenant on Civil and Political Rights (CCPR). However, for citizens to effectively exercise that right, they must first enjoy other rights such as freedom of expression,
assembly and association, and basic economic and social rights. Institutions making possible the people's participation and control are a further prerequisite. Parliaments — sovereign bodies constituted through regular, free and fair elections to ensure government
of the people, for the people and by the people — are therefore a key institution in a democracy. As the body competent to legislate and to keep the policies and actions of the
executive branch under constant scrutiny, parliament also plays a key role in the promotion
and protection of human rights. Furthermore, parliaments establish the legal framework that guarantees the independence of the judiciary and, therefore, the rule of law, a cornerstone of democracy and human rights protection. For all these reasons, parliaments
are crucial to democracy and human rights.

"As an ideal, democracy aims essentially to preserve and promote the dignity and fundamental rights of the individual, to achieve social justice, foster the economic and social development of the community, strengthen the cohesion of society and enhance national tranquillity, as well as to create a climate that is favourable for international peace. As a form of government, democracy is the best way of achieving these objectives; it is also the only political system that has the capacity for self-correction."
Inter-Parliamentary Union, Universal Declaration on Democracy,
Cairo September 1997, paragraph 3.

CHAPTER 2:
WHAT STATE OBLIGATIONS ARISE
FROM HUMAN RIGHTS?

Although in principle human rights can be violated by any person or group, and in fact human rights abuses committed against the backdrop of globalization by non-State actors
(transnational corporations, organized crime, international terrorism, guerrilla and paramilitary
forces and even intergovernmental organizations) are on the increase, under present international law, *only States assume direct obligations in relation to human rights.*

By becoming parties to international human rights treaties, States incur three broad obligations: the duties to respect, to protect and to fulfil. While the balance between these
obligations or duties may vary according to the rights involved, they apply in principle to all civil and political rights and all economic, social and cultural rights. Moreover, States have a duty to provide a remedy at the domestic level for human rights violations.

What does the "obligation to respect" mean?

The State "obligation to respect" means that the State is obliged to refrain from interfering.

It entails the prohibition of certain acts by Governments that may undermine the enjoyment
of rights. For example, with regard to the right to education, it means that Governments must respect the liberty of parents to establish private schools and to ensure the religious and moral education of their children in accordance with their own convictions.

What does the "obligation to protect" mean?

The "obligation to protect" requires States to protect individuals against abuses by non-State actors. Once again, the right to education can serve as an example. The right of children to education must be protected by the State from interference and indoctrination
by third parties, including parents and the family, teachers and the school, religions, sects, clans and business firms. States enjoy a broad margin of appreciation with respect to

this obligation. For instance, the right to personal integrity and security obliges States to combat the widespread phenomenon of *domestic violence* against women and children: although
not every single act of violence by a husband against his wife, or by parents against their children, constitutes a human rights violation for which the State may be held ac-

The State's obligation to respect, to protect and to fulfil: examples

Right to life

Respect The police shall not intentionally take the life of a suspect to prevent his or her escape in the event of a minor offence, such as theft.

Protection Life-threatening attacks by an individual against other persons (attempted homicide)
shall be crimes carrying appropriate penalties under domestic criminal law.

The police shall duly investigate such crimes in order to bring the perpetrators to justice.

Fulfilment The authorities shall take legislative and administrative measures to reduce progressively
child mortality and other types of mortality whose underlying causes
can be combated.

Prohibition of torture or cruel, inhuman or degrading treatment or punishment

Respect The police shall not use torture in questioning detainees.

Protection The authorities shall take legislative and other measures against domestic violence.
Fulfilment The authorities shall train police officers in acceptable methods of questioning.

Right to vote
Respect The authorities shall not interfere with the voting procedure and shall respect the
election results.
Protection The authorities shall organize voting by secret ballot to preclude threats by persons
in power (such as politicians, heads of clan or family or employers).
Fulfilment The authorities shall organize free and fair elections and ensure that as many citizens
as possible can vote.

Right to health
Respect The authorities shall not restrict the right to health (inter alia through forced sterilization or medical experimentation).
Protection Female genital mutilation (FGM) shall be prohibited and eradicated.
Fulfilment An adequate number of hospitals and other public health-care facilities shall provide
services equally accessible to all.

Right to food
Respect The authorities shall refrain from any measures that would prevent access to adequate
food (for instance, arbitrary eviction from land).
Protection The authorities shall adopt laws or take other measures to prevent powerful people
or organizations from violating the right to food (examples: a company polluting
the water supply, or a landowner evicting peasants).
Fulfilment The authorities shall implement policies — such as agrarian reform — to ensure
the population's access to adequate food and the capacity of vulnerable groups to feed themselves.

Box 9

countable, Governments have a responsibility to take positive measures — in the form of
pertinent criminal, civil, family or administrative laws, police and judiciary training or
general awareness raising — to reduce the incidence of domestic violence.

What does the "obligation to fulfil" mean?
Under the "obligation to fulfil", States are required to take positive action to ensure that
human rights can be exercised. In respect of the right to education, for instance, States

must provide ways and means for free and compulsory primary education for all, free secondary
education, higher education, vocational training, adult education, and the elimination of illiteracy (including such steps as setting up enough public schools or hiring and remunerating an adequate number of teachers).

The principle of progressive realization

Th e principle of progressive realization applies to the positive State obligations to fulfi l and
to protect. Th e right to health, for example, does not guarantee the right of everyone to be
healthy. However, it does oblige States, in accordance with their respective economic capabilities,
social and cultural traditions and observing international minimum standards, to establish and maintain a public health system that can in principle guarantee access to certain
basic health services for all. Progressive realization means that Governments should establish targets and benchmarks in order progressively to reduce the infant mortality rate, increase the number of doctors per thousand inhabitants, raise the percentage of the
population that has been vaccinated against certain infectious and epidemic diseases, or improve basic health facilities, etc. Obviously, the health standard in poor countries may

The right to obtain remedy under international and regional human rights treaties: examples

According to article 2 (3) of CCPR, States parties undertake "to ensure that (a) ... any person
whose rights or freedoms ... are violated shall have an eff ective remedy" and that (b) persons
claiming such a remedy shall have their "right thereto determined by competent judicial, administrative
or legislative authorities, or by any other competent authority provided for by the legal system of the State"; and "to develop the possibilities of judicial remedy".
Article 13 of the European Convention for the Protection of Human Rights and Fundamental
Freedoms stipulates that: "Everyone whose rights and freedoms as set forth in the Convention
are violated shall have an eff ective remedy before a national authority ..."
Article 25 (1) of the American Convention on Human Rights (also known as the Pact of San
Jose, Costa Rica) establishes this remedy as a separate human right: "Everyone has the right to
simple and prompt recourse, or any other eff ective recourse, to a competent court or tribunal
for protection against acts that violate his fundamental rights recognized by the constitution or

laws of the State concerned or by this Convention ..."

Box 10

be lower than in rich countries without any violation of Governments' obligations to fulfil the right to health. The total absence of positive measures to improve the public health system, retrogressive measures or the deliberate exclusion of certain groups (such as women and religious or ethnic minorities) from access to health services can, however, amount to a violation of the right to health.

What does the "obligation to provide domestic remedies" mean?

The very notion of rights entails, in addition to a substantive claim, the possibility to have recourse to a national — judicial, administrative, legislative or other — authority in the event that a right is violated. Every person who claims that his or her rights have not been respected must therefore be able to seek an *effective remedy* before a competent domestic body vested with the power to provide redress and to have its decisions enforced.

The right to recourse to a supranational court

The right to have recourse to an international human rights court once all avenues of seeking redress at the domestic level are exhausted has been accepted only partially. According to advanced procedures established under the European Convention for the Protection of Human Rights and Fundamental Freedoms, individuals may appeal to the permanent European Court of Human Rights, whose judgements are legally binding. Provision is made for the right of individuals to file petitions with an international human rights court under the American Convention on Human Rights, but this is not currently the case under United Nations treaties (for details see Chapters 5 and 9).

The right to reparations

The right to effective remedy implies that the victim of a human rights violation is entitled to reparations for the harm suffered. The State's obligation entails inter alia bringing to justice those responsible for the violation, including public officials or State agents, and taking measures to prevent its recurrence. Box 11 lists various forms of reparation.

Right of victims to reparation after human rights violations:

Restitution: release of detainees, restitution of property

Satisfaction: public apologies, truth commissions, criminal investigations against perpetrators of gross human rights violations

Rehabilitation: legal, medical, psychological and social measures to help victims recover (for
instance, setting up centres for rehabilitation from torture)

Compensation: indemnification for financial or non-financial damages

Guarantee of non-recurrence: legislative and administrative changes, disciplinary measures

Box 11

15

Remedies for violations of economic, social and cultural rights

The provisions for the right to a remedy cited above (see Box 10) refer primarily to civil and political rights, whereas most treaties relating to economic, social and cultural rights
— such as the International Covenant on Economic, Social and Cultural Rights (CESCR) and the European Social Charter — contain no similar provisions. The reason is that the domestic or international justiciability of economic, social and cultural human rights is still questioned by many Governments, and even by some human rights scholars. The distinction
between the two categories of rights dates back to the ideological debates of the cold war. Civil and political rights were then perceived as purely "negative" rights — directed
against State interference — whereas economic, social and cultural rights were seen as "programme rights" — political claims requiring positive State action - aimed, for instance,
at guaranteeing employment, good health and full social security for everyone. Such "programme rights" were considered unenforceable by the courts.
Supranational courts, such as the European or the Inter-American Court of Human Rights, have ruled that States must take action to ensure respect for civil and political rights. States must, for instance, establish a judicial system capable of fulfilling the obligation
to guarantee a fair trial within a reasonable time. In cases of allegations of torture, enforced disappearances or arbitrary executions, they must carry out full criminal investigations
to bring the perpetrators to justice and to provide compensation and other forms of reparation to victims and their families.
These same facilities may also be established with regard to economic, social and cultural
rights. As mentioned above, international courts are capable of deciding in a judicial procedure that a State has not fulfilled its positive obligation with regard to civil and political
rights, for example the obligation to organize a judicial system in accordance with the minimum guarantees set out in article 6 of the European Convention for the Protection of

Human Rights and Fundamental Freedoms (the right to fair trial). It can therefore be argued that the same court would also be fully empowered to decide whether States fulfilled their positive obligations to organize their school systems in accordance with the minimum guarantees of the right to education, as laid down in articles 13 and 14 of CESCR, or their public health systems in accordance with the minimum guarantees of the right to the enjoyment of the highest attainable standard of physical and mental health, as established under article 12 of CESCR.

Yet almost no international court has been mandated to rule on economic, social and cultural rights. The only exceptions are the Inter-American Court of Human Rights, which, by virtue of article 19 (6) of the 1988 Additional Protocol to the American Convention on Human Rights in the Area of Economic, Social and Cultural Rights, is authorized to decide on individual petitions relating to the right to education and the right to organize trade unions; and the Human Rights Chamber for Bosnia and Herzegovina, which, pursuant to annex 6 to the Dayton Peace Agreement of 1995, handed down decisions in many cases relating to alleged or apparent discrimination in the enjoyment of various economic, social and cultural rights. Although in 1993 the Vienna World Conference on Human Rights decided to speed up the drafting of an optional protocol to the International Covenant on Economic, Social and Cultural Rights in order to establish a right to submit individual complaints to the Committee on Economic, Social and Cultural Rights (which is, as the other United Nations treaty-monitoring bodies, only a quasi-judicial expert body — see Chapter 5), many Governments are still obstructing that important development.

It may still take years for the argument that economic, social and cultural rights are non-justiciable to be refuted, because of the following vicious circle: Governments refuse to authorize domestic and international courts to rule on economic, social and cultural rights; there is thus relatively little relevant judicial case law; and this fact is to some extent considered as evidence that these rights are not justiciable — or are less justiciable than civil and political rights.

Competence of domestic courts in the area of economic, social and cultural rights: an example

In some countries, domestic courts are mandated to rule on economic, social and cultural rights.

A pertinent example is provided by the jurisprudence of South Africa, where economic, social

and cultural rights, such as the rights to food, access to health care and housing, enshrined in
the Constitution, may be enforced by the courts. In the *Grootboom case* (*Government of the
Republic of South Africa v. Irene Grootboom and others*, CCT 11/00), the Constitutional Court
set a precedent. The case was appealed to the Court by the South African Government when the
Cape High Court ordered it to provide a group of homeless children and their parents with shelters
(tents, portable latrines and regular water supply). The group had lived in an informal settlement
that flooded when it rained, then moved to another site from which they were evicted, and their shacks there were burnt down. Completely homeless, as their initial settlement had
meanwhile been occupied by others, they squatted in a sports field and filed an application with
the High Court, invoking the right to housing and children's rights as enshrined in the Constitution.
The application on the basis of the right to housing failed, because the Court was satisfied that the State had taken "reasonable" measures towards the progressive realization of this
right within the State's "available resources". However, it held that — by virtue of the children's
constitutionally guaranteed right to shelter, and in accordance with the children's best interests
— the children and their parents were entitled to shelter provided by the State.

Box 12

CHAPTER 3:
INTERNATIONAL HUMAN RIGHTS INSTRUMENTS

The emergence of international human rights law

International human rights law emerged in the nineteenth century when international law
developed a doctrine under which "humanitarian intervention" was considered legitimate
in cases in which a State committed against its own subjects atrocities that "shocked the conscience of mankind". Later, the influence of the Red Cross Movement and the establishment
in 1919 of the International Labour Organization (ILO) led to the conclusion of, respectively, the Geneva Conventions6 and the first international conventions designed to
protect industrial workers from gross exploitation and to improve their working conditions.

The minority treaties concluded after the First World War sought to protect the rights of ethnic and linguistic minorities, and are therefore sometimes seen as precursors
of modern international human rights instruments. Strictly speaking, however, the first international human rights treaty — the Slavery Convention — was adopted in 1926 and entered into force the following year.

The International Bill of Human Rights

With the establishment in 1945 of the United Nations, *"promoting and encouraging respect*
for human rights and for fundamental freedoms for all without distinction as to race, sex,
*language, or religion"*7 became one of the fundamental goals pursued by the international
community. The Universal Declaration of Human Rights (1948) provides the first authoritative
interpretation of the term "human rights", as used in the Charter, and, although it was not drafted or voted upon as a legally binding instrument, the Declaration can now — more than 50 years later — be considered as *a general standard on human rights*.

6 For further information on the Geneva Conventions and humanitarian law, see *Respect for International Humanitarian Law:*
a Handbook for Parliamentarians, IPU, Geneva 1999.
7 *Charter of the United Nations*, Chapter I, Article 1, para.3.

18

The Universal Declaration of Human Rights was adopted in two years, but it took almost 20 years to agree on the text of the International Covenant on Civil and Political Rights (CCPR) and the International Covenant on Economic, Social and Cultural Rights (CESCR). After six years of drafting, they were finalized in the United Nations Commission
on Human Rights in 1954, but the General Assembly took 12 more years to adopt them. It took a further 10 years until the required 35 instruments of ratification were deposited
and the Covenants finally entered into force (1976). The Universal Declaration of Human Rights, and the two Covenants are the only general human rights instruments of the United Nations. Together with the two Optional Protocols to CCPR (1966 and 1989), they are usually referred to as the "International Bill of Human Rights".

"The Declaration is a timeless and powerful document that captures the
profound aspirations of humankind to live in dignity, equality and security. It
provides minimum standards and has helped turn moral issues into a legally
binding framework...."
Sergio Vieira de Mello, former United Nations High Commissioner for Human Rights,
Message delivered on Human Rights Day, 10 December 2002.

Core human rights treaties

The International Bill of Human Rights has been supplemented with a number of more

specifi c binding instruments. Some treaties are subject to supervision by monitoring bodies
and form, with the two Covenants, a set of instruments usually referred to as the core human rights treaties (see Chapter 5). Th ese additional instruments are:
Th e International Convention on the Elimination of All Forms of Racial Discrimination (CERD; adoption in 1965; entry into force in 1969);

The Universal Declaration of Human Rights
Under the leadership of such eminent personalities as Eleanor Roosevelt, Rene Cassin and
Charles Malik, the United Nations Commission on Human Rights succeeded in drafting the
Universal Declaration of Human Rights in two years. It was adopted by the General Assembly on
10 December 1948. Th e Declaration sets out civil, political, economic, social and cultural rights
and the right of everyone "to a social and international order in which the rights and freedoms
set forth in [the] Declaration can be fully realized". Although it is not a binding instrument, and
the Socialist States and South Africa abstained when it was adopted, the Declaration has risen,
morally and politically, to the status of an immensely authoritative instrument, expressing the
United Nations understanding of human rights. Today, it serves as the substantive foundation
of the charter-based system of human rights protection (see Chapter 8). Th e Declaration, together
with the International Covenant on Civil and Political Rights (CCPR), the International Covenant on Economic, Social and Cultural Rights (CESCR) and the two Optional Protocols to
CCPR, form the International Bill of Human Rights.

Box 13
19
Th e Convention on the Elimination of All Forms of Discrimination against Women (CEDAW; adoption in 1979; entry into force in 1981);
Th e Convention against Torture and Other Cruel, Inhuman or Degrading Treatment or Punishment (CAT; adoption in 1984; entry into force in 1987);
Th e Convention on the Rights of the Child (CRC; adoption in 1989; entry into force in 1990);
Th e International Convention on the Protection of the Rights of All Migrant Workers and Members of Th eir Families (known as the Migrant Workers Convention, or CMW; adoption in 1990; entry into force in 2003).

Other human rights instruments of the United Nations
Th e United Nations and its specialized agencies have adopted many other human rights

instruments devoted to specific groups, including women, refugees, aliens and stateless persons, minorities and indigenous peoples, prisoners, persons with disabilities, children and adolescents, and victims of crime. Further universal instruments deal with major hu-

Drafting and adopting international human rights treaties and related instruments

All human rights treaties and major declarations are adopted by the United Nations General Assembly, the only body where all — currently 191 — Member States are represented, with one vote each. The drafting process often begins with the adoption of a non-binding declaration, providing a common definition, and continues in the form of the more difficult task of developing legally binding standards.

The text of human rights instruments is generally first drafted by the United Nations Commission on Human Rights, which usually delegates the initial round of drafting to its standing Sub-Commission on the Promotion and Protection of Human Rights (see Chapter 8) or to an intersessional working group set up by the Commission for that purpose (for instance, at the time of writing, one such group was drafting a treaty on enforced disappearances). The drafting process in the Commission and its subsidiary bodies generally takes at least several years, and may even span two decades.

Once the text is adopted by the United Nations Commission on Human Rights, the drafting process usually speeds up. The text must then be approved by the Economic and Social Council. That is normally done within one session. Lastly, the draft must be discussed and formally adopted by the General Assembly, and in particular its Third Committee on Social, Humanitarian and Cultural Affairs. In the early years, it was not unusual for the Third Committee to redraft the text more or less from scratch. In recent years, however, the major political decisions are taken in the Commission, and work in the General Assembly is limited to solving a few remaining problems within one or two sessions.

Once a treaty is adopted by the General Assembly, usually by consensus, it is opened for *signature*

and ratifi cation by Member States. It enters into force after the deposit of a specifi c number
of instruments of ratifi cation or accession.

Box 14

20

man rights violations, such as slavery, torture, enforced disappearance, genocide, forced labour and religious intolerance, or focus on other specifi c human rights issues in the areas of education, employment, development, administration of justice, marriage, and the
freedoms of association and of information.

A detailed list of human rights instruments is provided in annex 4.

Steps in defi ning and implementing human rights standards

Declarations: setting non-binding standards

Universal Declaration of Human Rights (1948)

American Declaration of Human Rights (1948)

Binding international treaties and conventions

United Nations Covenants (1966-1976)

European Convention for the Protection of Human Rights and Fundamental Freedoms (1950- 1953)

American Convention on Human Rights (1969-1978)

African Charter on Human and Peoples' Rights (1981-1986)

Implementation: human rights treaty-monitoring bodies and mechanisms

Complaints procedure

Reporting procedure

Inquiry procedure

System of regular visits

Box 15

Human rights jurisprudence

Human rights treaties and conventions are living instruments, constantly developed through
the jurisprudence of the *international courts and expert bodies* responsible for international
monitoring. Th ese bodies have given the initial standards dynamic interpretations far beyond
their original meanings, adapting their provisions to current circumstances. For instance, the
prohibition of inhuman and degrading treatment and punishment under article 3 of the European
Convention for the Protection of Human Rights and Fundamental Freedoms (1950) was not initially meant to apply to minor forms of corporal punishment (such as those practised in
British schools); however, in the course of adaptation of the Convention as a living instrument,

the European Court of Human Rights has found that no form of corporal punishment is permitted
under article 3. Similarly, the United Nations Human Rights Committee (see Chapter 5) has found that the right to security of the person, guaranteed in article 9 of CCPR along with
the right to liberty, was not intended to be narrowed down to mere formal loss of liberty: in a
landmark decision (case of *Delgado Páez v. Colombia*, 195/1985), the Committee ruled that
States may not ignore threats to the personal security of non-detained persons within their
jurisdictions, and are obliged to take reasonable and appropriate measures to protect them.

Box 16

21

CHAPTER 4:
MAY GOVERNMENTS RESTRICT HUMAN RIGHTS?

Some human rights, such as the prohibition of torture and slavery, *are absolute*. The application
of interrogation techniques amounting to torture as defined under article 1 of CAT
— for instance electric shocks and other methods causing severe physical pain or mental suffering — is not justified on any grounds whatsoever, including — in the area of counterterrorism
— such circumstances as the need to extract from a detainee information about
an imminent terrorist attack.

States are allowed a *margin of appreciation* in relation to their obligations to respect, protect and fulfil most human rights. Most of these obligations are subject to progressive
realization, and the particular social, political, economic, religious and cultural circumstances
of every society must therefore be taken into account in assessing whether a State has violated its human rights obligations. Accordingly, the principle of the universality of human rights primarily applies to a core content of human rights, while Governments, by
virtue of reservations, derogation and limitation clauses, and the principle of progressive
realization, enjoy fairly broad powers to implement human rights in accordance with their
national interests.

Limitation clauses

Many obligations to respect human rights are subject to so-called limitation clauses. The
exercise of political freedoms, such as freedom of expression, assembly and association,

carries with it duties and responsibilities and may, therefore, be subject to certain formalities,
conditions, restrictions and penalties in the interests of national security, territorial integrity or public safety, the prevention of disorder or crime, the protection of public health or morals, or the protection of the reputation or rights and freedoms of others. If people misuse their freedom of speech and of participation in a demonstration for incitement
to racial or religious hatred, for war propaganda or for instigating others to commit crimes, Governments have an obligation to interfere with the exercise of these freedoms in

Rights, freedoms and prohibitions that are not subject to derogation even in times of war

Under article 4 of CCPR
- Right to life
- Prohibition of torture, or cruel, inhuman or degrading treatment or punishment
- Prohibition of slavery and servitude
- Prohibition of detention for debt
- Freedom from retroactive criminal laws
- Right to recognition as a person before the law
- Freedom of thought, conscience and religion

Under article 15 of the European Convention for the Protection of Human Rights and Fundamental Freedoms
- Right to life, except in respect of deaths resulting from lawful acts of war
- Prohibition of torture, cruel, inhuman and degrading treatment or punishment
- Prohibition of slavery and servitude
- Freedom from retroactive criminal laws

Under article 27 of the American Convention on Human Rights
- Right to legal personality
- Right to life
- Right to humane treatment
- Prohibition of slavery
- Freedom from retroactive criminal laws
- Freedom of conscience and religion
- Right to nationality
- Right to participate in government
- Right to judicial remedy
- Right to a name
- Rights of the family
- Rights of the child

Box 17
Legitimate restrictions
Reservations;
Derogation measures in cases of emergency;

Prohibition of human rights misuse;
Limitation clauses must:
- comply with domestic law;
- serve a legitimate purpose;
- be proportionate.

Box 18

order to protect the human rights of others. *Any interference, restriction or penalty must,*
however, be carried out in accordance with domestic law and must be necessary for achieving
the respective aims and national interests in a democratic society. States must in any case demonstrate the necessity of applying such limitations, and take only those measures
which are proportionate to the pursuance of the legitimate aims.

Derogation in a state of emergency

In times of war, rioting, natural disasters or other public emergencies (such as terrorist attacks)
that pose a serious threat to the life of a nation, Governments may take measures derogating
from their human rights obligations, provided the following conditions are met:
- A state of emergency must be declared;
- The specific measures derogating from an international treaty must be officially notified to the competent international organizations and other States parties;
- Derogation is permissible only to the extent strictly required by the situation;
- The derogation must be lifted as soon as the situation permits;
- The rights subject to derogation must not be among those that admit no derogation (see Box 17).

Reservations to international or regional human rights treaties

In certain cases, States issue statements upon signature, ratification, acceptance, approval
of, or accession to, a treaty. Such statements may be entitled "reservation", "declaration",
"understanding", "interpretative declaration" or "interpretative statement".
Article 19 of the 1969 Vienna Convention on the Law of Treaties specifies that a State may, when signing, ratifying, accepting, approving or acceding to a treaty, make a reservation,
unless:

Legitimate restrictions: examples of jurisprudence

It is the task of international human rights bodies to assess on a case-by-case basis whether a
particular form of interference serves a *legitimate purpose,* is based on a valid and foreseeable

domestic law, and is *proportional.* The European Court of Human Rights, for instance, has interpreted the relevant limitation clauses in ECHR in a way that on the one hand provides Governments with a fairly broad margin of appreciation, while on the other hand requiring them to show a *pressing social need* in order to justify restrictions. For instance, the Court did not accept the argument given by the Irish Government that the general prohibition of homosexuality under Irish criminal law was necessary in a democratic society for the protection of public morals, since in the absence of any comparable legislation in other European societies, there was no pressing social need for such a far-reaching restriction of the right to privacy.

Box 19

24

1. The reservation is prohibited by the treaty;
2. The treaty provides that only specified reservations, which do not include the reservation in question, may be made; or
3. In cases not falling under the above two categories, the reservation is incompatible with the object and purpose of the treaty.

Where a treaty is silent on reservations and a reservation is formulated and subsequently circulated, the States concerned have 12 months to object to the reservation, beginning on the date of the depositary notification or the date on which the State expressed its consent to be bound by the treaty, whichever is later (see article 20(5) of the Vienna Convention 1969).

A State may, unless the treaty stipulates otherwise, withdraw its reservation or objection to a reservation, either completely or partially, at any time.

Counter-terrorism measures and human rights

The *Digest of Jurisprudence of the United Nations and Regional Organizations on the Protection of Human Rights while Countering Terrorism*, published by the Office of the UN High Commissioner for Human Rights (OHCHR) in September 2003, presents a collection of excerpts from the jurisprudence of human rights bodies of the United Nations and other organizations (in particular, African, American and European regional organizations). The *Digest* shows that during counter-terrorism activities, some issues have been found to be of particular relevance to the question of the protection of human rights and fundamental freedoms. One such issue is the definition of terrorism. Although the term has not yet been authoritatively defined, States have agreed on some key elements of its definition.

On 9 December 1994, the United Nations General Assembly adopted the Declaration on Measures to Eliminate International Terrorism (A/RES/49/60). It states that terrorism includes *"criminal acts intended or calculated to provoke a state of terror in the general public, a group of persons or particular persons for political purposes"* and further holds that such acts *"are in any circumstances unjustifiable, whatever the considerations of a political, philosophical, ideological, racial, ethnic, religious or any other nature that may be invoked to justify them."*

The issue of terrorism and human rights has long been a matter of concern to the United Nations human rights programme, but dealing with it became more urgent after the attacks of 11 September 2001 and the worldwide surge in terrorist acts. At a special meeting of the Security Council's Counter-Terrorism Committee with international, regional, and subregional organizations on 6 March 2003, Secretary-General Kofi Annan stated:

"Our responses to terrorism, as well as our efforts to thwart it and prevent it, should uphold the human rights that terrorists aim to destroy. Respect for human rights, fundamental freedoms and the rule of law are essential tools in the effort to combat terrorism — not privileges to be sacrificed at a time of tension."

Some United Nations human rights bodies have expressed concern that counter-terrorism measures may infringe on human rights. For example, United Nations special rapporteurs and independent experts, at their tenth annual meeting, held in Geneva in June 2003, stated:

"Although they [special rapporteurs and independent experts] share in the unequivocal condemnation of terrorism, they voice profound concern at the multiplication of policies, legislation and practices increasingly being adopted by many countries in the name of the fight against terrorism, which affect negatively the enjoyment of virtually all human rights — civil, cultural, economic, political and social.

"They draw attention to the dangers inherent in the indiscriminate use of the term 'terrorism', and the resulting new categories of discrimination. [They] deplore the fact that, under the pretext of combating terrorism, human rights defenders are threatened and vulnerable groups are targeted and discriminated against on the basis of origin and socio-economic status, in particular migrants, refugees and asylum-seekers, indigenous peoples and people fighting for their land rights or against the negative effects of economic globalization

policies."

Under very specific conditions, terrorism may justify a state of emergency, in which some rights may be subject to derogation in accordance with CCPR and regional human rights instruments. Under the same provisions, however, certain human rights are not subject to suspension under any circumstances (see Box 17).

Under CCPR and regional human rights instruments, derogation from rights other than the above is permitted only in special circumstances; they must be exceptional, strictly limited in time and, to the extent required by the exigencies of the situation, subject to regular review, and consistent with other obligations under international law; and they must not entail discrimination. It is furthermore required that the State inform the Secretary-General of the United Nations or the relevant regional organization of the provisions from which it has derogated, and the grounds for the derogation.

Building on States' other obligations under international law, the Human Rights Committee has developed a list of elements that, in addition to the rights specified in article 4 of CCPR, cannot be subject to derogation. These elements include the following:

- All persons deprived of liberty must be treated with respect for their dignity; hostage-taking, abduction and unacknowledged detention are prohibited;
- Persons belonging to minorities are to be protected;
- Unlawful deportations or forcible transfers of population are prohibited; and
- "No declaration of a state of emergency ... may be invoked as justification for a State party to engage itself ... in propaganda for war, or in advocacy of national, racial or religious hatred that would constitute incitement to discrimination, hostility or violence".

Furthermore, as the right to a fair trial during armed conflict is explicitly guaranteed under international humanitarian law, the Human Rights Committee found that the principles of legality and the rule of law require that fundamental fair trial requirements be respected during a state of emergency. The Committee stressed that it is inherent in the protection of those rights that are explicitly recognized as not being subject to derogation that they be secured by procedural guarantees, including, often, judicial guarantees.

Under CCPR and the regional human rights instruments, the principles of necessity and proportionality apply when it is exceptionally permissible to limit some rights for specific, legitimate and well-defined purposes other than emergencies. The measures taken must be appropriate and must be the least intrusive possibility to achieve their objectives. The discretion given to authorities to act in that connection must not be unfettered. In all cases, the principle of non-discrimination must be respected and special efforts must be made to safeguard the rights of vulnerable groups. Counter-terrorism measures targeting specific ethnic or religious groups are contrary to human rights, and may kindle an upsurge in discrimination and racism.

CHAPTER 5:
UNITED NATIONS HUMAN RIGHTS TREATY-MONITORING BODIES

Compliance of States parties with their respective obligations under the seven United Nations core human rights treaties (see Chapter 3) is monitored by seven expert organs, which are known as treaty-monitoring bodies or treaty bodies.

- The Human Rights Committee (CCPR);
- The Committee on Economic, Social and Cultural Rights (CESCR);
- The Committee on the Elimination of Racial Discrimination (CERD);
- The Committee on the Elimination of Discrimination against Women (CEDAW);
- The Committee against Torture, and its Subcommittee on Prevention (CAT);
- The Committee on the Rights of the Child (CRC);
- The Committee on the Protection of the Rights of All Migrant Workers and Members of Their Families (CMW).

With the exception of the CESCR Committee, which was created by a resolution of the Economic and Social Council in 1985, the above bodies were established by their respective instruments, and were set up as soon as the respective treaties entered into force.

Membership and functioning

The Committees for the CCPR, CESCR, CERD and CRC have 18 members each, the CAT and CMW Committees 10, and the CEDAW Committee consists of 23 experts. Their members are elected by the States parties to the respective treaties (with the exception of the CESCR Committee, which is elected by the Economic and Social Council), with due regard for equitable geographic distribution. The CCPR and CRC Committees meet three times a year, the CMW Committee once and the other treaty bodies twice. With the exception of the CEDAW Committee, which is serviced by the United Nations Division for the Advancement of Women (UNDAW) of the Department of Economic and Social Affairs (DESA) of the United Nations at its New York Headquarters, all these treaty bodies are serviced by OHCHR in Geneva.

Reporting procedure
OBLIGATIONS OF STATES

The State reporting procedure is the only mandatory procedure common to all seven core human rights treaties. Governments have an obligation to submit to each treaty-monitoring

body an initial report, followed by periodic reports, and emergency or other reports requested by the treaty-monitoring body. Th e treaty bodies provide States with guidelines
aimed at assisting them in the preparation of the reports.
Generally speaking, the reports are expected to provide the following minimum information:
• All measures adopted by a State to give eff ect to the rights provided for in the treaty;
• Progress made in the enjoyment of those rights;
• Relevant empirical information, including statistical data;
• All problems and diffi culties aff ecting the domestic implementation of the treaty.
As a rule, State reports are drafted by the respective Governments. However, to ensure completeness and objectivity, the involvement in report preparation of other State institutions
(above all parliament), national human rights commissions and ombudsmen and relevant non-governmental organizations (NGOs) and civil society organizations (CSOs) is considered advisable.

EXAMINATION OF STATE REPORTS

Treaty bodies analyse State reports and discuss them in public sessions, in the presence of State representatives. Although the Committees aim at a constructive dialogue with Governments, State representatives may be confronted with highly critical questions and
remarks formulated by Committee members. At the end of the examination of each State
report, the treaty bodies adopt concluding observations and comments and recommendations
that are subsequently released at the end of the session and published in the bodies' annual reports. States are expected to implement those recommendations and to provide,
in their next reports, information on the measures taken to that end. Occasionally, the Committees request specifi c reports, particularly in emergency situations or other cases involving major human rights violations.

THE ROLE OF NGOS AND OTHER ORGANIZATIONS

International and domestic NGOs closely follow the examination of State reports and provide
the experts with relevant information, or even shadow reports. Th e CCPR, CESCR
and CRC Committees allow NGOs to play a relatively active role, and to take the fl oor in special meetings. United Nations specialized agencies, such as ILO and UNESCO, and other United Nations organs are invited to assist in monitoring treaty implementation. Th e United Nations Children's Fund (UNICEF), in particular, with its worldwide network of country offi ces, provides the CRC Committee with active and valuable assistance in the
ambitious task of monitoring compliance in 192 States parties.

GENERAL COMMENTS ISSUED BY TREATY MONITORING BODIES

Treaty bodies adopt and publish *general comments* or *general recommendations* concerning
the provisions and obligations contained in their respective treaties. These documents reflect the Committees' experience in the reporting procedure and constitute an authoritative
source of interpretation of human rights instruments.

Individual complaints procedure

The Optional Protocols to CCPR and CEDAW, and optional clauses in CERD, CAT and the Migrant Workers Convention provide for procedures for individual complaints (called
"communications"). A similar procedure is expected to figure in the optional protocol to the International Covenant on Economic, Social and Cultural Rights that is currently being
drafted in the United Nations Commission on Human Rights.

Under those provisions, which are accepted by an ever greater number of States parties (see Box 22), any individual subject to the jurisdiction of a State party who (a) claims to be a victim of a human rights violation and (b) has exhausted all domestically available possibilities of seeking effective remedy is entitled to file a complaint with the competent
treaty-monitoring body. The committees examine such complaints under a quasijudicial,
confidential procedure culminating in a final, non-binding decision (called "final views, suggestions or recommendations") that declares the complaint either inadmissible

Where to obtain information on the work of treaty-monitoring bodies

Detailed information on all treaty bodies and access to their general comments or recommendations
is provided at http://www.ohchr.org/english/bodies/index.htm. Considerable guidance is also offered at http://www.ohchr.org/english/contact.

OHCHR contact information:

Mailing address: OHCHR – Palais des Nations
8-14 avenue de la Paix
CH – 1211 Geneva 10
Switzerland
Tel.: +41 (22) 917 9000
Fax: +41 (22) 917 9008

Box 20

30

(if formal requirements are not met) or admissible, and — in the latter case — issues an opinion on the merits (determining whether the complainant's human rights have been violated).

Inter-State complaints procedure

CCPR, CERD, CAT and the Migrant Workers Convention provide for inter-State complaints

procedures, under which a State party is entitled to submit a complaint to the respective
committee, claiming that another State party is not fulfilling its treaty obligations. The procedure is based on the precept that under international law every State party has a legal interest in the fulfilment of the obligations of every other State party.

Complaints procedures

Example of the First Optional Protocol to CCPR
Communication from an individual claiming to be a victim of a violation of CCPR
Human Rights Committee
Admissibility procedure
- Recognition of the competence of the Committee by the States parties
(article 1 of the Optional Protocol);
- Exhaustion of domestic remedies
(article 2, 5 (2) (b) of the Optional Protocol);
- Non-anonymous and non-abusive character of the communication
(article 3 of the Optional Protocol);
- Compatibility (*ratione temporis, personae, loci, materiae*) with CCPR provisions
(article 3 of the Optional Protocol);
- Absence of a concurrent examination under another international procedure
(article 5 (2) (a) of the Optional Protocol)
- Substantiation of allegations (prima facie case, article 2 of the Optional Protocol)

Proceedings on the merits
Examination and deliberation (confidential)
Decision

Box 21

Inadmissible
State/individual
Individual State party

Acceptance of individual complaints procedures by States, and effectiveness of the procedures

Ratification of the First Optional Protocol to CCPR (104 States parties as of November 2004)

Algeria, Angola, Argentina, Armenia, Australia, Austria, Azerbaijan, Barbados, Belarus, Belgium, Benin, Bolivia, Bosnia and Herzegovina, Bulgaria, Burkina Faso, Cameroon, Canada,
Cape Verde, Central African Republic, Chad, Chile, Colombia, Congo, Costa Rica, Cote d'Ivoire,
Croatia, Cyprus, Czech Republic, Democratic Republic of the Congo, Denmark, Djibouti, Dominican Republic, Ecuador, El Salvador, Equatorial Guinea, Estonia, Finland, France, Gambia, Georgia, Germany, Ghana, Greece, Guatemala, Guinea, Guyana, Hungary, Iceland,
Ireland, Italy, Kyrgyzstan, Latvia, Lesotho, Libyan Arab Jamahiriya, Liechtenstein, Lithuania,

Luxembourg, Madagascar, Malawi, Mali, Malta, Mauritius, Mexico, Mongolia, Namibia, Nepal,
Netherlands, New Zealand, Nicaragua, Niger, Norway, Panama, Paraguay, Peru, Philippines,
Poland, Portugal, Republic of Korea, Romania, Russian Federation, Saint Vincent and the Grenadines, San Marino, Senegal, Serbia and Montenegro, Seychelles, Sierra Leone, Slovakia,
Slovenia, Somalia, South Africa, Spain, Sri Lanka, Suriname, Sweden, Tajikistan, the former
Yugoslav Republic of Macedonia, Togo, Turkmenistan, Uganda, Ukraine, Uruguay, Uzbekistan,
Venezuela and Zambia.

Ratifi cation of the Optional Protocol to CEDAW (68 States parties as of November 2004)

Albania, Andorra, Austria, Azerbaijan, Bangladesh, Belarus, Belgium, Belize, Bolivia, Bosnia
and Herzegovina, Brazil, Canada, Costa Rica, Croatia, Cyprus, Czech Republic, Denmark,
Dominican Republic, Ecuador, Finland, France, Gabon, Georgia, Germany, Greece, Guatemala,
Hungary, Iceland, Ireland, Italy, Kazakhstan, Kyrgyzstan, Lesotho, Libyan Arab Jamahiriya,
Liechtenstein, Lithuania, Luxembourg, Mali, Mexico, Mongolia, Namibia, Netherlands, New
Zealand, Niger, Norway, Panama, Paraguay, Peru, Philippines, Poland, Portugal, Romania,
Russian Federation, Senegal, Serbia and Montenegro, Slovakia, Slovenia, Solomon Islands,
Spain, Sri Lanka, Sweden, Th ailand, the former Yugoslav Republic of Macedonia, Timor-Leste,
Turkey, Ukraine, Uruguay and Venezuela.

Acceptance of individual complaints procedure under article 22 of CAT
(56 States parties as of November 2004)

Algeria, Argentina, Australia, Austria, Azerbaijan, Belgium, Bosnia and Herzegovina, Bulgaria,
Burundi, Cameroon, Canada, Chile, Costa Rica, Croatia, Cyprus, Czech Republic, Denmark,
Ecuador, Finland, France, Germany, Ghana, Greece, Guatemala, Hungary, Iceland, Ireland,
Italy, Liechtenstein, Luxembourg, Malta, Mexico, Monaco, Netherlands, New Zealand,
Norway, Paraguay, Peru, Poland, Portugal, Russian Federation, Senegal, Serbia and Montenegro,
Seychelles, Slovakia, Slovenia, South Africa, Spain, Sweden, Switzerland, Togo, Tunisia, Turkey,
Ukraine, Uruguay and Venezuela.

**Acceptance of individual complaints procedure under article 14 of CERD
(45 States parties as of November 2004)**
Algeria, Australia, Austria, Azerbaijan, Belgium, Brazil, Bulgaria, Chile, Costa Rica, Cyprus, Czech Republic, Denmark, Ecuador, Finland, France, Germany, Hungary, Iceland, Ireland, Italy, Liechtenstein, Luxembourg, Malta, Mexico, Monaco, Netherlands, Norway, Peru, Poland,

Box 22

In general comment No. 31 on the nature of the general legal obligation imposed on States parties to CCPR, the Human Rights Committee commends to States parties the view that violations of the rights guaranteed under CCPR by any State party deserve their
attention. It points out that "to draw attention to possible breaches of Covenant obligations
by other State parties and to call on them to comply with their Covenant obligations should, far from being regarded as an unfriendly act, be considered as a reflection of legitimate
community interest".

The committees are expected to examine the complaints in closed meetings and, if necessary,
to appoint an ad hoc conciliation commission to investigate and settle the matter between the States concerned. Although the inter-States complaint procedure before CERD is mandatory (which means that any of the 162 States parties is entitled to file a complaint alleging racial discrimination by any other State party), no inter-State complaint
has so far been brought before any United Nations treaty-monitoring bodies.

**Inquiry procedures under CAT and
the Optional Protocol to CEDAW**

CAT and the Optional Protocol to CEDAW provide for a procedure of *suo moto* inquiry by the respective treaty bodies (also known as "inquiry of its own motion"). This may be initiated if the committees receive reliable and plausible information to the effect that torture or discrimination against women, respectively, is being systematically practised in
the territory of a State party. A treaty body that launches such an inquiry may carry out a
fact-finding mission to the country concerned, subject to approval by its Government. All
proceedings are confidential, but the committees may include a summary account of the
Portugal, Republic of Korea, Romania, Russian Federation, Senegal, Serbia and Montenegro,
Slovakia, Slovenia, South Africa, Spain, Sweden, Switzerland, the former Yugoslav Republic of

Macedonia, Ukraine, Uruguay and Venezuela.

Effectiveness:
- Recourse to an individual complaints procedure has been most effective under the First Optional Protocol to CCPR: as of November 2004, after 27 years of existence, the Human Rights Committee (the body monitoring CCPR) had registered more than 1,300 cases and rendered decisions in about 480;
- In April 2004, the CAT Committee, established in 1987, had registered 242 cases and rendered decisions on more than 90. Most of the cases, however, did not involve direct allegations of torture in a State party, but rather violations of the principle of non-refoulement (or "non-repatriation", laid down in article 3 of the Convention) in relation to aliens' claims that expulsion or extradition by (most often European) States would expose them to torture in their countries of origin or destination;
- In March 2004, the CERD Committee, the oldest of the treaty bodies (established in 1970), had registered only 33 cases, and rendered decisions on 15.

33

results of their inquiries in their annual reports. The CAT Committee has so far conducted six inquiries (concerning Egypt, Mexico, Peru, Serbia and Montenegro, Sri Lanka, and Turkey). The CEDAW Committee has initiated an inquiry procedure concerning Mexico.

The system of regular visits to detention centres established under the Optional Protocol to CAT

The Optional Protocol to CAT of December 20028 provides for a system of regular visits to places of detention by an international body, the Subcommittee on Prevention of the Com-

A summary of procedures

**Treaty Date of Body Member- Members State Inter-State Individual *Suo moto*
adoption/ ship elected by reporting complaints complaints inquiry
Entry into
force**

CAT 12 December Committee 10 States Mandatory Optional Optional Mandatory
1984/ against parties article 19 article 21 article 22 (possibility
26 June 1987 Torture to opt out)
articles 20
and 28

Treaty	Date	Committee	Reporting	State reports	Inter-state complaints	Individual complaints
CCPR	16 December 1966/ 23 March 1976	Human Rights Committee	18 States parties	Mandatory article 40	Optional articles 41 and 42	First Optional Protocol
CEDAW	18 December 1979/ 3 September 1981	Committee on the Elimination of Discrimination against Women	23 States parties	Mandatory article 18	Optional Protocol articles 8 and 10 (possibility to opt out)	Optional Protocol
CERD	21 December 1965/ 4 January 1969	Committee on the Elimination of Racial Discrimination	18 States parties	Mandatory article 9	Mandatory articles 11, 12 and 13	Optional article 14
CESCR	16 December 1966/ 3 January 1976	Committee on Economic, Social and Cultural Rights	18 Economic and Social Council (1985)	Mandatory articles 16 and 17		Draft optional protocol
CMW	18 December 1989/ 1 July 2003	Committee on Migrant Workers	10 States parties	Mandatory article 73	Article 76 (not yet in force)	Article 77 (not yet in force)
CRC	20 November 1989/ 2 September 1990	Committee on the Rights of the Child	18 States parties	Mandatory article 44		

Box 23

8 By August 2005, the Optional Protocol had been ratified by 11 States; 20 ratifications are required for the Protocol to enter into force.

34

mittee against Torture, and by national bodies. The system is designed to prevent torture and other cruel, inhuman or degrading treatment or punishment. The international body and the national bodies formulate recommendations and issue them to the Government concerned. While the recommendations of the national bodies may be published in their annual reports, the recommendations and observations of the international Subcommittee may be made public only if a State party does not comply with its treaty obligations.

35

CHAPTER 6:
CHARTER-BASED SYSTEM OF HUMAN RIGHTS PROTECTION UNDER THE UNITED NATIONS

COMMISSION ON HUMAN RIGHTS

The United Nations Commission on Human Rights is the most important political organ of the United Nations in the area of human rights. It has developed gradually, and has over the years established various procedures to deal with important human rights issues and respond to the thousands of petitions that it receives regularly from NGOs and individuals with regard to alleged human rights violations.

The confidential "1503 procedure"

Under this confidential procedure (referred to as the "1503 procedure" because Economic and Social Council resolution 1503 (XLVIII) of 27 May 1970 forms its legal basis), every year, a special working group of the Sub-Commission on the Promotion and Protection of Human Rights studies thousands of individual petitions, seeking to determine whether any countries display "a consistent pattern of gross and reliably attested violations of human rights". Such "country situations" are forwarded to a pre-sessional working group and ultimately to the Commission meeting in plenary. In a private session, attended only by the representatives of the Member States, the Commission may then decide to conclude the examination, to keep the respective country under surveillance (possibly for a number of years), to carry out a full, confidential investigation with the assistance of a special rapporteur or an ad hoc committee, or, as a measure of last resort, if the situation has not improved and/or the respective Government has refused to cooperate, "to go public". "Going public" consists of pursuing the examination of the country situation under one of the special procedures described below.

The special procedures

Pursuant to Economic and Social Council resolution 1235 (XLII) of 6 June 1967, the United Nations Commission on Human Rights has established a number of special procedures to deal with allegations of human rights violations. These procedures consist in examining, reviewing and publicly reporting on either human rights situations in specific countries or territories (under country mandates) or alleged major human rights violations worldwide (under thematic mandates).

The United Nations Commission on Human Rights

The United Nations Commission on Human Rights is one of the Economic and Social Council's functional commissions. As a United Nations political body, the Commission comprises representatives of States Members, elected by the Economic and Social Council, whose number has increased over the years (it is currently 53). However, other States, various intergovernmental organizations and many NGOs participate in the meetings of the Commission as observers, and may take the floor and submit written observations. The annual session of the Commission is held at the Palais des Nations in Geneva in March and April, lasts six weeks and is in fact a major human rights conference attended by some 3,000 delegates, including many heads of State and Government, ministers, human rights defenders and journalists, who participate in public discussions on all crucial human rights issues. Since the 1990s, the Commission has also held emergency sessions concerning the human rights situations in the former Yugoslavia, Rwanda, East Timor and the occupied Palestinian territories. It has set up the Sub-Commission on the Promotion and Protection of Human Rights, which consists of 26 independent experts and functions as the Commission's think tank (see Chapter 6).

In recent years there has been increasing criticism of the Commission's capacity to perform its tasks. As United Nations Secretary-General Kofi Annan put it in his report on the reform of the United Nations,9 "States have sought membership of the Commission not to strengthen human rights but to protect themselves against criticism or to criticize others". He has therefore proposed to replace the Commission with a smaller permanent Human Rights Council, the members of which are to be elected directly by the General Assembly. The Council would function as a chamber of peer review and be mandated to evaluate all States' fulfilment of all their human rights obligations.

In 2005, the following States were members of the Commission: Argentina, Armenia, Australia, Bhutan, Brazil, Burkina Faso, Canada, China, Congo, Costa Rica, Cuba, Dominican Republic, Ecuador, Egypt, Eritrea, Ethiopia, Finland, France, Gabon, Germany, Guatemala, Guinea,

Honduras, Hungary, India, Indonesia, Ireland, Italy, Japan, Kenya, Malaysia, Mauritania, Mexico, Nepal, Netherlands, Nigeria, Pakistan, Paraguay, Peru, Qatar, Republic of Korea, Romania, Russian Federation, Saudi Arabia, South Africa, Sri Lanka, Sudan, Swaziland, Togo,
Ukraine, United Kingdom, United States of America and Zimbabwe.

Box 24

9 A/59/2005, page 45, paragraphs 182 and 183.

37

**Thematic monitoring mechanisms of
the United Nations Commission on Human Rights
(April 2005)**

Box 25

Th eme Since Mandate

Enforced or involuntary disappearances 1980 Working Group
Extrajudicial, summary or arbitrary executions 1982 Special Rapporteur
Torture 1985 Special Rapporteur
Freedom of religion or belief 1986 Special Rapporteur
Use of mercenaries 1987 Special Rapporteur
Sale of children, child prostitution
and child pornography 1990 Special Rapporteur
Arbitrary detention 1991 Working Group
Internally displaced persons 1992 Representative of the Secretary-General
Racism, racial discrimination, xenophobia
and related intolerance 1993 Special Rapporteur
Promotion and protection of the right to
freedom of opinion and expression 1993 Special Rapporteur
Missing persons in former Yugoslavia 1994-1997 Expert
Violence against women 1994 Special Rapporteur
Independence of judges and lawyers 1994 Special Rapporteur
Illicit movement and dumping of toxic and
dangerous products and wastes 1995 Special Rapporteur
Human rights and extreme poverty 1998 Independent Expert
Right to education 1998 Special Rapporteur
Human rights of migrants 1999 Special Rapporteur
Structural adjustment policies 2000 Independent Expert
Human rights defenders 2000 Special Representative of the Secretary-General
Right to housing 2000 Special Rapporteur
Right to food 2000 Special Rapporteur
Human rights and fundamental
freedoms of indigenous peoples 2001 Special Rapporteur
Legal questions related to disappearances 2001 Independent Expert
Right to health 2002 Special Rapporteur
Problems of racial discrimination
faced by people of African descent 2002 Working Group

Options regarding the elaboration
of an optional protocol to CESCR 2003 Open-ended Working Group
Impunity 2004 Independent Expert
Terrorism 2004 Independent Expert
Trafficking in persons 2004 Special Rapporteur
Human rights and international solidarity 2005 Independent Expert
Promotion and protection of human rights
while countering terrorism 2005 Special Rapporteur
Use of mercenaries as a means of violating
human rights and impeding the exercise of
the right of the people to self-determination
2005 Working Group
Human rights of migrants 2005 Special Rapporteur

38

These procedures may take the form of a mandate implemented by a special rapporteur,
representative of the United Nations Secretary-General, independent expert or working group. Special procedure tasks include making urgent appeals, conducting country visits and drawing up standards.

COUNTRY MANDATES

If the situation in a specific country is considered to indicate that there is a pattern of gross and systematic human rights violations, the Commission may adopt a resolution condemning the country concerned and/or may authorize a thorough investigation of the country situation by an expert. Country mandates are reviewed annually by the Commission.

THEMATIC MANDATES

A thematic special rapporteur, representative of the Secretary-General, expert or working
group may investigate the occurrence of violations of specific human rights in all countries,
and — subject to approval by the States concerned — may carry out on-site missions. Thematic mandates are reviewed by the Commission every three years.

**The Sub-Commission on the Promotion and
Protection of Human Rights**

The Sub-Commission on the Promotion and Protection of Human Rights, the Commission's
think tank, prepares studies, assists in drafting new standards and conducts investigations.
Every August, it convenes in Geneva for three weeks, and States, intergovernmental organizations and NGOs participate in its meetings as observers. Many of its tasks are assigned to individual experts, who are designated to serve as rapporteurs on specific
issues, or to working groups.
In addition to the Working Group on Communications, which plays a key role in the

confidential "1503 procedure", and the long-standing working groups on contemporary forms of slavery, indigenous peoples and minorities, which serve as forums for the discussion
of substantive issues among Governments, NGOs, victims and representatives of the groups concerned, new working groups have been set up on transnational corporations and the administration of justice.

CHAPTER 7:
THE OFFICE OF THE UNITED NATIONS HIGH COMMISSIONER FOR HUMAN RIGHTS

The Office of the United Nations High Commissioner for Human Rights (OHCHR), similar to the Office of the United Nations High Commissioner for Refugees (UNHCR), was established at the repeated request of leading NGOs, such as Amnesty International, and
some Governments. Consensus was reached on the establishment of this Office by the delegates of the 171 States participating in the World Conference on Human Rights (Vienna,
1993), and on 20 December 1993 the General Assembly adopted resolution 48/141, creating the post of the High Commissioner for Human Rights, with the rank of Under-Secretary-General, as the "United Nations official with principal responsibility for United
Nations human rights activities".

In the same resolution, the General Assembly listed the High Commissioner's specific responsibilities, which inter alia are:
- To promote and protect the effective enjoyment by all of all civil, cultural, economic, political and social rights, including the right to development;
- To provide advisory services, technical and financial assistance in the field of human rights to States that request them;
- To coordinate United Nations education and public information programmes in the field of human rights;
- To play an active role in removing the obstacles to the full realization of human rights and in preventing the continuation of human rights violations throughout the world;
- To engage in a dialogue with Governments in order to secure respect for human rights;
- To enhance international cooperation for the promotion and protection of human rights;
- To coordinate human rights promotion and protection activities throughout the United Nations system;
- To rationalize, adapt, strengthen and streamline the United Nations machinery in the field of human rights in order to improve its efficiency and effectiveness.

Accordingly, OHCHR's mission consists in protecting and promoting all human rights, for all. It aims to strengthen the United Nations human rights programme and provide

the United Nations treaty-monitoring bodies and special mechanisms established by the United Nations Commission on Human Rights with quality support. OHCHR cooperates with other United Nations bodies to integrate human rights standards into the work of the
United Nations system as a whole.

OHCHR engages in dialogue with Governments on human rights issues with a view to building national capacities in the area of human rights and enhancing respect for human
rights. It also provides advisory services and technical assistance when requested, and encourages Governments to pursue the development of effective national institutions and
procedures for the protection of human rights.

A number of OHCHR field presences have been established to ensure that international human rights standards are progressively implemented and realized at the country level, both in law and in practice. This goal too is pursued by building national human rights capacities and institutions. It is also addressed by following up on the recommendations of

Human rights in action: OHCHR in the field

Main field presences:
Bosnia and Herzegovina, Burundi, Cambodia, Colombia, Democratic Republic of the Congo,
and Serbia and Montenegro

Human rights components of United Nations peace missions:
Abkhazia/Georgia, Afghanistan, Central African Republic, Cote d'Ivoire, Democratic Republic
of the Congo, Ethiopia/Eritrea, Guinea-Bissau, Iraq (to be established), Liberia, Sierra Leone,
Tajikistan and Timor-Leste

Regional offices:
Addis Ababa, Ethiopia; Almaty, Kazakhstan; Bangkok, Thailand; Beirut, Lebanon; Pretoria,
South Africa; Santiago, Chile; Tashkent, Uzbekistan (to be established); and Yaounde, Cameroon

Technical cooperation:
Angola, Azerbaijan, Brazil, Ecuador, El Salvador, Guatemala, Mexico, Mongolia, Nepal, Nicaragua, Palestine, Philippines, Somalia, Sri Lanka and Sudan

Box 26

human rights treaty-monitoring bodies and the mechanisms of the United Nations Commission
on Human Rights, and by promoting a culture of human rights.

An essential condition for the success of field presences is that Governments, national institutions, NGOs and the United Nations country teams must be increasingly empowered to take on rights-related activities on their own, within the context of regional or subregional strategies.

United Nations High Commissioners for Human Rights

After a career in the diplomatic service of Ecuador, Jose Ayala-Lasso became the first United Nations High Commissioner for Human Rights in 1994. He was succeeded in 1997 by Mary Robinson, a former President of Ireland. She became responsible for the United Nations human rights programme at a time of structural reform: when she was appointed, her staff and the Centre for Human Rights were consolidated into a single Office of the High Commissioner for Human Rights (OHCHR). Under her leadership, the Office geared up to face existing and emerging human rights challenges more effectively and to harness the energies of new actors in the global quest for a universal culture of respect for fundamental rights and freedoms. On 12 September 2002, Sergio Vieira de Mello, after an impressive United Nations track record in tackling some of the world's most complicated humanitarian and peacekeeping challenges, became the third High Commissioner. In May 2003, he was asked by the Secretary-General to take a four-month leave of absence from OHCHR to serve as Special Representative of the Secretary-General in Iraq, where he was tragically killed on 19 August 2003. Until the appointment of a new High Commissioner, the Office was led by Acting High Commissioner Bertrand Ramcharan from Guyana. Since 1 July 2004, OHCHR has been headed by Louise Arbour, a former Justice of the Supreme Court of Canada and, from 1996 to 2000, Chief Prosecutor for the International Criminal Tribunals for the former Yugoslavia and for Rwanda. In her capacity as prosecutor, she indicted, among others, former Yugoslav and Serbian President Slobodan Milosevic for war crimes and crimes against humanity related to atrocities committed in Kosovo. The incrimination of Slobodan Milosevic was the first indictment of a serving head of State.

Box 27

CHAPTER 8:

INTEGRATING HUMAN RIGHTS INTO THE WORK OF THE UNITED NATIONS

Promoting human rights and fundamental freedoms is a key objective of the United Nations. To that end, the Organization has adopted the policy of "integrating human rights", namely, ensuring that human rights — as a cross-cutting theme — are taken into consideration by all organs of the United Nations system. Accordingly, in addition to the United Nations Commission on Human Rights, which remains the main human rights body, a steadily growing number of specialized agencies, programmes, funds and other United Nations bodies have been developing human rights promotion and protection activities.

The Vienna World Conference on Human Rights (1993), and subsequent resolutions of the General Assembly and the United Nations Commission on Human Rights called upon the United Nations to make available, at the request of the Governments concerned, certain
assistance programmes. These should address the reform of national legislation and the establishment and/or strengthening of national institutions and related structures to
uphold human rights, the rule of law and democracy, the provision of electoral assistance
and the promotion of human rights awareness through training, teaching and education,
popular participation and the involvement of a vibrant civil society.

The United Nations Secretary-General's reform programme, launched in 1997, called for the integration of human rights into the work of the United Nations system as a whole
and the development of practical tools to implement the Vienna blueprint. The result has
been progress in the human rights policies and activities of several United Nations agencies
and programmes.

The publication of the United Nations Secretary-General's 2001 report entitled *Strengthening of the United Nations: An agenda for further change* (A/57/387) represented
a further important development. In that second reform report, the Secretary-General reiterated that the promotion and protection of human rights constitutes "a bedrock
requirement for the realization of the Charter's vision of a just and peaceful world". The main goal consists in building the capacities of United Nations humanitarian and development
operations to enable them to support States Members' efforts to establish and strengthen national human rights promotion and protection systems, consistent with international human rights norms and principles. Paragraph 50 of the report reads as follows:

"In paragraphs 25 and 26 of the Millennium Declaration, Member States resolved to

strengthen their capacity at the country level to implement the principles and practices of
human rights, including minority rights, the rights of women, the rights of children and the rights of migrants. Building strong human rights institutions at the country level is what in the long run will ensure that human rights are protected and advanced in a sustained
manner. The emplacement or enhancement of a national protection system in each country, reflecting international human rights norms, should therefore be a principal objective
of the Organization. These activities are especially important in countries emerging from conflict."

Human rights in the General Assembly and its permanent programmes

The General Assembly, the highest United Nations law-making body, not only has ensured
the adoption of an impressive set of human rights conventions, declarations, principles, rules and other instruments, but also discusses at every session, particularly in its Third Committee, which is responsible for social, humanitarian and cultural affairs, the factual human rights situation in many States, and adopts corresponding resolutions.

Many of the Organization's programmes, funds and institutes, such as the United Nations
Development Programme (UNDP), the World Food Programme (WFP), the United Nations Children's Fund (UNICEF), the United Nations Human Settlements Programme (UN-HABITAT), the United Nations University (UNU), the Office of the United Nations High Commissioner for Refugees (UNHCR) and the Office of the United Nations High Commissioner for Human Rights (OHCHR - see Chapter 7) carry out important activities in the field of human rights.

Human rights and the Security Council

The Security Council, the sole United Nations body that is competent to adopt legally binding resolutions and enforce them when States Members fail to comply, has in recent
years assumed an increasingly active role in the area of human rights. Human rights today form an essential component of peacekeeping and peacebuilding operations, and many human rights experts are deployed in the field to monitor the human rights situations
in post-conflict contexts and assist the countries concerned in promoting the rule of law, in building an independent judiciary, in supporting law enforcement, in organizing
prison administration, and in setting up national human rights commissions and other institutions necessary for the protection of human rights. In addition, the Security Council, in an increasing number of cases, has considered gross and systematic human
rights violations as a threat to the peace and, consequently, acted under Chapter VII of the Charter of the United Nations by imposing economic and other sanctions,

authorizing military force and establishing ad hoc international criminal tribunals (see Chapter 10).

Human rights and the "United Nations family"

The United Nations system, informally referred to as the "United Nations family", consists
of the United Nations and a growing number of specialized agencies that are legally independent intergovernmental organizations maintaining a special relationship with the
Organization on the basis of agreements concluded with the Economic and Social Council
under Article 63 of the Charter of the United Nations. Accordingly, the United Nations policy of "human rights integration" applies also to the specialized agencies, many of which have a long history of activity related to specific human rights.

Key United Nations bodies active in the area of human rights

Specialized agencies

International Labour Organization (ILO)
Food and Agriculture Organization of the United Nations (FAO)
United Nations Educational, Scientific and Cultural Organization (UNESCO)
World Health Organization (WHO)

Programmes and funds

United Nations Children's Fund (UNICEF)
United Nations Development Programme (UNDP)
United Nations Development Fund for Women (UNIFEM)
United Nations Human Settlement Programme (UN-HABITAT)
United Nations Relief and Works Agency for Palestine Refugees in the Near East (UNRWA)
World Food Programme (WFP)

Research and training institutes

United Nations Institute for Training and Research (UNITAR)
United Nations International Research and Training Institute for the Advancement of Women (INSTRAW)
United Nations Research Institute for Social Development (UNRISD)

Bodies established by the Security Council

International Criminal Tribunal for the former Yugoslavia (ICTY)
International Criminal Tribunal for Rwanda (ICTR)

Other United Nations entities

Office of the United Nations High Commissioner for Human Rights (OHCHR)
Office of the United Nations High Commissioner for Refugees (UNHCR)
United Nations University (UNU)

Box 28

The **International Labour Organization** (ILO) is the main agency dealing with economic rights such as the rights to work, to equal and fair treatment and to healthy working

conditions, with trade union rights, including the right to strike and to engage in collective
bargaining, and with related provisions, such as the prohibition of forced labour, the worst
forms of child labour and discrimination in hiring and the workplace. ILO, established in
1919 and run on the basis of a "tripartite system" which places employers' and employees'
representatives on a more or less equal footing with Government representatives, has developed
many fundamental international treaties, recommendations and procedures for
the protection of economic and other human rights.

The **United Nations Educational, Scientific and Cultural Organization** (UNESCO)
is the main agency in the area of cultural rights (especially the right to education) and has
developed various instruments and procedures for their protection. It also played a key
role in the implementation of the United Nations Decade for Human Rights Education
(1995 to 2004) and the promotion of a universal culture of human rights and peace.

Technical assistance to States and parliaments

OHCHR technical assistance in the area of human rights

The United Nations Technical Cooperation Programme in the Field of Human Rights assists
States, at their request, in building and strengthening national structures that have a direct
impact on the observance of human rights in general and the maintenance of the rule of law.
Components of the programme focus on the incorporation of international human rights standards
in national laws and policies; building or strengthening national institutions capable of promoting
and protecting human rights, democracy and the rule of law; formulating national plans
of action for the promotion and protection of human rights; providing human rights education
and training; and promoting a human rights culture. Such assistance takes the form of expert
advisory services, training courses, workshops and seminars, fellowships, grants, the provision
of information and documentation, and the assessment of domestic human rights needs.

The United Nations regards technical cooperation as a complement to, but never a substitute
for, monitoring and investigation under the human rights programme. As emphasized in relevant
reports of the Secretary-General and resolutions of the United Nations Commission on

Human Rights, the provision of advisory services and technical assistance does not reduce a
Government's responsibility to account for the human rights situation in its territory, nor does
it exempt it from monitoring under the appropriate United Nations procedures.

IPU technical assistance

IPU provides advisory services on the entire spectrum of parliamentary life, in particular on
the role, structure and working methods of a national parliament. Its programme comprises
projects for training parliamentary staff, providing material resources and equipment and organizing
seminars on topics of specifi c interest to parliamentarians. Most of those projects address inter alia human rights and gender issues. In that connection, IPU cooperates closely
with UNDP and OHCHR. More information on IPU technical assistance can be obtained from
the IPU Secretariat.

Box 29

Th e **World Health Organization** (WHO) is the main agency for the promotion and protection of the right to health, and has developed, inter alia, a successful global programme
on HIV/AIDS.

Th e **Food and Agriculture Organization of the United Nations** (FAO) is the biggest of the specialized agencies, and is the major actor in the promotion and protection of the right to food, which is one of the most important elements in the global fi ght against
poverty. Th is major development goal was agreed upon by some 150 heads of State and
Government during the Millennium Summit, held in September 2000.

CHAPTER 9:
REGIONAL HUMAN RIGHTS TREATIES AND MONITORING

In addition to the United Nations charter-based system of human rights protection, which
applies to all States, and the United Nations treaty-based system, which applies only to States parties, many States in Africa, the Americas and Europe have also assumed binding
human rights obligations at the regional level and have accepted international monitoring.
No regional human rights treaty and monitoring mechanism has yet been adopted in the

Asian and Pacific region.
Africa
In 1981, the member States of the Organization of African Unity, which has since become
the African Union (AU), adopted the African Charter on Human and Peoples' Rights, which entered into force in October 1986. It is a general human rights treaty and has been ratified by all 53 States members of the African Union. As its title implies, this regional treaty, in addition to a number of civil, political, economic, social and cultural rights, also provides for collective rights of peoples to equality, self-determination, discretion
over their wealth and natural resources, development, national and international peace and security and "a general satisfactory environment". Although such solidarity rights of the so-called "third generation" of human rights are of considerable political importance, their legal significance in a binding treaty is disputed (see Chapter 2). In addition to the Charter, AU has adopted treaties in the areas of refugee protection and children's rights.

The Charter provides for a complaints procedure before the African Commission on Human and Peoples' Rights, headquartered in Banjul, Gambia. Since complaints (or "communications") may be submitted by any person (including States, which may file inter-State complaints, and any individual or collective entity, such as NGOs, families, clans, communities or other groups), the legal question of the status of the victim does

50

not arise. The African Commission does not hear isolated complaints, but only communications
suggesting the existence of a pattern of serious or massive violations of human and peoples' rights. In such cases, the African Commission may undertake an in-depth study only at the request of the Assembly of Heads of State and Government, the highest
political body of AU. In addition to this complaints procedure, the Commission also examines
State reports under a procedure similar to the one followed by the United Nations treaty bodies.
An Additional Protocol to the African Charter, adopted in 1998 and providing for the establishment of an African Court on Human and Peoples' Rights, entered into force on 25 January 2004.

Regional human rights treaties
Council of Europe
European Convention for the Protection of Human Rights and Fundamental Freedoms (1950-1953) and Additional Protocols
European Social Charter (1961-1965), Additional Protocols and
Revised European Social Charter (1996-1999)
European Convention on the Legal Status of Migrant Workers (1977-1983)
European Convention for the Prevention of Torture and Inhuman or Degrading Treatment or Punishment (1987-1989)

European Charter for Regional or Minority Languages (1992-1998)
Framework Convention for the Protection of National Minorities (1995-1998)
European Convention on the Exercise of Children's Rights (1996-2000)
Convention on Human Rights and Biomedicine (1997-1999)
European Convention on Nationality (1997-2000)

Organization of American States
American Convention on Human Rights (1969-1978) and Additional Protocols
Inter-American Convention to Prevent and Punish Torture (1985-1987)
Inter-American Convention on the Prevention, Punishment and Eradication of Violence against Women (1994-1995)
Inter-American Convention on the Forced Disappearance of Persons (1994-1996)
Inter-American Convention on International Traffic in Minors (1994-1997)
Inter-American Convention on the Elimination of All Forms of Discrimination against Persons with Disabilities (1999-2001)

African Union (formerly Organization of African Unity)
African Charter on Human and Peoples' Rights (1981-1986)
Convention Governing the Specific Aspects of Refugee Problems in Africa (1969-1974)
Convention on the Rights and Welfare of the African Child (1990-1999)

Box 30

The Americas

The inter-American system for the protection of human rights comprises two distinct processes, based on the one hand on the Charter of the Organization of American States (OAS), and on the other hand on the Pact of San Jose, Costa Rica (the American Convention
on Human Rights). While the charter-based process is applicable to all OAS member States, the American Convention on Human Rights is legally binding only on States parties.

The Convention, adopted in 1969 and in force since 1978, focuses on civil and political rights, but is supplemented with an Additional Protocol (1988-1999) addressing economic,
social and cultural rights. Furthermore, OAS has adopted special treaties on enforced disappearances,
torture, violence against women, international trafficking in minors and discrimination against persons with disabilities.

The Convention provides for an inter-State and an individual complaints procedure before
the Inter-American Commission on Human Rights (IACHR), a quasi-judicial monitoring body located in Washington, DC, and the Inter-American Court of Human Rights, located in San Jose (Costa Rica). Of the 35 States members of OAS, only 25 are parties to the
Convention. For the 10 States that have not ratified the Convention, only the weaker, charter-
based system before the Inter-American Commission applies; and even for the States

that are party to the Convention, the jurisdiction of the Inter-American Court is optional. The overwhelming majority of the thousands of complaints that are filed under this system are dealt with only by the Inter-American Commission, which either declares them
inadmissible, facilitates an amicable settlement or publishes its conclusions on the merits
of the cases in a report. Such reports contain non-binding recommendations that are in practice all too often ignored by the respective Governments. The applicants themselves
are not entitled to bring their cases before the Inter-American Court of Human Rights; only the States concerned and the Commission may do so. Although the Commission, in accordance with its recently revised rules of procedure, has begun to refer an increasing number of cases to the Court, only about 50 individual petitions have so far given rise to final and legally binding judgements of the Court. Those cases addressed human rights violations in certain South and Central American countries. In most of them, it was established
that gross and systematic human rights violations (including torture, arbitrary executions
and enforced disappearances) had taken place, and the Court granted far-reaching measures of reparation beyond monetary compensation to the victims and their families.
In addition to its "contentious jurisdiction" (competence to hear cases between contending
parties), the Court is also competent to render advisory opinions interpreting international
human rights treaties (especially the American Convention on Human Rights) and assessing the compatibility of domestic laws with these treaties.

Arab region

On 15 September 1994, the States members of the Arab League adopted the Arab Charter
on Human Rights, but none of the League's 22 member States signed it. In March 2003, 52
the Arab League Council decided to redraft the Charter in line with international human rights law and standards. A committee of experts, consisting of Arab members of the United Nations treaty-monitoring bodies, was formed on the basis of a memorandum of understanding signed by the League of Arab States and OHCHR in April 2002 to assist the
Arab League in that exercise. The draft proposed by the experts was subsequently taken
up by the Standing Committee on Human Rights of the Arab League in its redrafting exercise.
The draft was then presented for final discussion and adoption at a Summit of the League of Arab States in May 2004, where it was endorsed. A number of Arab States are in

the process of ratifying the Charter.

Although OHCHR has voiced concern about some of the provisions of the Charter in its current form, the new provisions are much more advanced than the previous version in respect of such issues as states of emergency, fair trial guarantees, slavery, sexual violence, disabilities and trafficking. As the Charter also provides for a monitoring mechanism similar to the UN Human Rights Committee, the instrument's adoption paves the way for the establishment of one more regional human rights protection and promotion mechanism.

However, this new system does not envisage any individual complaints procedure, but article 52 of the Charter provides for the possibility of adopting optional protocols.

Asia and the Pacific

There is no Asian and Pacific regional convention on human rights. Through OHCHR, however, the countries of the region have focused on strengthening regional cooperation to promote respect for human rights. In a series of Asian and Pacific regional workshops, notably a workshop held in Tehran in 1998, a framework of cooperation was established and a consensus was reached on principles and a "step-by-step", "building-block" approach that could lead to regional arrangements through extensive consultations among Governments.

It has been agreed that the regional arrangements must address the needs and priorities defined by the Governments of the region. Roles, functions, tasks, outcomes and achievements are to be determined by consensus.

Europe

The primary goal of the Council of Europe is the protection of human rights and fundamental freedoms. As soon as it was established in 1949, the Council began to draw up the European Convention for the Protection of Human Rights and Fundamental Freedoms, which was signed in 1950 and came into force in 1953. The European Convention and its Additional Protocols constitute a general human rights treaty focused on civil and political rights. Social, economic and cultural rights are enshrined in the European Social Charter (1961-65) and its Additional Protocols and revisions (the Revised European Social Charter, 1996-99). Furthermore, the Council of Europe has adopted special treaties in the areas of data protection, migrant workers, minorities, torture prevention and biomedicine.

Today, the European Convention provides for the most advanced system of human rights monitoring at the supranational level. Under article 34 of the European Convention, any person, NGO or group of individuals claiming to be a victim of a human rights violation, under the Convention and its protocols, committed by one of the currently 46 member States of the Council of Europe is entitled, once all domestically available possibilities of seeking remedy have been exhausted, to file a petition to the European Court of Human Rights, whose seat is in Strasbourg (France). If a violation is found, the Court may provide satisfaction to the injured party. Its decisions are final and legally binding on the States parties. Their implementation is monitored by the Committee of Ministers, the highest political body of the Council of Europe.

Under a Protocol to the European Social Charter that entered into force in 1998, some organizations may lodge complaints with the European Committee on Social Rights. Once a complaint has been declared admissible, a procedure is set in motion, leading to a decision on the merits by the Committee. The decision is transmitted to the parties concerned and the Committee of Ministers in a report, which is made public within four months. Lastly, the Committee of Ministers adopts a resolution, in which it may recommend that the State concerned take specific measures to ensure that the situation is brought into line with the Charter.

CHAPTER 10:
COMBATING IMPUNITY:
THE INTERNATIONAL CRIMINAL COURT (ICC)

An appalling series of the worst crimes known to humanity — war crimes, genocide, crimes against humanity, including systematic practices of torture, extrajudicial executions and enforced disappearances — were committed throughout the world in the twentieth century, during international wars, in regional conflicts and in times of peace. The vast majority of the perpetrators of such crimes — "that deeply shock the conscience of humanity" [10] — were not punished.

The first efforts to end such impunity followed in the aftermath of the Second World War, when the Allies set up at Nuremberg and Tokyo international military tribunals whose exclusive task was to bring major war criminals to justice. The tribunals therefore were strongly related to the application of international humanitarian law, the law of armed conflict. Since then, the focus has gradually shifted. Today international criminal law covers both war crimes (which can be committed only during armed conflict) and major "human rights crimes": genocide and crimes against humanity (which can be committed in peacetime as well as in war). Although the creation of an "international penal tribunal" was envisaged as early as 1948 under article 6 of the United Nations Convention on the Prevention and Punishment of the Crime of Genocide, the first such tribunal was established only in 1993, by means of a Security Council resolution adopted under Chapter VII of the Charter of the United Nations and relating exclusively to the former Yugoslavia.

The International Criminal Tribunal for the former Yugoslavia (ICTY) and the International Criminal Tribunal for Rwanda (ICTR)

Under Security Council resolution 827 (1993), the competence of the International Criminal Tribunal for the former Yugoslavia to prosecute crimes against humanity is restricted

10 *Rome Statute of the International Criminal Court* (ICC), preamble.

56

to acts committed during armed conflict. Security Council resolution 955 (1994) established the International Criminal Tribunal for Rwanda one year later and gave it competence to prosecute the main perpetrators of the Rwandan genocide and related crimes against humanity, without making any reference to armed conflict.

The International Criminal Court (ICC)

The competence of the International Criminal Court (ICC), like that of the International Criminal Tribunal for Rwanda, is not restricted to armed conflict. Established pursuant to the adoption of the Rome Statute of the International Criminal Court on 17 July 1998, ICC, in addition to war crimes, deals with genocide and a broad range of crimes against humanity, irrespective of the existence of an armed conflict. The Rome Statute builds upon the concept of State responsibility for human rights violations, by adding the individual responsibility of both State and non-State agents for such violations when they are gross and systematic. It can therefore be considered an important victory in the fight against impunity — a major reason such violations occur — and thus one of the most significant and innovative developments in the protection of human rights at the international level.

"Successive generations have for over a century progressively weaved an impressive fabric of legal and moral standards based on respect for the dignity of the individual. But the Court is the first and only permanent international body with the power to bring to justice individuals — whoever they are — responsible for the worst violations of human rights and international humanitarian law. We are finally acquiring the tools to translate fine-sounding words into action...."

Sergio Vieira de Mello,
former United Nations High Commissioner for Human Rights,

Statement on the occasion of the inauguration of ICC on 11 March 2003.

Rome Statute of the International Criminal Court (ICC):
- Adopted on 17 July 1998 by 120 votes to 7 (China, Iraq, Israel, Libyan Arab Jamahiriya, Qatar, United States of America, Yemen), with 21 abstentions
- Signed by 139 States
- Ratified by 99 States (as of June 2005)

Significant dates:
- Entry into force: 1 July 2002
- Election of the Court's 18 judges by the Assembly of States Parties: February 2003
- Election of the Court's Prosecutor, Luis Moreno Ocampo, by the Assembly of States Parties:
21 April 2003

Box 31

ICC concept and jurisdiction

Why was ICC created?
- To end impunity;
- To help end conflicts;
- To deter future perpetrators;
- To take over when national criminal justice bodies are unable or unwilling to act and to
make up for any shortcomings of ad hoc tribunals (such as those established for the former
Yugoslavia and Rwanda).

How is ICC's jurisdiction defined in the Rome Statute?
Article 5: Crimes within the jurisdiction of ICC are: genocide,[11] crimes against humanity[12]
and war crimes;
Article 25: Every (natural) person shall be responsible for a crime within the jurisdiction of
ICC, if he or she — as an individual, jointly or through another person — commits, orders or
solicits such a crime or induces, aids, abets or otherwise assists in its commission;
Article 11: ICC has jurisdiction only with respect to crimes committed after the entry into
force of the Statute (1 July 2002) on the territory of a State party or by nationals of a State
party anywhere in the world.

Who can refer cases to the court ?
- A State party (article 14);
- The United Nations Security Council (article 13 (b));
- The ICC Prosecutor, initiating on his/her own initiative investigations based on credible
information received from States, NGOs, victims, or any other source (article 15).

Relationship between ICC and other courts
ICC and national courts: National courts have jurisdiction in all relevant cases and, under the principle of "complementarity", ICC may act only when national courts are unable or unwilling to prosecute;
ICC and the International Court of Justice (ICJ): ICJ deals only with disputes between States,
not criminal acts committed by individuals;

Box 32
11 Genocide occurs when acts are "committed with intent to destroy, in whole or in part, a national, ethnical, racial or religious
group", *Rome Statute of the International Criminal Court*, article 6.
12 Crimes against humanity are crimes "committed as part of a widespread or systematic attack directed against any civilian
population". They include murder, extermination, enslavement, deportation, forcible transfer of population, imprisonment,
torture, rape, sexual slavery, enforced prostitution, forced pregnancy, enforced sterilization, other forms of sexual violence,
persecution against any identifiable group or category of people, enforced disappearance of persons, apartheid, and similar
inhuman acts intentionally causing suffering or serious injury to the body or to mental or physical health. Ibid., article 7.

➡

STATE OBLIGATIONS UNDER THE ROME STATUTE OF ICC
By ratifying the Statute, States assume the following three fundamental obligations, in whose fulfilment parliaments play a key role:13
1. *An obligation resulting from ICC's complementary nature*: Since ICC may act only when States are unable or unwilling to do so, they carry primary duty for bringing to justice those responsible for crimes under international law. States must therefore enact
and enforce national legislation ensuring that such crimes are also crimes under their national law - irrespective of where they were committed, who committed them or who are the victims.
2. *An obligation to cooperate fully*: Under article 86 of the Statute, States parties shall "cooperate fully with the Court in its investigation and prosecution of crimes within the *ICC and the ad hoc international tribunals (ICTY and ICTR):* Ad hoc tribunals are subject to
time and place limits ("selective justice"), while a permanent court such as ICC can operate
with greater consistency.

The agreement on the privileges and immunities of the Court
Under article 48 of the Rome Statute, the Court shall "enjoy in the territory of each State

Party such privileges and immunities as are necessary for the fulfilment of its purposes."

An agreement on ICC privileges and immunities concluded concurrently with the Statute's adoption provides for appropriate protection and assurances and, specifically, for the protection of the ICC staff, defence counsel, victims and witnesses during an investigation. Although by ratifying the Statute States parties are bound to respect ICC staff privileges and immunities and ICC documents, only 16 States had ratified the agreement as of 20 October 2004.

➡

Challenges for ICC

Failure to reach a consensus in Rome, and measures taken by the Government of the United States of America to conclude bilateral agreements with States parties exempting its nationals from the jurisdiction of ICC;

Presence of indicted criminals in the territory of States which have not ratified the ICC Statute or refuse to cooperate with ICC;

Narrow definition of crimes against humanity committed in peacetime;

Role of the Security Council;

Weakness in the principle of complementarity: How is ICC to determine that national courts are unwilling or unable to prosecute?

Box 33

13 Source: Amnesty International, *The International Criminal Court: Checklist for effective implementation* (AI Index: IOR 40/011/2000).

jurisdiction of the Court". States must therefore enable the Prosecutor and the defence to conduct effective investigations in their jurisdictions and ensure that their courts and other authorities cooperate fully in the areas of obtaining documents, conducting searches, locating and protecting witnesses and arresting and surrendering persons indicted by ICC. States should also cooperate with ICC on sentence enforcement and in developing and implementing public information initiatives and training programmes for officials on Statute implementation.

3. *An obligation to ratify the agreement on ICC privileges and immunities*, thus enabling ICC to function independently and unconditionally.

In a study on action taken by States parties to enact effective implementing legislation,14

Amnesty International identified the following most frequent inadequacies of draft national
legislation:
a. Weak definition of crimes;
b. Unsatisfactory principles of criminal responsibility and defence;
c. Failure to provide for universal jurisdiction to the full extent permitted by international
law;
d. Political control over the initiation of prosecution;
e. Failure to provide for the speediest and most efficient procedures of compensating victims;
f. Inclusion of provisions that prevent, or could potentially prevent, cooperation with ICC;
g. Failure to provide for persons condemned by ICC to serve their sentence in national prisons;
h. Failure to establish training programmes for national authorities on the effective implementation of the Rome Statute.

**The Set of Principles for the protection and promotion of
human rights through action to combat impunity**

Since 1991, the United Nations has accomplished considerable work on the issue of combating
impunity, mainly through the United Nations Commission on Human Rights and
the Sub-Commission on the Promotion and Protection of Human Rights. Amnesty laws,
which in the 1970s were invoked for the release of political prisoners and symbolized freedom,
were later used to ensure the impunity of perpetrators of human rights violations.
Aware of this problem, the Vienna World Conference on Human Rights (1993) supported,
in its Declaration and Programme of Action, the efforts of the Commission and the
Sub-Commission to examine all aspects of the issue. Accordingly, the Sub-Commission
14 AI Index: IOR 40/019/2004.

requested one of its members, Mr. Louis Joinet, to prepare a set of principles for the protection
and promotion of human rights through action to combat impunity. The expert
submitted his report and the set of principles to the Sub-Commission in 1997.15 Under
those principles, victims have the following rights:

• *The right to know*: This is not merely the right of any individual victim, or persons
closely related to a victim, to know what happened, i.e., a right to the truth. It is also a
collective right to draw on history in order to prevent the recurrence of violations. Its
corollary is a State's "duty to remember" (paragraph 17 of the report).

• *The right to justice*: This right implies that all victims shall have an opportunity to
assert their rights and receive a fair and effective remedy, ensuring that their oppressors

stand trial and that the victims can obtain reparations.
* *Th e right to reparation*: Th is right entails individual and general collective measures. Details are laid down in a document entitled *Basic principles and guidelines on the right to reparation for victims of gross violations of human rights and humanitarian law*, drawn
up by Mr. Th eo van Boven for the Sub-Commission in 1996, and further developed by Mr. M. Cherif Bassiouni in 2000 at the request of the United Nations Commission
on Human Rights.16 Th ese principles and guidelines are still pending before the Commission.

ICC at work: examples
In December 2003, the Government of Uganda referred the situation concerning the Lord's
Resistance Army, which operates in northern Uganda, to the Prosecutor of ICC. In July 2004,
the Prosecutor determined that there was a suffi cient basis to start an investigation into this
situation.
In March 2004, the Government of the Democratic Republic of the Congo referred to the Prosecutor
the situation of crimes within ICC's jurisdiction allegedly committed in the country since the entry into force of the Rome Statute. Based on this request and information referred to the
Court previously by NGOs, the Prosecutor decided in June 2004 to open an investigation into
this situation, which involves mass murder, summary executions and a pattern of rape, torture,
forced displacement and the illegal use of child soldiers.
In January 2005, the Government of the Central African Republic (CAR) referred to the Prosecutor
the situation of crimes committed anywhere on its territory since the entry into force of the Rome Statute.
On 31 March 2005, the UN Security Council referred to the Prosecutor the document archive
of the International Commission of Inquiry on Darfur. In addition, the Offi ce of the Prosecutor
requested information from a variety of sources, leading to the collection of thousands of documents.
After a thorough analysis, the Prosecutor concluded that the statutory requirements for initiating an investigation were satisfi ed.

Box 34
15 E/CN.4/Sub.2/1997/20/Rev.1.
16 E/CN.4/Sub.2/1996/17 and E/CN.4/2000/62, respectively.

Although the above set of principles has not yet been adopted by the United Nations

Commission on Human Rights and the General Assembly, a report drawn up in 2004 at the request of the United Nations Commission on Human Rights on best practices and recommendations to assist States in strengthening their domestic capacity to combat all aspects of impunity 17 shows that the principles in question have already had a profound
impact on eff orts to combat impunity and are used as a key reference by regional and international
supervisory bodies and by national authorities.
17 E/CN.4/2004/88.

CHAPTER 11:
THE ROLE OF PARLIAMENTARIANS
IN THE PROTECTION AND PROMOTION
OF HUMAN RIGHTS

Basic principles

When it comes to human rights promotion and protection, parliaments and members of parliament are essential actors: parliamentary activity as a whole — legislating, adopting the budget and overseeing the executive branch — covers the entire spectrum of political,
civil, economic, social and cultural rights and thus has an immediate impact on the enjoyment
of human rights by the people. As the State institution which represents the people and through which they participate in the management of public aff airs, parliament is indeed
a guardian of human rights. Parliament must be aware of this role at all times because the country's peace, social harmony and steady development largely depend on the extent
to which human rights permeate all parliamentary activity.
For parliaments to fulfi l eff ectively their role as guardians of human rights, specifi c criteria
must be met and safeguards established.

ENSURING THE REPRESENTATIVE NATURE OF PARLIAMENT

Parliament's authority derives to a large extent from its capacity to refl ect faithfully the diversity of all components of society. Th ese include, inter alia, men and women, various
political opinions, ethnic groups, and minorities. To achieve this, members of parliament must be chosen by the sovereign people in free and fair elections by universal, equal and
secret suff rage, in accordance with the principles set forth in article 21 of the Universal Declaration of Human Rights and article 25 of CCPR.

GUARANTEEING THE SOVEREIGNTY OF PARLIAMENT BY PROTECTING THE FREEDOM OF EXPRESSION OF ITS MEMBERS

Parliament can fulfil its role only if its members enjoy the freedom of expression necessary in order to be able to speak out on behalf of constituents. Members of parliament must be free to seek, receive and impart information and ideas without fear of reprisal. They are therefore generally granted a special status, intended to provide them with the requisite independence: they enjoy parliamentary privilege or parliamentary immunities.

Parliamentary immunities ensure the independence and dignity of the representatives of the nation by protecting them against any threat, intimidation or arbitrary measure directed against them by public officials or other citizens. They thus ensure the autonomy

Protecting parliamentarians' human rights:
the IPU Committee on the Human Rights of Parliamentarians

- If parliamentarians are to defend the human rights of the people they represent, they must themselves be able to exercise their human rights, most importantly the right to freedom of expression. Noting that this often is not the case, IPU in 1976 adopted a procedure for the examination and treatment of alleged violations of the human rights of parliamentarians.
- It entrusted a Committee on the Human Rights of Parliamentarians with the task of examining complaints concerning parliamentarians "who are or who have been subjected to arbitrary actions during the exercise of their mandate, whether parliament is sitting, [is] in recess or has been dissolved as the result of unconstitutional or extraordinary measures." The procedure applies to members of the national parliament of any country.
- The Committee is composed of five full members and five substitutes, each elected on an individual basis to represent a geopolitical region for five years. It holds four closed meetings per year.
- Once it has found that a complaint is admissible, the Committee examines the case in the light of national, regional and international human rights law. The procedure is mainly based on comparative verification of all information referred to the Committee by the authorities of the country concerned, particularly parliament, and the complainants. All evidence before the Committee is dealt with confidentially.

- The Committee also holds hearings with the parties and — subject to approval by the State
concerned and fulfilment of certain minimum conditions — may carry out on-the-spot missions.
- The Committee may bring a case to the attention of all IPU members in public reports. It
does so to enable parliaments and their members to take action in favour of the colleagues
concerned.
- The Committee pursues cases as long as it considers that their examination can help to
find solutions respectful of human rights. When this is no longer applicable, it may close a case and recommend that the IPU Governing Council pronounce a condemnation of the
authorities concerned.

Box 35

65

and independence of the institution of parliament. The scope of immunities varies. The minimum guarantee, which applies to all parliaments, is *non-accountability*. Under this guarantee, parliamentarians in the exercise of their functions may say what they please without the risk of sanctions, other than that of being disavowed by the electorate, which
may eventually not renew their mandates. In many countries, members of parliament also
enjoy *inviolability*: it is only with the consent of parliament that they may be arrested, detained and subjected to civil or criminal proceedings. Inviolability is not equivalent to impunity. It merely entitles parliament to verify that proceedings brought against its members
are legally founded.

"The protection of the rights of parliamentarians is the necessary prerequisite
to enable them to protect and promote human rights and fundamental freedoms in
their respective countries; in addition, the representative nature of a parliament
closely depends on the respect of the rights of the members of that parliament."
Inter-Parliamentary Council,
Resolution establishing the procedure for the examination and treatment of communications
concerning violations of the human rights of parliamentarians, Mexico City, April 1976.

UNDERSTANDING THE LEGAL FRAMEWORK, IN PARTICULAR PARLIAMENTARY PROCEDURE

It is essential that members of parliament be fully familiar with the constitution and the State's human rights obligations, the functioning of government and public administration
and, of course, parliamentary procedure. Certain parliaments, for instance the Parliament

of South Africa, organize seminars for newly elected parliamentarians to enable them to familiarize
themselves with the legal framework of their work and parliamentary procedure.
To fulfi l their functions, members of parliament must be provided with adequate resources.
Technical assistance can enhance the knowledge of parliamentarians in the area of human rights and help to overcome the inadequacy of available resources (see Part I, Box 29).

DETERMINING PARLIAMENT'S ROLE IN STATES OF EMERGENCY

When a state of emergency is declared, the fi rst victim is often the parliament: its powers
may be drastically reduced, or it may even be dissolved. To avoid such an eventuality, the
parliament should ensure that:

- States of emergency do not open the door to arbitrary measures;
- Th e parliament is responsible for declaring and lifting a state of emergency in accordance with international human rights principles, including the fact that specifi c human rights are not subject to derogation (see Chapter 4);
- Th e dissolution or even suspension of parliament in a state of emergency is prohibited by law;
- In states of emergency, parliament closely monitors the activities of the authorities — particularly law enforcement agencies — invested with special powers;
- States of emergency are defi ned in constitutions or in laws having constitutional status,
so that they are sheltered from opportunistic reforms.

Parliamentary action to promote and protect human rights

RATIFYING HUMAN RIGHTS TREATIES

Th e ratifi cation of human rights treaties is an important means of demonstrating to the international community and domestic public opinion a State's commitment to human rights. Ratifi cation — an expression of the State's resolve to implement the obligations laid
down in the treaty and to allow international scrutiny of its progress in human rights promotion
and protection — has far-reaching consequences for the ratifying State.
Human rights treaties are signed and ratifi ed by a representative of the executive, usually
the head of State or Government or the minister for foreign aff airs. Th e ultimate decision,
however, on whether or not a treaty should be ratifi ed rests in most countries with the parliament, which must approve ratifi cation. Ratifi cation renders the international human
rights norms guaranteed in a treaty legally eff ective in the ratifying country and obliges it

to report to the international community on measures adopted to align its legislation with
treaty norms.

Involvement of parliament in the negotiation and drafting of treaties

Members of national parliaments are generally not directly involved in drafting international
or regional treaties or in the related political decision-making processes. Only the Parliamentary
Assembly of the Council of Europe, a regional parliamentary assembly established in 1949,
plays an increasingly important role in human rights monitoring and in the drafting of new
instruments. Its Committee on Legal Affairs and Human Rights cooperates closely with the
Committee of Ministers (consisting of the ministers for foreign affairs of the Council's member
States, which currently number 46) and the Steering Committee for Human Rights when new
instruments are drawn up or major human rights problems emerge. For instance, the Committee
of Ministers has invited the Parliamentary Assembly to assist it in addressing the problem
posed by the steadily increasing number of applications referred to the European Court of Human
Rights.

IPU has consistently called for greater involvement of members of parliament in negotiating international
human rights instruments, insisting that parliament, since it must eventually enact relevant legislation and ensure its implementation, should intervene long before the ratification
stage and participate, along with Government representatives, in the drafting of new instruments
within international deliberative bodies.

Box 36

What you can do as a parliamentarian

❑ Check whether your Government has ratified (at least) the seven core treaties (see Part I,
Chapters 3 and 5) and the existing regional treaties on human rights.

❑ If not, ascertain whether the Government has the intention of signing those instruments.
If not, use parliamentary procedure to determine the reasons for such inaction and to encourage the Government to start the signing and ratification process without delay.

❑ If a signing procedure is under way, check whether the Government intends to make reservations to the treaty and, if so, determine whether the reservations are necessary and compatible with the content and purpose of the treaty (see Chapter 4). If you conclude
that they are groundless, take action to ensure that the Government reverses its position.

❑ Check whether any reservations made by your country to treaties already in force are still
necessary. If you conclude that they are not, take action for their withdrawal.

❑ Check whether your Government has made the necessary declarations or ratified the
relevant Optional Protocols (see Part I, Chapter 5) with a view to:

(a) Recognizing the competence of treaty bodies to receive individual complaints (under
CCPR, CEDAW, CERD, CAT and the Migrant Workers Convention);

(b) Recognizing the competence of treaty-monitoring bodies (CAT and CEDAW) to institute
an inquiry procedure;

(c) Ratifying the Optional Protocol to CAT (the Optional Protocol provides for a system of
regular visits to detention centres).

❑ If not, take action to ensure that the declarations are made or the Optional Protocols are
ratified.

❑ Make sure that public officials, State agents and the general public are aware of ratified
human rights treaties and their provisions.

❑ If your country has not yet signed and ratified the ICC Statute, take action to ensure that
it does, and that it abstains from any agreements reducing the force of the Statute and undermining the Court's authority.

Parliamentary action to preserve the integrity of the ICC Statute

Reacting to the proposal put forward by the Government of the United States of America to
conclude bilateral agreements exempting United States nationals from ICC jurisdiction, many
parliaments (for instance, the parliaments of Uruguay and Switzerland) have addressed messages
to their Governments urging them to reject that proposal and to abstain from concluding
any agreement implying a deviation from the Statute. Others have refused to ratify such bilateral

agreements.

Box 37

The Inter-Parliamentary Council "calls on all Parliaments and their members to take action at the national level to ensure that international and regional human rights treaties are ratified or acceded to promptly by their countries, in case they have not already done so, and that reservations are withdrawn whenever they conflict with the object and purpose of the treaty"
Resolution adopted on the occasion of the 50th anniversary of the Universal Declaration of Human Rights,
Cairo, September 1997, paragraph 3 (i).

ENSURING NATIONAL IMPLEMENTATION

Adopting the budget

Guaranteeing enjoyment of human rights by all is not costless. Effective measures for human
rights protection and, especially, for preventing human rights violations require considerable
funds. In approving the national budget, thereby setting national priorities, the parliament must ensure that sufficient funds are provided for human rights implementation.
Then, in monitoring Government spending, the parliament can, if necessary, hold the Government accountable for inadequate performance in the area of human rights.

Overseeing the executive branch

Through their oversight function, subjecting the policies and acts of the executive to constant
scrutiny, parliaments and members of parliament can and must ensure that laws are actually implemented by the administration and any other bodies concerned. Under parliamentary procedure, the means available to members of parliament for scrutinizing Government action include:

- Written and oral questions to ministers, civil servants and other executive officials;
- Interpellations;
- Fact-finding or investigation committees or commissions;
- Votes of no confidence, if the above attempts fail.

Following up on recommendations and decisions

Recommendations formulated by United Nations treaty-monitoring bodies and special rapporteurs and by other international or regional monitoring bodies (see Part I, Chapters
5, 6 and 9) can be effectively used by members of parliament to scrutinize the compliance
of executive action with the human rights obligations of the State.

The 100th Inter-Parliamentary Conference "calls on Parliaments to work actively to ensure ... that national Governments fulfil their reporting responsibilities towards the human rights treaty bodies in a timely and effective way and that the

competent government agencies cooperate fully with the United Nations Special
Rapporteurs so that they receive the necessary support to carry out their work
effectively."
Resolution on "Strong action by national parliaments in the year of the 50th anniversary
of the Universal Declaration of Human Rights to ensure the promotion and
protection of all human rights in the 21st century", Moscow, September 1998, paragraph
4 (ii).

Establishing parliamentary human rights bodies

Human rights should thoroughly permeate parliamentary activity. Within its area of competence,
each parliamentary committee should consistently take into consideration human
rights and assess the impact of bills and other proposed legal norms on the enjoyment
of human rights by the population. To ensure that human rights are duly taken into account
in parliamentary work, ever more parliaments set up specialized human rights bodies
or entrust existing committees with the task of considering human rights issues. Many
parliaments have also established committees for specific human rights issues, such as
gender equality or minority rights. Moreover, informal groups of members of parliament
are active in the area of human rights.

Parliamentary human rights bodies are assigned various tasks, including — almost
always — assessing the conformity of bills or legislation with human rights obligations. In
some cases such bodies are competent to receive individual petitions.

Adopting enabling legislation

If international legal obligations are not implemented at the domestic level, the respective
treaties become dead letters. Parliaments and parliamentarians have a key role to play

Implementing recommendations of a regional treaty body: An example

Parliaments, particularly their human rights committees, can be instrumental in ensuring the
implementation of decisions or recommendations of international or regional human rights
bodies. For instance, the Human Rights Committee of the House of Representatives of Brazil
played a decisive role in the implementation of the first decision of the Inter-American Commission
on Human Rights in a case against Brazil: the case of Joao Canuto, Chairman of the
Rural Labour Union of Rio Maria, State of Para, who was assassinated in 1985. In 1998, the
Commission concluded that the State of Brazil had violated the American Convention on Human
Rights by failing to provide Mr. Canuto with due protection when he reported that he had

received death threats, and by failing to conduct an effective investigation and initiate judicial
proceedings in relation to his assassination. It recommended that Brazil should streamline
criminal procedures and pay the victim's family compensation for physical and moral loss. In
1999, the Human Rights Committee of the House of Representatives organized a national campaign
to make the authorities aware of the decision and the importance of implementing it. The
decision was implemented soon thereafter.

Box 38

What you can do as a parliamentarian

Parliaments should regularly follow and contribute to the work of treaty-monitoring bodies.
Accordingly, you may wish to:

❏ Verify the status of cooperation between your State, the United Nations treaty bodies
and other international or regional monitoring mechanisms (see Part I, Chapters 5, 6 and
9) by requesting information from your Government. You may wish to put a question to your Government on this subject;

❏ Ensure that the parliament is kept abreast of the work of the treaty bodies and related
mechanisms, and that relevant information is regularly made available to it by the parliamentary
support services;

❏ Follow up on the recommendations, concluding observations and other comments formulated
by treaty bodies regarding your country;

❏ Study the recommendations formulated by United Nations special rapporteurs, particularly
those addressing the situation in your country, if applicable;

❏ Check whether any action has been taken to implement these recommendations and, if not,
use parliamentary procedure to determine the reasons and to initiate follow-up action;

❏ Make sure that special rapporteurs conducting on-site missions visit your parliament or
the competent parliamentary committees, and that the parliament receives a copy of their reports;

❏ Make sure that standing invitations to visit your country are extended to special rapporteurs;

❏ Use your powers to carry out on-the-spot visits to schools, hospitals, prisons and other
places of detention, police stations and private companies to personally ascertain whether human rights are respected.

To monitor your State's compliance with its obligations under human rights treaties, you may wish to ensure that:

❏ The required national reports are submitted regularly, by enquiring after your country's
reporting timetable and ensuring that the Government respects it. When reporting is delayed, you may request an explanation and, if necessary, use parliamentary procedure
to urge the Government to comply with its obligation;

❏ Complete reports are submitted.

To that end, make sure that:

❏ The parliament (through the competent committees) is involved in the preparation of
the State report, provides input in terms of information, ensures that its action is properly
included in the report and in any case is informed of its contents;

❏ The report complies with guidelines on reporting procedures (see Part I, Chapter 5) and
takes account of the treaty bodies' general recommendations and concluding observations
on preceding reports, with reference to any related lessons learned;

❏ A member of your parliament is present when the report is presented to the relevant treaty
body. If this is not possible, recommend that your country's permanent mission to the United
Nations (either in New York or Geneva, depending on where the treaty body meets) follow
the work of the treaty body and ensure that its report is forwarded to your parliament.

71

when it comes to adopting the necessary implementing legislation in any area (civil, criminal,
administrative or labour law, education, health care or social security law).

Th e procedure for translating international treaties into national law is generally laid down in a State's constitution, which determines the extent to which individuals may

Ideal competence of a parliamentary human rights committee

To be fully eff ective, a parliamentary human rights body should:

• Have a comprehensive human rights mandate, encompassing legislative and oversight functions;

• Be competent to deal with any human rights issue it deems important, take legislative and

other initiatives in the area of human rights and address human rights problems and concerns
referred to it by third parties;
• Be competent to advise other parliamentary bodies on human rights issues;
• Have the power to send for persons and documents and to carry out on-site missions.

Box 39
What you can do as a parliamentarian
You may:
❏ Ensure that international human rights provisions are incorporated into national law and,
if possible, given constitutional status so that they enjoy maximum protection under national
law;
❏ Ensure that bills brought before your parliament and the parliamentary committees on
which you sit are consistent with the human rights obligations of your country, and review
existing legislation to determine whether it is compatible with those obligations;
❏ To this end, familiarize yourself with the work of the treaty bodies, the recommendations
formulated by them and other international or regional monitoring mechanisms (see Part I, Chapters 5, 6 and 9), and with the work of national or international human rights NGOs and national human rights institutions. If you find lack of conformity, take action to redress the situation by ensuring that amendments or new bills are drafted or that a petition is filed with the constitutional court or a similar judicial body in your country;
❏ Ensure that Government decrees issued under existing legislation do not run counter to the spirit of the laws and the human rights guarantees that they are intended to provide;
❏ Ensure that public officials, particularly law enforcement agencies, are aware of their duties
under human rights law and receive appropriate training;
❏ In view of the importance of public awareness of human rights, ensure that human rights
education is part of the curricula in your country's schools;
❏ Ensure that human rights obligations under constitutional and international law are implemented
openly, constructively, innovatively and proactively.

directly invoke treaty provisions before national courts. There are basically two types of approaches:
(a) The system of automatic incorporation, under which treaties upon ratification or accession become part of domestic law and may therefore be invoked by individuals. In some cases, publication of the treaties in the official gazette or enactment of national

implementing legislation is required before the treaties have the force of national law and individuals are able to invoke their provisions before domestic courts;

(b) The dualistic system, under which treaties become part of the national legal system only through actual enactment. Under this system, an individual may not invoke treaty provisions that are not part of national legislation. They do not prevail over contrary domestic law.

In civil law countries, it is essential that human rights be enshrined in the constitution, as that instrument sets the norms and serves as the framework for all other national legislation,
which must be in conformity with its spirit and principles.

The Inter-Parliamentary Council "calls on all Parliaments and their members
to take action at the national level to ensure that enabling legislation is enacted
and that the provisions of national laws and regulations are harmonized with the
norms and standards contained in these (international) instruments with a view to
their full implementation."
Resolution adopted on the occasion of the 50th anniversary of
the Universal Declaration of Human Rights,
Cairo, September 1997, paragraph 3 (ii).

Parliamentary action to promote the justiciability of economic,
social and cultural rights

In many States, individuals may not claim their economic, social and cultural rights before a
court of law. Parliaments can remedy that situation by enacting domestic laws enabling courts
to rule on individual complaints regarding such rights. In practice, this may not require major
reforms. For instance, most countries have labour courts competent to hear cases of arbitrary
dismissal, discriminatory recruitment practices or unsafe working conditions. In that context,
the main difference is that very few laws refer explicitly to the rights to work and to just and
favourable working conditions as laid down in articles 6 and 7 of CESCR, and few judges realize
that they are in fact implementing and enforcing those fundamental economic rights. Similarly,
since most States implement laws ensuring free and compulsory primary education, parents
whose children are denied access to schools on arbitrary or discriminatory grounds ought to
have recourse to domestic administrative and judicial bodies. It should not be difficult to relate
such claims and remedies to the human right to education, thereby ensuring the justiciability

of that right.

Box 40

The legislative process and international human rights standards: an example

The legislative process in Finland — in particular the work of the parliamentary Constitutional Law Committee — exemplifies frequent use of international standards (including the output of treaty bodies) in drafting and scrutinizing legislative proposals. The framework for such use is laid down in section 22 of the Constitution (2000), which stipulates that "the public authorities shall guarantee the observance of basic rights and liberties and (international) human rights", and section 74, which provides that "the Constitutional Law Committee shall issue statements on the constitutionality of legislative proposals and other matters brought for its consideration, as well as on their relation to international human rights treaties". The mandate of the Constitutional Law Committee is to review the consistency of proposed bills with the Constitution and human rights standards, and to address relevant opinions to the parliament and other institutions. The Committee relies heavily on external academic expertise. The types of treaty body output — particularly the output of the Human Rights Committee — which are used extensively in the Finnish legislative process include primarily decisions on individual cases and general comments, but also concluding observations, reporting guidelines and other material. The country-specific material includes references not only to Finland, but to other countries as well. In some cases the reference to the treaty body source results directly from an international or constitutional legal obligation to comply. This may be done in response to a specific finding by a treaty body that a violation has occurred, or it may result from the general constitutional requirement to ensure compliance with human rights provisions.[18]

[18] International Law Association (ILA), *Final report of the Committee on International Human Rights Law and Practice of the International Law Association on the impact of UN human rights treaty bodies findings on the work of national courts and tribunals*, 71st Biennial ILA Conference, Berlin, August 2004, pp.36-38.

Box 41
The Paris Principles
In 1993, the United Nations General Assembly adopted a set of principles applicable to the
establishment of national human rights institutions (see next page). Known as the "Paris Principles",
these have become the internationally accepted benchmark setting out core minimum standards for the role and functioning of such institutions. According to these principles, national
human rights institutions must:
- Be independent, and their independence must be guaranteed either by statutory law or
constitutional provisions;
- Be pluralistic in their roles and memberships;
- Have as broad a mandate as possible;
- Have adequate powers of investigation;
- Be characterized by regular and eff ective functioning;
- Be adequately funded;
- Be accessible to the general public.

Box 42

CREATING AND SUPPORTING AN INSTITUTIONAL INFRASTRUCTURE
National human rights institutions (NHRIs)
Over the past 20 years, there has been growing awareness of the need to strengthen, at the national level, concerted action aimed at implementing and ensuring compliance with
human rights standards. One of the means used to that end has been the establishment of national human rights institutions (NHRIs). While the term covers a range of bodies whose legal status, composition, structure, functions and mandates vary, all such bodies are set up by Governments to operate independently — like the judiciary — with a view to
promoting and protecting human rights.
NHRIs, often called human rights commissions, should have the capacity and authority to:
- Submit recommendations, proposals and reports to the Government or parliament on any matter relating to human rights;
- Promote the conformity of national laws and practices with international standards;
- Receive and act upon individual or group complaints of human rights violations;
- Encourage the ratifi cation and implementation of international human rights standards
and contribute to reporting procedures under international human rights treaties;

Countries that have established national human rights institutions
Countries with national institutions accredited by the International Coordinating Committee of National Institutions for the Promotion and Protection of Human Rights:

Asia and the Pacific: Australia, Fiji, India, Indonesia, Malaysia, Mongolia, Nepal, New Zealand, Philippines, Republic of Korea, Sri Lanka, Thailand
Africa: Algeria, Cameroon, Ghana, Malawi, Mauritius, Morocco, Niger, Nigeria, Rwanda, Senegal, South Africa, Togo, Uganda
Americas: Argentina, Bolivia, Canada, Colombia, Costa Rica, Ecuador, Guatemala, Honduras, Mexico, Panama, Paraguay, Peru, Venezuela
Europe: Albania, Bosnia and Herzegovina, Denmark, France, Germany, Greece, Ireland, Luxembourg, Poland, Portugal, Spain, Sweden

Others:

Asia and the Pacific: Hong Kong Special Administrative Region of China, Islamic Republic of Iran
Africa: Benin, Burkina Faso, Chad, Madagascar, Namibia, United Republic of Tanzania, Zambia
Americas: Antigua and Barbuda, Barbados
Europe: Austria, Belgium, Netherlands, Norway, Russian Federation, Slovakia, Slovenia and United Kingdom

Box 43

75

• Promote awareness of human rights through information and education, and carry out research in the area of human rights;
• Cooperate with the United Nations, regional institutions, national institutions of other countries and NGOs.

Relations between NHRIs and parliaments have great potential for human rights protection
and promotion at the national level. They were discussed at an international workshop entitled *National Human Rights Institutions and Legislatures: Building an Effective Relationship*,
which was held in Abuja, Nigeria, from 22 to 25 March 2004 .19
A set of guidelines for strengthening cooperation between NHRIs and parliaments, known as the Abuja Guidelines, was drawn up during the above workshop.

Recommendations for parliamentarians from the Abuja Guidelines

• Parliaments should produce an appropriate legislative framework for the establishment of
NHRIs in accordance with the Paris Principles.
• Parliaments and NHRIs should evolve an effective working relationship to better promote
and protect human rights.
• Parliaments should ensure that adequate resources and facilities are provided to NHRIs
to enable them to perform their functions effectively. Parliaments should also ensure that
resources are in fact made available to the NHRIs.
• NHRIs' annual reports and other reports should be debated — and the Government's response

presented — in parliament promptly.
- An all-party parliamentary committee should have specific responsibility for overseeing
and supporting the work of NHRIs. In smaller States, this function might be undertaken by an existing parliamentary standing committee.
- Members of NHRIs should be invited to appear regularly before the appropriate parliamentary
committees to discuss the bodies' annual reports and other reports.
- Parliamentarians should invite members of NHRIs to meet regularly with them to discuss
matters of mutual interest.
- Parliamentarians should ensure that sufficient time is given to the consideration of the
work of NHRIs.
- Parliamentarians should ensure that their constituents are made aware of the work of NHRIs.
- Parliamentarians should scrutinize carefully any Government proposals that might adversely
affect the work of NHRIs, and seek the views of NHRI members on such proposals.
- Parliamentarians should ensure that NHRI recommendations for action are followed up
and implemented.

Box 44
19 The workshop was organized by the National Human Rights Commission of Nigeria, the Committee on Human Rights of the
Nigerian House of Representatives, the Legal Resources Consortium of Nigeria and the British Council, and was supported by
the United Kingdom's Foreign and Commonwealth Office.

Ombudsman's office

The ombudsman's office is a national institution found in many countries. There is some
overlap between the activities of an ombudsman's office and those of a national human rights commission, but the ombudsman's role is usually somewhat more restricted, consisting
generally speaking in ensuring fairness and legality in public administration. Ombudsmen
generally report to parliament. Only an ombudsman with a specific human rights mandate can be properly described as a national human rights institution.

National human rights action plans

No State in the world has a perfect human rights record. Moreover, since every country must develop its human rights policy in the light of its specific political, cultural, historical
and legal circumstances, there is no single approach for countries to tackle human

rights problems. Accordingly, the Vienna World Conference on Human Rights, held in 1993, encouraged States to draw up national human rights action plans to develop a human rights strategy suited to their own situations. The adoption of national action plans should be a truly national endeavour, free from partisan political considerations. A national action plan must be supported by the Government and involve all sectors of society, because its success largely depends on the extent to which the population takes ownership of it.

The main function of such a plan is to improve the promotion and protection of human rights. To that end, human rights improvements are expressed as tangible objectives of public policy, which are to be attained through the implementation of specific programmes, the participation of all relevant sectors of Government and society, and the
allocation of sufficient resources. The plan should be based on a solid assessment of a country's human rights needs. It should provide guidance to Government officials, NGOs,
professional groups, educators and advocates and other civil society members on human
rights promotion and protection tasks. It should also promote the ratification of human rights instruments and awareness of human rights standards, with particular regard for the human rights situation of vulnerable groups. Detailed information on national human
rights action plans and how to develop them can be found in OHCHR's *Handbook on National Human Rights Plans of Action,* Professional Training Series No. 10, which is

A national action plan requires considerable organizational effort. Some of the factors that have a direct positive impact on its effectiveness are:
• Steady political support;
• Transparent and participatory planning;
• Comprehensive assessment of the human rights situation;
• Realistic prioritization of problems to be solved, and action-oriented approach;
• Clear performance criteria and strong participatory mechanisms for monitoring and evaluation;
• Adequate commitment of resources.

MOBILIZING PUBLIC OPINION

Parliaments can contribute enormously to raising public awareness of human rights and mobilizing public opinion on related issues — all the more so since political debate often focuses on such questions as discrimination against various groups, gender equality, minority rights or social issues. Parliamentarians should at all times be sensitive to the

impact that their public statements on a human rights issue can have on the public's perception
of the issue in question.

To raise general human rights awareness in their country, parliamentarians should work with other national actors involved in human rights activities, including NGOs.

Establishing a national human rights action plan: an example

In Lithuania, the parliament, the parliamentary Committee on Human Rights and UNDP jointly developed a national human rights action plan. The process consisted of three phases.

First, priority issues were identified through a participatory process, and experts prepared a
baseline study on human rights in Lithuania. In a second phase, the study was then validated
in a national conference and regional workshops. Lastly, the plan was drawn up on the basis of
the baseline study and the broad consultation. The plan was debated in parliamentary committees
and approved by the parliament on 7 November 2002. Subsequent analysis of the process
showed that the leading role played by the parliamentary Committee on Human Rights had
been instrumental, inasmuch as it had ensured broad public involvement.

Box 45

What you can do as a parliamentarian

In view of the importance of parliamentary and non-parliamentary human rights mechanisms
for human rights promotion and protection and for raising public awareness, you may wish to:

❑ Promote the establishment in your parliament of a parliamentary committee specializing
in human rights;

❑ Promote in your country the establishment of a national human rights institution in accordance
with the Paris Principles, and take action to implement the Abuja Guidelines (see Boxes 42 and 44);

❑ Propose the development of a national human rights action plan and, if such a decision
is taken, ensure that the parliament participates in all stages of preparation, drafting and
implementation.

"Non-governmental organizations such as trade unions, private associations
and human rights organizations constitute an invaluable source of information and

expertise for parliamentarians who, in many countries, lack the resources and assistance needed if they are to be effective in monitoring the policy and practice of the Government in the field of human rights."
IPU Symposium on "The Parliament: Guardian of Human Rights",
Budapest, May 1993, Deliberations.

PARTICIPATING IN INTERNATIONAL EFFORTS

Parliaments and parliamentarians can contribute significantly to international human rights protection and promotion efforts. As discussed earlier, respect for human rights is
a legitimate concern of the international community and, under international law, States
parties to human rights treaties have a legal interest in the fulfilment of the obligations by
other States parties. In accordance with the inter-State complaints procedure provided for
in some of the core human rights treaties (see Chapter 5), a State may therefore call attention
to acts committed by another State in breach of a treaty. Parliaments, through their human rights bodies, may raise human rights issues involving such possible breaches and
thereby promote compliance with human rights norms worldwide.

Parliaments and parliamentarians can support international human rights organizations by securing the funding that they require. They should participate actively in the

work of the United Nations Commission on Human Rights and in drawing up new international
human rights instruments that they will eventually be called upon to ratify.

In our increasingly globalized world, decisions taken at the international level have an ever greater impact on national politics and limit the scope of national decision-making. Ever more frequently, major economic decisions affecting citizens' lives are taken outside
their country's borders by international bodies that are not accountable, but that have an
impact on the ability of the State to ensure the exercise of human rights, particularly economic,
social and cultural rights.

There is consequently a need to "democratize" these institutions if individual countries are to maintain their capacity to ensure human rights, especially economic, social and cultural rights. Parliaments and their members must therefore take a more active part in the deliberations of these institutions so as to make their voices heard.

International trade agreements, human rights and the obligations of States

At the request of the United Nations Commission on Human Rights, OHCHR issued several
reports on human rights and trade, in particular on the human rights implications of the WTO
Agreement on Trade-Related Aspects of Intellectual Property Rights, known as the TRIPS Agreement,[20] the WTO Agreement on Agriculture[21] and the WTO General Agreement on
Trade in Services, or GATS.[22] The reports point out that all WTO members have ratified at least
one human rights instrument, most of them have ratified CESCR and all but one have ratified
CRC. They also affirm that WTO members should therefore ensure that international rules on
trade liberalization do not run counter to their human rights obligations under those treaties.
Trade law and policy should therefore "focus not only on economic growth, markets or economic
development, but also on health systems, education, water supply, food security, labour,
political processes and so on". States have a responsibility to ensure that the loss of autonomy
which they incur when they enter into trade agreements "does not disproportionately reduce
their capacity to set and implement national development policy". All this requires "constant
examination of trade law and policy as it affects the enjoyment of human rights. Assessing the
potential and real impact of trade policy and law on the enjoyment of human rights is perhaps
the principal means of avoiding the implementation of any retrogressive measure that reduces
the enjoyment of human rights".[23]
In the same vein, CESCR general comment No. 14 on the right to health stipulates that States
parties should ensure that the right to health is given due consideration in international agreements,
and take steps "to ensure that these instruments do not adversely impact upon the right to health. Similarly, States parties have an obligation to ensure that their actions as members of
international organizations take due account of the right to health…." (paragraph 39).

Box 46

20 E/CN.4/Sub.2/2001/13.
21 E/CN.4/2002/54.
22 E/CN.4/Sub.2/2002/9.
23 E/CN.4/Sub.2/2002/9, paragraphs 7, 9 and 12.

In that context, IPU has embarked on a process of bringing parliaments closer to institutions
such as the World Trade Organization (WTO).

*The 107th Inter-Parliamentary Conference "calls on parliaments to play an
active role in monitoring decisions taken and activities carried out by the multilateral
institutions, in particular those affecting the development of nations; in bringing
trade- and fi nance-related multilateral institutions closer to the peoples they
are meant to serve; and in making multilateral institutions more democratic,
transparent and equitable".
Resolution on "Th e role of parliaments in developing public policy in an era of
globalisation, multilateral
institutions and international trade agreements", Marrakech, March 2002, paragraph 9.*

What you can do as a parliamentarian

Parliaments and parliamentarians should contribute to the promotion and protection of human rights at the international level and make their voices heard.
To this end, you may wish to:

❏ Establish contacts with parliamentarians in other countries in order to (a) share experiences,
success stories and lessons learned, and (b) discuss possibilities of bilateral or multilateral
cooperation, particularly regarding human rights violations that require crossborder cooperation (such as traffi cking, migration and health issues);

❏ Ensure that your parliament participates (through the competent committees) in the work of the United Nations Commission on Human Rights, or at least is kept abreast of your Government's positions on the various issues debated in the Commission. If appropriate,
you may address questions to your Government regarding the grounds for its positions;

❏ Ensure that your parliament is informed of any ongoing negotiations on new human rights treaties, and that it has the opportunity to contribute to such negotiations;

❏ Ensure that your parliament (through the competent committees) draws attention to breaches of human rights treaties in other countries and, if appropriate, invite your Government
to lodge an inter-State complaint (see Part I, Chapter 5);

❏ Participate in electoral observer missions and other international human rights missions;

❏ Ensure that your parliament is informed of any international negotiations whose outcome may negatively impact on your country's ability to comply with its human rights obligations and, if appropriate, ask the Government how it intends to safeguard such compliance.

CHAPTER 12:
WHAT PARLIAMENTARIANS SHOULD KNOW ABOUT THE CIVIL AND POLITICAL RIGHTS CONTAINED IN THE UNIVERSAL DECLARATION OF HUMAN RIGHTS (UDHR)

The right to life

Article 3 of UDHR

"Everyone has the right to life, liberty and security of the person."

Article 6 (1) of CCPR

"Every human being has the inherent right to life. Th is right shall be protected by law. No one shall be arbitrarily deprived of his life."

Th e right to life is the most fundamental human right and cannot be subject to derogation even in war or in states of emergency. Unlike the prohibition of torture or slavery, however, the right to life is not an absolute right. Th e death of a combatant as a result of a "lawful act of war" within the meaning of international humanitarian law does not constitute a violation of the right to life. Similarly, if law enforcement agents take a person's life, that act may not violate the right to life either, for example if the death results from a use of force that was absolutely necessary for such legitimate purposes as self-defence or the defence of a third person, or from a lawful arrest, or from actions taken to prevent the escape of a person legally detained or to put down a riot or insurrection. Such absolute necessity can be determined only by a competent judicial body, on a case-by-case basis, taking into account the principle of proportionality and, in the fi nal instance, by a treaty body. In addition, the right to life cannot be considered absolute in legal systems that authorize capital punishment (see below).

THE RIGHT TO LIFE AND STATE OBLIGATIONS

As all other human rights, the right to life does not only protect individuals against arbitrary interference by Government agents, but also obliges States to take **positive measures** in order to provide protection from arbitrary killings, enforced disappearances and similar violent acts committed by paramilitary forces, organized crime or any private individual.

States must therefore outlaw such acts as crimes, and must implement appropriate legislation.

The right to life and supranational jurisprudence

In 1995, hearing the case of *McCann and others v. the United Kingdom*, the European Court of
Human Rights found that a military operation in which three terrorist suspects — whom British
soldiers claimed they were attempting to arrest — were shot dead had been insufficiently
planned, and hence amounted to a violation of the right to life.

In many cases, the European and Inter-American Courts of Human Rights and the UN Human
Rights Committee have ruled that summary and arbitrary killings are by definition a violation
of the right to life.

Furthermore, since the landmark judgement of the Inter-American Court of Human Rights in
the 1988 case of *Velásquez Rodríguez v. Honduras*, it has also been established that the practice
of enforced disappearances constitutes a violation of, or at least a grave threat to, the right to
life.

Box 47

The case of Osman v. the United Kingdom (1998)

The European Court of Human Rights heard a claim filed by the relatives of Ahmed Osman
— shot dead by his son's schoolteacher — that there had been a violation of the man's right to
life. The Court considered that the following two conditions had to be met in order to substantiate
the allegation according to which the authorities, by failing to take measures to protect a
person whose life was endangered by the criminal acts of another, had violated their positive
obligation to safeguard the victim's right to life:

(a) The authorities had known or ought to have known beforehand that there was a real and
immediate risk to the victim's life from a third party's criminal behaviour; and
(b) The authorities had failed to take measures which were within their power and could
reasonably have been expected to avoid that risk.

The Court found that in this case there had been no violation of the right to life, since the applicants
did not show that the police knew or ought to have known that the lives of the Osman

family were at real and immediate risk from the schoolteacher, or that the measures that the
police could have taken would have produced any tangible results.

Box 48

Accordingly, States have a duty to ensure that:
- A homicidal attack against a person by another person is an offence carrying appropriate penalties under domestic criminal law;
- Any violent crime is thoroughly investigated in order to identify the perpetrators and bring them to justice;
- Measures are taken to prevent and punish arbitrary killing by law enforcement officers;
- Effective procedures are provided by law for investigating cases of persons who have been subjected to an enforced disappearance.

The Human Rights Committee has held that States often interpret the right to life too narrowly, and that their obligation to protect and fulfil it is broader than merely incriminating murder, assassination and homicidal attacks. In general comment No. 6, it affirmed that States should "take all possible measures to reduce infant mortality and to increase life expectancy, especially in adopting measures to eliminate malnutrition and epidemics" — which implies that States have a duty to take all possible measures to ensure an adequate standard of living — and that they have "a supreme duty to prevent wars, acts of genocide and other acts of mass violence causing arbitrary loss of life".

In that vein, parliamentarians can contribute to the realization of the right to life by ensuring that:
- Measures are taken to improve the situation with regard to the rights to food, health, security, peace and an adequate standard of living, all of which contribute to protecting the right to life;
- The Government adopts and implements policies to provide staff such as police officers and prison guards with training in order to minimize the probability of violations of the right to life;
- Measures are taken to reduce infant mortality and increase life expectancy, especially by eliminating malnutrition and epidemics.

CONTROVERSIAL ISSUES RELATED TO THE RIGHT TO LIFE

Capital punishment

The issue of the death penalty is central to the right to life. The legal history of that issue and the related debates share many similarities with the history of — and debates on — two other practices: slavery and torture. Slavery, widely practised in the world

throughout history, was abolished in law only in the nineteenth century, and torture was
routinely accepted as part of criminal procedure until the Enlightenment. While both practices are now absolutely forbidden under customary and treaty-based international law, there has been only comparatively slow progress towards abolition of the death penalty.

84

In 1984, the United Nations Economic and Social Council adopted, and the United Nations General Assembly endorsed,24 Safeguards guaranteeing protection of the rights of those facing the death penalty (sometimes referred to as the "ECOSOC Safeguards"). Although these safeguards — largely reflecting CCPR provisions — are minimum standards, they continue to be violated. Some pertinent considerations are outlined below.

Specific categories of offenders are or should be exempt from capital punishment. They
include:

- *Minors*: CCPR and CRC clearly state that a person under 18 years of age at the time he or she commits an offence should not be subjected to the death penalty. That rule has become part of customary international law;
- *Elderly persons*: Neither CCPR nor the Safeguards provide for such exemption, although in 1988 the United Nations Committee on Crime Prevention and Control recommended to the Economic and Social Council that the States Members should be advised to establish a maximum age for sentencing or execution; article 4 (5) of ACHR provides that capital punishment shall not be imposed on persons who, at the time the crime was committed, were over 70 years of age;
- *Pregnant women*: The Safeguards preclude the execution of pregnant women, thereby
protecting the unborn child (in conformity with article 6 of CCPR);
- *Mentally impaired persons:* The principle that people of unsound mind should not be sentenced or put to death — absent from CCPR and regional human rights treaties — is included in the Safeguards guaranteeing protection of the rights of those facing the death penalty.

Arguments and counter-arguments concerning capital punishment

Arguments and justifications Counter-arguments

for the death penalty

Deterrence The deterrent effect of the death penalty
has not been supported by evidence

Retribution and justice for the victims Modern standards of justice favour the rehabilitation and reintegration of offenders

Limitation of appeals and habeas corpus reform This increases the risk of judicial error and
of the execution of innocent persons

Explicit exception to the right to life under This would endorse a form of cruel, inhuman
international law and degrading punishment

Box 49
24 General Assembly resolution 39/118, 14 December 1984.
85
Moreover, international law provides for procedural requirements applicable to all death
penalty cases: fair trial guarantees, the possibility of appeal to a higher court, and clemency.
Under article 6 (4) of CCPR, amnesty, pardon or commutation of a death sentence may be granted at all times. Clemency may postpone or set aside a death sentence — for
instance, by commuting it to life imprisonment — and can be used to make up for errors,
mitigate a harsh punishment or compensate for any criminal law provisions that may disallow
consideration of relevant factors. Th e right of any death convict to seek clemency is clearly affi rmed in international human rights law.
Where it has not been abolished, the death penalty should constitute exceptional punishment,
always meted out in accordance with the principle of proportionality. Article 6 of CCPR refers to "the most serious crimes" and, under the Safeguards, the defi nition of the
"most serious crimes" punishable by death "should not go beyond intentional crimes, with
lethal or other extremely grave consequences". Th is restriction is in line with the goal of total abolition of the death penalty. As the United Nations General Assembly affi rmed in
1971, the right to life can be fully guaranteed only if the number of off ences for which the
death penalty may be imposed is progressively restricted, "with a view to the desirability of
abolishing it in all countries".25

Movement towards the abolition of capital punishment
At the end of the Second World War, when international human rights standards were being
drawn up, the death penalty was still applied in most States. Consequently, article 2 of ECHR, article 6 of CCPR and article 4 of ACHR provide for an exception to the principle of the right to life in the case of capital punishment. Since then, however, a clear trend for
abolishing and prohibiting the death penalty has emerged, mainly in Europe and Latin America.

Abolition of capital punishment in Europe
Th e Sixth Additional Protocol to ECHR, adopted in 1983 and ratifi ed by all Council of Europe States members with the exception of Monaco and the Russian Federation, forbids

the death penalty in peacetime, and the thirteenth Additional Protocol to the European Convention, adopted in 2002, provides for an absolute prohibition of capital punishment in Europe (i.e., even in war). Since the abolition of capital punishment was adopted as an
integral part of European Union and Council of Europe policy (and also as an admission requirement for new member States), Europe can today be considered a death penalty free
zone.

Eff orts to abolish capital punishment in the Americas and worldwide
A similar development can be observed in the Americas and on a global scale. In 1990, OAS
adopted a Protocol to the American Convention on Human Rights abolishing the death
25 General Assembly resolution 2857 (XXVI), 20 December 1971.
86
penalty, but only eight States (Brazil, Costa Rica, Ecuador, Nicaragua, Panama, Paraguay, Uruguay and Venezuela) have ratifi ed it so far. Similarly, the Second Optional Protocol to
CCPR (1989), which aims at the universal abolition of the death penalty, has been ratifi ed
by only 54 — predominantly European and Latin American — States. However, powerful countries such as the United States of America and China and many Islamic States not only continue to apply capital punishment, but also strongly oppose its abolition under international law.

Abortion
Whereas article 4 of ACHR generally protects the right to life from the moment of conception,
article 6 of CCPR and article 2 of ECHR do not explicitly determine the point at which the protection of life begins. Invoking a 1973 judgement of the United States Supreme

Trends in jurisprudence in support of non-extradition
and the abolition of capital punishment
• In 1989, hearing the case of *Soering v. the United Kingdom,* the European Court of Human
Rights decided that the extradition by the United Kingdom of a German citizen to the United
States of America, where he would remain on death row for many years, constituted inhuman
treatment under article 3 of ECHR.
• In 1993, in *Ng v. Canada,* another extradition case involving the United States of America,
the Human Rights Committee decided that execution by gas asphyxiation, as practised in
California, constituted inhuman punishment under article 7 of CCPR.
• In a landmark judgement of 1995, the South African Constitutional Court concluded that

capital punishment as such, irrespective of the method of execution or other circumstances,
was inhuman and violated the prohibition of inhuman punishment in South Africa.
- In 2003, hearing the case of *Judge v. Canada*, the UN Human Rights Committee considered
"that Canada, as a State party which has abolished the death penalty, irrespective of whether it
has not yet ratified the Second Optional Protocol to the Covenant Aiming at the Abolition of
the Death Penalty, violated the author's right to life under article 6, paragraph 1, by deporting
him to the United States of America, where he is under sentence of death, without ensuring
that the death penalty would not be carried out".
- In the case of *Öcalan v. Turkey* (2003), the European Court of Human Rights held that the
imposition of the death penalty after an unfair trial amounted to inhuman treatment and
violated article 3 of ECHR.
- On 1 March 2005, the United States Supreme Court ruled that capital punishment of persons
convicted of crimes committed when they were minors was unconstitutional. The Court cited
the "overwhelming weight of international opinion against the juvenile death penalty" as providing
"respected and significant confirmation" of its decision, stating that "It does not lessen
fidelity to the Constitution or pride in its origins to acknowledge that the express affirmation
of certain fundamental rights by other nations and peoples underscores the centrality of those
same rights within our own heritage of freedom."

Box 50

The world situation with respect to capital punishment

According to Amnesty International, in 2004, at least 3,797 people were executed in 25 countries
and at least 7,395 people were sentenced to death in 64 countries. These figures include
only cases known to Amnesty International; actual figures are probably higher.26

Abolitionist and retentionist countries

Abolitionist for all crimes: 85
Abolitionist for all but exceptional crimes such as wartime crimes: 11
Abolitionist in practice: 24
Total of countries that are abolitionist in law or practice: 120

Retentionist (countries and territories): 76

1. Abolitionist for all crimes

Countries and territories where the law does not provide for capital punishment for any crime:

Andorra, Angola, Armenia, Australia, Austria, Azerbaijan, Belgium, Bhutan, Bosnia and Herzegovina, Bulgaria, Cambodia, Canada, Cape Verde, Colombia, Costa Rica, Cote d'Ivoire,

Croatia, Cyprus, Czech Republic, Denmark, Djibouti, Dominican Republic, Ecuador, Estonia,

Finland, France, Georgia, Germany, Greece, Guinea-Bissau, Haiti, Holy See, Honduras, Hungary,

Iceland, Ireland, Italy, Kiribati, Liechtenstein, Lithuania, Luxembourg, Malta, Marshall Islands, Mauritius, Mexico, Micronesia (Federated States of), Monaco, Mozambique, Namibia,

Nepal, Netherlands, New Zealand, Nicaragua, Niue, Norway, Palau, Panama, Paraguay, Poland,

Portugal, Republic of Moldova, Romania, Samoa, San Marino, Sao Tome and Principe, Senegal,

Serbia and Montenegro, Seychelles, Slovakia, Slovenia, Solomon Islands, South Africa, Spain,

Sweden, Switzerland, the former Yugoslav Republic of Macedonia, Timor-Leste, Turkey, Turkmenistan, Tuvalu, Ukraine, United Kingdom, Uruguay, Vanuatu, Venezuela.

2. Abolitionist for ordinary crimes only

Countries where the law provides for capital punishment only for such crimes as may be committed

under military law or other exceptional circumstances:

Albania, Argentina, Armenia, Bolivia, Brazil, Chile, Cook Islands, El Salvador, Fiji, Greece, Israel, Latvia, Mexico, Peru and Turkey.

3. Abolitionist in practice

Countries which retain the death penalty for ordinary crimes such as murder, but which can be

considered abolitionist in practice, insofar as they have not executed anyone during the past 10

years and are believed to have a policy or established practice of not carrying out executions, and

countries which have made an international commitment not to use the death penalty:

Box 51

➡

26 Detailed information may be found at the website of Amnesty International under http://web.amnesty.org/pages/deathpenalty-

facts-eng.

Court in the case of *Roe v. Wade,* the domestic courts in other countries and some legal scholars have maintained that legal protection of the right to life begins when the foetus is able to survive on its own. Under this interpretation, persons who carry out abortion before approximately the end of the first trimester of pregnancy may be exempted from criminal responsibility for their actions. A law that exempts them would thus be consistent with the positive obligation of States to protect the foetus's right to life against interference by the parents or the physician, as the foetus's right to life would emerge only after it is able to survive without its mother. However, after the first trimester, the positive obligation of the State would arise, and the right of the unborn child to life must be balanced against other human rights, in particular the mother's rights to life, and possibly her right to health and privacy as well.

Genetic engineering

The Council of Europe plays a pioneering role in this controversial field, which is on the borderline between ethics, human rights and modern developments in biotechnology. In 1997, the Committee of Ministers adopted the Convention for the Protection of Human Rights and Dignity of the Human Being with regard to the Application of Biology and Medicine (Convention on Human Rights and Biomedicine). The Convention reaffirms the principle of free and informed consent for every intervention in the health field (article 5); stipulates that an intervention seeking to modify the human genome may be undertaken only for preventive, diagnostic or therapeutic purposes, and solely if its aim is not to introduce any modification in the genome of any descendants (article 13); and provides that the human body and its parts shall not, as such, give rise to financial gain (article 21). The Algeria, Benin, Brunei Darussalam, Burkina Faso, Central African Republic, Congo, Gambia, Grenada, Kenya, Madagascar, Maldives, Mali, Mauritania, Nauru, Niger, Papua New Guinea, Russian Federation, Sri Lanka, Suriname, Togo, Tonga and Tunisia.

4. Retentionist

Countries and territories which retain the death penalty for ordinary crimes:
Afghanistan, Antigua and Barbuda, Bahamas, Bahrain, Bangladesh, Barbados, Belarus, Belize, Botswana, Burundi, Cameroon, Chad, China, Comoros, Cuba, Democratic People's Republic of Korea, Democratic Republic of the Congo, Dominica, Egypt, Equatorial Guinea, Eritrea,

Ethiopia, Gabon, Ghana, Guatemala, Guinea, Guyana, India, Indonesia, Islamic Republic of
Iran, Iraq, Jamaica, Japan, Jordan, Kazakhstan, Kuwait, Kyrgyzstan, Lao People's Democratic
Republic, Lebanon, Lesotho, Liberia, Libyan Arab Jamahiriya, Malawi, Malaysia, Mongolia,
Morocco, Myanmar, Nigeria, Oman, Pakistan, Palestine, Philippines, Qatar, Republic of Korea, Rwanda, Saint Kitts and Nevis, Saint Lucia, Saint Vincent and the Grenadines, Saudi
Arabia, Sierra Leone, Singapore, Somalia, Sudan, Swaziland, Syrian Arab Republic, Tajikistan,
Th ailand, Trinidad and Tobago, Uganda, United Arab Emirates, United Republic of Tanzania,
United States of America, Uzbekistan, Viet Nam, Yemen, Zambia and Zimbabwe.

fi rst Additional Protocol to the Convention, adopted a year later, aims at the prohibition of
cloning human beings, and the second Additional Protocol, adopted in 2002, concerns the
transplantation of organs and tissues of human origin.

Euthanasia

Doubtlessly, the obligation of States to protect the right to life applies especially to the incurably
ill, to persons with disabilities and to other people who are particularly vulnerable
to imposed measures of euthanasia. But in the case of a terminally ill person who explicitly
and seriously wishes to die, the obligation to protect the right to life must be weighed
against other human rights enjoyed by that person, above all the right to privacy and dignity.
Domestic laws on active or passive euthanasia (such as the relevant legislation in the
Netherlands) that limit criminal responsibility by providing for careful consideration of all
rights involved and take adequate precautions against potential abuse are not inconsistent
with the positive State obligation to protect the right to life. Yet, faced with diffi cult questions
on the borderline between ethics and medicine, States may also decide to prohibit
euthanasia, as the judgement of the European Court of Human Rights in the case of *Pretty
v. the United Kingdom* (2002) shows (see Box 52).

The case of Pretty v. the United Kingdom (2002)

Dianne Pretty was terminally ill, and paralysed from the neck down from motor neurone disease.

Her intellectual and decision-making capacity, however, was unimpaired and she wanted to commit suicide, but her condition prevented her from performing this act alone. She therefore sought a guarantee from the Director of Public Prosecutions that her husband would not be prosecuted if he assisted her in ending her life. Her request was rejected pursuant to the relevant provisions of English law, which prohibit any assistance in committing suicide, and this decision was upheld in the last instance at the national level. In its decision on her application, which claimed that this judgement violated inter alia her right to life, the European Court held that the right to life, guaranteed under article 2 of ECHR, could not be interpreted as conferring the diametrically opposite right, the right to die, whether at the hands of another person or with the assistance of a public authority. As a consequence of that judgement, a private member bill (known as the Patient Assisted Dying Bill) was subsequently introduced in the British Parliament with the aim of making it lawful for a physician to assist a person to die under very stringently defined conditions and circumstances. The authors of the Bill, which is still being debated, consider that the right to assist a person to die derives from article 8 (1) of ECHR, an article that stipulates inter alia that everyone has the right to respect for his private and family life. In their view, it is not incompatible with the positive obligation of the State to protect life.

Box 52

90

Prohibition of torture and cruel, inhuman or degrading treatment or punishment: the right to personal integrity and dignity

Article 5 of UDHR

"No one shall be subjected to torture or to cruel, inhuman or degrading treatment or punishment."

Article 7 of CCPR

"No one shall be subjected to torture or to cruel, inhuman or degrading treatment or punishment. In particular, no one shall be subjected without his free consent to medical or scientific experimentation."

Torture is one of the most serious human rights violations, as it constitutes a direct attack on

the personality and dignity of the human being. The prohibition of torture and other forms
of physical and mental ill-treatment, i.e., the right to personal integrity and dignity, is an *absolute*
human right and is therefore not subject to derogation under any circumstances. This also means that no one may invoke an order from a superior as a justification of torture.

WHAT IS TORTURE?
Article 1 of CAT defines torture as any act — committed by a public official or other person
acting in an official capacity or at the instigation of or with the consent of such a person — by which severe physical or mental pain or suffering is intentionally inflicted on a person for a specific purpose, such as extortion of information or confession, punishment,
intimidation or discrimination.

Codification of the prohibition of torture
The prohibition of torture is codified in the Universal Declaration of Human Rights (article 5),
CCPR (article 7) and CAT, and also in regional treaties such as ECHR (article 3), the European
Convention for the Prevention of Torture and Inhuman or Degrading Treatment or Punishment,
ACHR (article 5), the Inter-American Convention to Prevent and Punish Torture and the African Charter on Human and Peoples' Rights (article 5), and in some legally non-binding but
morally authoritative instruments, including the Standard Minimum Rules for the Treatment
of Prisoners, the Basic Principles for the Treatment of Prisoners, the Body of Principles for the
Protection of All Persons under Any Form of Detention or Imprisonment, the United Nations
Rules for the Protection of Juveniles Deprived of their Liberty, and the Principles on the Effective
Investigation and Documentation of Torture and Other Cruel, Inhuman or Degrading Treatment
or Punishment. Torture is also absolutely prohibited by various provisions of the 1949 Geneva Conventions, in particular their common article 3. Furthermore, the Rome Statute of
ICC defines torture as a "crime against humanity" when it is knowingly committed as part of a
widespread or systematic attack against any civilian population.

Box 53

Actions that lack one of the essential elements of torture — perpetration by or with the

consent of a public official, intent, specific purpose and intensity of suffering — are considered,
depending on the form, purpose and severity of suffering, as cruel, inhuman or degrading treatment or punishment. Since all punishment inflicts suffering and contains
an element of humiliation, an additional element must be present in order for it to qualify
as cruel, inhuman or degrading punishment.

"Torture is intended to humiliate, offend and degrade a human being and turn him or her into a 'thing'".
Antonio Cassese, former President of the Council of Europe's Committee for the Prevention of Torture, in Inhuman States: Imprisonment, Detention and Torture in Europe Today, *Cambridge Polity Press, 1996, p. 47.*

"The legal and moral basis for the prohibition of torture and other cruel, inhuman or degrading treatment or punishment is absolute and imperative and must under no circumstances yield or be subordinated to other interests, policies and practices."
Theo van Boven, Special Rapporteur of the Commission on Human Rights on torture and other cruel, inhuman or degrading treatment or punishment.

WHAT STATE OBLIGATIONS ARISE FROM THE PROHIBITION OF TORTURE?
Governments must not restrict or allow derogations from the right to personal integrity and dignity, even in war and in states of emergency. The CAT Committee has ruled that even when a suspect is believed to hold information about imminent attacks that could endanger the lives of civilians, the State thus threatened may not employ methods of in-

Procedural safeguards during police custody
It is widely recognized that torture and ill-treatment occur mostly during police custody. The following
procedural safeguards limit considerably the exposure of arrested persons to that risk:
• Notification of custody: The right of arrested persons to have the fact of their detention
notified to a third party of their choice (family member, friend or consulate);
• The right of detainees to have access to a lawyer;
• The right of detainees to request a medical examination by a physician of their choice (in
addition to any medical examination carried out by a physician called by the police authorities);
• Availability of centralized registers of all detainees and places of detention;
• Exclusion of evidence elicited through torture or other forms of compulsion;
• Audio- or videotaping of all police interrogations.

Box 54

terrogation violating the prohibition of torture and ill-treatment, such as restraining a person under painful conditions, hooding, prolonged exposure to loud music or sleep deprivation, threats, violent shaking or use of cold air to chill the detainee. The absolute

prohibition of torture and ill-treatment is founded on the premise that if limited exceptions
are permitted, experience has shown that the use of torture tends to spread like a cancer.
The absolute character of the prohibition of torture must be guaranteed. States are therefore forbidden from derogating from rights which, if suspended, would result in a risk
of torture, such as the right not to be held in detention for prolonged periods incommunicado
and the right of arrested persons to have prompt access to a court. States have an obligation
to prevent, investigate, prosecute and punish any act of torture. They must provide reparation to victims, including medical and psychological rehabilitation and compensation
for material and moral damages (see Box 55).

State obligations under CAT

States parties to the Convention have a duty to:

- Enact legislation to punish torture, empower the authorities to prosecute and punish the
crime of torture wherever it has been committed and whatever the nationality of the perpetrator
or victim, and prevent these practices (principle of universal jurisdiction);
- Ensure that education and information regarding the prohibition of torture are fully included
in the training of civil or military law enforcement personnel, medical staff, public
officials and other persons who may be involved in the custody, interrogation or treatment
of arrested, detained or imprisoned individuals;
- Ensure that interrogation rules, instructions, methods and practices and the arrangements
for the custody and treatment of persons subjected to any form of arrest, detention or imprisonment
are systematically reviewed by independent bodies;
- Ensure that complaints of torture and ill-treatment are investigated thoroughly by competent
authorities, that torturers are brought to justice, that effective remedies are available to victims, and that laws are drawn up to implement measures that prevent torture and ill-treatment during detention;
- Refrain from expelling or returning ("refoulement") or extraditing a person to another State where it is likely that he or she will be exposed to torture (principle of "non-refoulement"
or "non-repatriation");
- Submit periodic reports to the CAT Committee on the measures taken to give effect to the

Convention, or other reports that the Committee may request;
• Establish independent national commissions (consisting of members of the judiciary, law
enforcement officials, lawyers and physicians, independent experts and civil society representatives)
to carry out preventive visits to all places of detention (Optional Protocol to
CAT, adopted in 2002).

Box 55

PROHIBITION OF CRUEL, INHUMAN OR DEGRADING PUNISHMENT

Since any punishment implies suffering and humiliation, an additional element must be present for it to qualify as cruel, inhuman or degrading punishment. Minimum standards in this area vary from country to country. In Europe, the death penalty and all forms of corporal punishment are today considered as inhuman or degrading punishment, and are
therefore prohibited, and in many countries life imprisonment is considered in the same vein. The Human Rights Committee has considered corporal punishment, such as chastisement
of prisoners in Jamaica and in Trinidad and Tobago, as degrading punishment under article 7 of CCPR. Furthermore, it has maintained that certain methods of execution such
as gas asphyxiation constitute inhuman punishment, and thus violate international law.

THE RIGHT OF DETAINEES AND PRISONERS TO BE TREATED WITH HUMANITY

Article 10 of CCPR guarantees the right of all persons deprived of their liberty to be treated
with humanity and with respect for their inherent dignity. According to the Human Rights Committee, people deprived of their liberty may not be "subjected to any hardship
or constraint other than that resulting from the deprivation of their liberty."
A number of soft law instruments specify minimum standards applicable to detention.

United Nations minimum standards in respect of detention and the conduct of law enforcement

• Safeguards Guaranteeing Protection of the Rights of Those Facing the Death Penalty, 1948
• Standard Minimum Rules for the Treatment of Prisoners, 1955
• Code of Conduct for Law Enforcement Officials, 1979
• Principles of Medical Ethics relevant to the Role of Health Personnel, particularly Physicians, in the Protection of Prisoners and Detainees against Torture and Other Cruel, Inhuman or Degrading Treatment or Punishment, 1982
• Safeguards guaranteeing Protection of the Rights of those facing the Death Penalty, 1984
• United Nations Standard Minimum Rules for the Administration of Juvenile Justice ("The
Beijing Rules"), 1985

- Body of Principles for the Protection of All Persons under Any Form of Detention or Imprisonment, 1988
- Basic Principles on the Use of Force and Firearms by Law Enforcement Officials, 1990
- Basic Principles for the Treatment of Prisoners, 1990
- United Nations Guidelines for the Prevention of Juvenile Delinquency ("The Riyadh Guidelines"), 1990
- United Nations Standard Minimum Rules for Non-Custodial Measures ("The Tokyo Rules"), 1990
- United Nations Rules for the Protection of Juveniles Deprived of their Liberty, 1990

Box 56

The right to personal liberty

Article 3 of UDHR

"Everyone has the right to life, liberty and security of the person"

Article 9 of UDHR

"No one shall be subjected to arbitrary arrest, detention or exile"

Article 9 (1) of CCPR

"Everyone has the right to liberty and security of person. No one shall be subjected to arbitrary arrest or detention. No one shall be deprived of his liberty except on such grounds and in accordance with such procedure as are established by law."

27 E/CN.4/Sub.2/1993/21.

28 See, for instance, *CorpWatch*, "Prison privatization: the bottom line", 21 August 1999.

Human rights and privatization of prisons

Private sector involvement in prison operations — construction of penitentiaries, transport of
prisoners, procurement of supplies and even full management of detention centres — has been
steadily increasing since the 1980s, when it was reintroduced first in the United States of America
(where it had been abandoned half a century earlier). Prison privatization has reduced the
States' ability to ensure respect for prisoners' rights. In a study carried out for the Sub-Commission
on the Promotion and Protection of Human Rights,27 Ms. Claire Palley, expert, set out the
following five principled policy arguments against contracting out prison management:

a. Only the State should have the power to administer justice and enforce it by coercion, because
the legitimacy of such inherently governmental powers with which, in a democracy,
the people entrust the State depends on their exercise by the State;

b. Disciplinary powers and functions should be exercised only by the State, because such functions
can result in the diminution of residual liberty or the prolongation of confinement;

c. Force in restraining prisoners should be exercised only by the State, the sole entity that
may legitimately administer justice and enforce it by coercion;
d. Liability for human rights violations must be a State responsibility;
e. Th e State must ensure the accountability and public visibility of the criminal justice system
and the public's access to information.

Th e study also addresses the problem of the creation of large prison trusts that are set up by
building industry enterprises and security companies, and the interests that such trusts may
have in infl uencing penal policy in general. Some have raised the question whether privatization
of prisons may not be tantamount to privatizing prisoners.28

Box 57

95

Th e right to personal liberty aims at providing protection against arbitrary or unlawful arrest and detention. Th is basic guarantee applies to everyone, including persons held on
criminal charges or on such grounds as mental illness, vagrancy or immigration control. Other restrictions of movement, such as banishment to an island or a certain area of a country, curfews, expulsion from a county or prohibition to leave a country, do not constitute
interference with personal liberty, although they may violate other human rights, such as freedom of movement and residence (article 14, UDHR).

WHEN IS ARREST OR DETENTION LAWFUL?

An individual may be deprived of his or her liberty only on legal grounds and under a procedure
established by law. Th e procedure must conform not only to domestic law, but also to international standards. Th e relevant domestic law must not be arbitrary, i.e., it must not
be tainted by inappropriateness, injustice or unpredictability. Moreover, law enforcement

Article 5 of the European Convention for the Protection of Human Rights and Fundamental Freedoms: permissible grounds for arrest and detention

- Imprisonment of a person after conviction for a criminal off ence
- Police custody and pre-trial detention of a criminal suspect in order to prevent fl ight, interference with evidence or recurrence
- Detention in a civil context to ensure that a witness appears in court or undergoes a paternity test
- Detention of aliens in connection with immigration, asylum, expulsion and extradition
- Detention of minors for the purpose of educational supervision
- Detention of persons with mental disabilities in a psychiatric hospital
- Quarantine of sick persons in order to contain infectious diseases

– Detention of alcoholics, drug addicts and vagrants

Box 58
Human Rights Committee jurisprudence on pretrial detention
According to the Human Rights Committee, pretrial detention must be not only lawful, but
also necessary and reasonable under given circumstances. The Human Rights Committee has
recognized that CCPR allows authorities to hold a person in custody as an exceptional measure,
if it is necessary in order to ensure that person's appearance in court, but has interpreted the
"necessity" requirement narrowly: suspicion that a person has committed a crime does not by
itself justify detention pending investigation and indictment. The Human Rights Committee
has also held, however, that custody may be necessary to prevent flight, avert interference with
witnesses and other evidence, or prevent the commission of further offences.

Box 59

in any given case must not be arbitrary or discriminatory, but should be proportionate to
all of the circumstances surrounding the case.

Typical examples of *permissible grounds for arrest and detention* are to be found in article 5 of ECHR, which is understood to provide an exhaustive list of cases of lawful deprivation of liberty in Europe (see Box 58) and can serve as a basis for the interpretation of the term "arbitrary deprivation of liberty" in article 9 of CCPR. Any imprisonment on mere grounds of inability to fulfil a contractual obligation, such as reimbursing a debt, is explicitly prohibited by article 11 of CCPR, article 7 (7) of ACHR and article 1 of the Fourth Additional Protocol to ECHR.

WHAT RIGHTS DOES A PERSON HAVE WHILE IN CUSTODY?

• Arrested persons have the *right to be informed* promptly of the reasons for their arrest
and detention, and of their right to counsel. They must be promptly informed of any charges brought against them in order to be able to challenge the lawfulness of their arrest or detention and, if they are indicted, to prepare their defence.

• Persons facing a possible criminal charge have the *right to be assisted by a lawyer* of their choice. If they cannot afford a lawyer, they should be provided with a qualified and effective counsel. Adequate time and facilities should be made available for communication with their counsel. Access to the counsel should be immediate.

• Persons in custody have the *right to communicate with the outside,* and in particular to have prompt access to their family, lawyer, physician, a judicial official and, if the detainee is a foreign national, to consular staff or a competent international organization. Access to the outside is an essential safeguard against such human rights violations as "disappearances", torture and ill-treatment, and is vital to obtaining a fair trial.

• Persons arrested on suspicion of a criminal offence have the *right to be brought promptly before a judge* or other judicial officer who must (a) assess whether there are sufficient legal grounds for the arrest, (b) assess whether detention before trial is necessary, (c) safeguard the well-being of the detainee and (d) prevent violations of the detainee's fundamental rights.

• Persons in pretrial detention have the *right to be tried within a reasonable time or else be released.* In accordance with the presumption of innocence, people awaiting trial on criminal charges should not be held in custody, as a general rule.

• Persons deprived of their liberty on whatever grounds have the *right to habeas corpus,* i.e., they may challenge the lawfulness of their detention before a court and have their detention regularly reviewed. The court must decide without delay, normally within a few days or weeks, on the lawfulness of the detention and order immediate release if the detention is unlawful. If detention for an unspecified period of time is ordered (for instance, in a psychiatric hospital), the detainee has a right to periodic review, normally every few months. Lastly, any victim of unlawful arrest or detention has an enforceable *right to compensation.*

Administration of justice: the right to a fair trial

Article 6 of UDHR

"Everyone has the right to recognition everywhere as a person before the law."

Article 7 of UDHR

"All are equal before the law and are entitled without any discrimination to equal protection of the law."

Article 8 of UDHR

"Everyone has the right to an effective remedy by the competent national tribunals for acts violating the fundamental rights granted him by the constitution or by law."

Article 10 of UDHR

"Everyone is entitled in full equality to a fair and public hearing by an independent and impartial tribunal, in the determination of his rights and obligations and of any criminal charge against him."

Article 11 of UDHR

"(1) Everyone charged with a penal offence has the right to be presumed innocent until proven guilty according to law in a public trial at which he has had all the guarantees necessary for his defence.

(2) No one shall be held guilty of any penal offence on account of any act that did not constitute

a penal off ence, under national or international law, at the time when it was committed.
Nor shall a heavier penalty be imposed than the one that was applicable at the time the penal off ence was committed."
Articles 14, 15 and 16 of CCPR also enshrine the right to a fair trial.
Articles 6 to 11 of UDHR can be grouped under a common heading: administration of justice. Th e right to a fair trial, guaranteed also under CCPR and regional human rights treaties, is a basic human right and requires procedural guarantees.

EQUALITY BEFORE THE LAW AND THE COURTS

Fair trial guarantees presuppose equality before the law and the courts. Th e right to equality
before the law means that laws must not be discriminatory and that judges and offi cials must not enforce the law discriminatorily. Th e right to equality before the courts means that all persons are equally entitled to access to a court and have a right to equal treatment
by that court.

CORE ELEMENTS OF THE RIGHT TO A FAIR TRIAL

In criminal, civil and other proceedings the basic elements of the right to a fair trial are the
principle of "equality of arms" between the parties, and the requirement of a fair and public
hearing before an independent and impartial tribunal.

- *"Equality of arms"* means that both parties — the prosecution and the accused in criminal proceedings, or the plaintiff and the defendant in civil proceedings — have equal rights and opportunities to be present at the various stages of the proceedings, to be kept informed of the facts and arguments of the opposing party and to have their arguments heard by the court *(audiatur et altera pars)*. In principle, therefore, the principle of "equality of arms" requires adversarial proceedings.
- Court hearings and judgements must in general be public: not only the parties to the case, but also the general public, must have a right to be present. Th e idea behind the principle of a *public hearing* is transparency and control by the public, a key prerequisite for the administration of justice in a democratic society: *"Justice must not only be done; it must be seen to be done"*. It follows that, as a general principle, trials must not be conducted by a purely written procedure in camera, but by oral hearings to which the public has access. Not all stages of the proceedings, in particular at the appeal level, require public hearings; and the public, including the media, may be excluded for reasons of morals, public order, national security, private interests and, in exceptional cases, the interests of justice. However, every judgement must be made public, by full oral delivery or by written announcement.

THE RIGHTS OF THE ACCUSED IN CRIMINAL TRIALS

In addition to the right to "equality of arms" and to a public hearing, international human
rights law provides for a number of specifi c rights that persons charged with a criminal

off ence should enjoy:
Independent and impartial tribunals: independence of the judiciary
Tribunals (courts) must be constituted in a way ensuring their independence and impartiality.
Independence entails safeguards relating to the manner of appointment of judges, the duration
of their office and the provision of guarantees against outside pressure. Impartiality means that,
in hearing the cases before them, judges must not be biased or guided by personal interests or
political motives. The United Nations Basic Principles on the Independence of the Judiciary
provide clear guidelines in that area.
The prerequisites for legal provisions ensuring court independence and impartiality are the
following:
- First and foremost, the independence of the judiciary should be enshrined in the constitution
or in national law;
- The method of selection of judicial officers should be characterized by balance between the
executive and an impartial body, many of whose members should be appointed by professional
organizations, such as law societies;
- The tenure of judges should be guaranteed up to a mandatory retirement age or the expiry
of their terms of office;
- Decisions on disciplinary action, suspension or removal of a judge should be subject to an
independent review.

Box 60

- The right to be presumed innocent. The prosecution must prove the person's guilt, and,
in case of doubt, the accused should not be found guilty, but must be acquitted;
- The right not to be compelled to testify or to confess guilt. This prohibition is in line with the presumption of innocence, which places the burden of proof on the prosecution, and with the prohibition of torture and ill-treatment. Evidence elicited by torture or ill-treatment may not be used in court;
- The right to defend oneself in person or through counsel of one's own choosing, and the right to be provided with legal assistance free of charge;
- The right to have adequate time and facilities for one's defence, and the right to communicate with one's counsel;
- The right to be tried without undue delay, as "justice delayed is justice denied". In

principle, criminal proceedings must be conducted more speedily than other proceedings, particularly if the accused is in detention;
- The right to be present at one's trial;
- The right to call and examine witnesses;
- The right to be provided with language interpretation free of charge if the accused cannot understand or speak the language used in court;
- The right to appeal to a higher tribunal;
- The right not to be tried and sentenced twice for the same offence (prohibition of double jeopardy, or principle of *ne bis in idem*);
- The right to receive compensation in the event of a miscarriage of justice;
- The principles of *nullum crimen sine lege* and *nulla poena sine lege* prohibit the enactment of retroactive criminal laws and ensure that convicted persons benefit from lighter penalties if they are enacted after the commission of the offence.

SPECIAL COURTS AND MILITARY COURTS

Special, extraordinary or military courts have been set up in many countries to try specific types of offences or to try people with special legal statuses. Frequently, such courts offer fewer guarantees of fair trial than ordinary courts and, as noted by the Human Rights Committee, "quite often the reason for the establishment of such courts is to enable
exceptional procedures to be applied which do not comply with normal standards of justice".29
Most international standards do not prohibit the establishment of special courts per se, but require that they be competent, independent and impartial, and that they afford
judicial guarantees ensuring fair proceedings.

29 HRC, *general comment* No. 13, para. 4.

THE RIGHT TO FAIR TRIAL IN A STATE OF EMERGENCY AND IN ARMED CONFLICT

As stated in Part I, some human rights may not be suspended under any circumstances. Some of these rights — such as the right to protection against torture and retroactive criminal laws — are part of fair trial guarantees. There is, moreover, a growing international
consensus that derogation from habeas corpus should not be possible either. The United
Nations Commission on Human Rights has called on all States "to establish a procedure such as habeas corpus or a similar procedure as a personal right not subject to derogation,
including during states of emergency".32
It is precisely during a national emergency that States are most likely to violate human rights. *Parliaments should use their powers to ensure that fair trial guarantees and the independence of the judiciary, which are vital to the protection of human rights, apply also
in states of emergency.*

International humanitarian law governs conduct during armed confl ict. Th e Geneva Conventions
of 1949 set out fair trial guarantees for people charged with criminal off ences.

The right to privacy and the protection of family life

Article 12 of UDHR

"No one shall be subjected to arbitrary interference with his privacy, family, home or correspondence, nor to attacks upon his honour and reputation. Everyone has the right to the protection of the law against such interference or attacks."

Article 16 of UDHR

"1. Men and women of full age, without any limitation due to race, nationality or religion,
have the right to marry and to found a family. Th ey are entitled to equal rights as to marriage, during marriage and at its dissolution.

Trials of military personnel in military courts for common crimes

Trials of military personnel in military courts for ordinary crimes and human rights violations
often result in impunity. Th e United Nations Special Rapporteur on extrajudicial, summary or arbitrary
executions has expressed concern over reports of "trials of members of the security forces
before military courts, where, it is alleged, they evade punishment because of an ill-conceived
esprit de corps, which generally results in impunity".30 Th e Inter-American Commission of Human
Rights has considered that the extension of military jurisdiction to include common crimes
solely on the grounds that they have been committed by military personnel does not off er the
guarantees of an independent and impartial court as laid down in article 8 (1) ACHR.31

Box 61

30 UN Doc.A/51/457, para. 125, October 1996.
31 IACHR, *Annual report*, 1993.
32 Commission resolution 1994/32.

101

2. Marriage shall be entered into only with the free and full consent of the intending spouses.
3. Th e family is the natural and fundamental group unit of society and is entitled to protection by society and the State."

Article 17 of CCPR

"1. No one shall be subjected to arbitrary or unlawful interference with his privacy, family,
home or correspondence, nor to unlawful attacks on his honour and reputation.
2. Everyone has the right to the protection of the law against such interference or attacks."

Article 23 of CCPR

"1. The family is the natural and fundamental group unit of society and is entitled to protection by society and the State.
2. The right of men and women of marriageable age to marry and to found a family shall
be recognized.
3. No marriage shall be entered into without the free and full consent of the intending spouses.
4. States Parties to the present Covenant shall take appropriate steps to ensure equality of rights and responsibilities of spouses as to marriage, during marriage and at its dissolution. In the case of dissolution, provision shall be made for the necessary protection
of any children."

The right to privacy is central to the notion of freedom and individual autonomy. Many of
the controversial issues that have arisen in the context of privacy litigation, such as State interference with homosexuality, transsexuality, prostitution, abortion, (assisted) suicide,
dress codes and similar codes of conduct, private communication, marriage and divorce, reproductive rights, genetic engineering, cloning and the forced separation of children from their parents, touch upon fundamental moral values and ethical issues, which are viewed differently in various societies. Furthermore, the liberal concept of privacy is based
on the private versus public dichotomy, and on the philosophy that Governments should not interfere with essentially private and family matters. However, it is precisely that dichotomy
that is challenged directly, above all by modern feminist theory, and blamed for major violations of the human rights of women and children, including domestic violence
and female genital mutilation (FGM).

THE RIGHT TO PRIVACY: A COMPLEX AND MULTIFACETED HUMAN RIGHT

This right guarantees
• respect for the individual existence of the human being, i.e., his or her particular nature, idiosyncrasy, appearance, honour and reputation.
• It protects individual autonomy and entitles individuals to isolate themselves from their fellow human beings and withdraw from public life into their own private spheres in order to shape their own lives according to their personal wishes and expectations. Certain institutional guarantees, such as protection of *home, family, marriage* and the *secrecy of correspondence* support this aspect of the right to privacy.

• It includes the right to be different and to manifest one's difference in public by behaviour that runs counter to accepted morals in a given society and environment. Government authorities and international human rights bodies, therefore, face
a delicate and difficult task of *striking a balance* between the right to privacy and

legitimate public interests, such as the protection of public order, health, morals and the rights and freedoms of others.

The following paragraphs touch upon only some of the more salient aspects of the right to privacy. In view of the controversial nature of most of the issues involved, it is often impossible to provide definite answers, as they depend on carefully weighing countervailing interests on a case-by-case basis, taking into account the special circumstances prevailing in a given society.

MAJOR ASPECTS OF THE RIGHT TO PRIVACY

Preservation of individual identity and intimacy

Privacy starts with respect for an individual's specific identity, which includes one's name, appearance, clothing, hairstyle, gender, feelings, thoughts and religious and other convictions. Mandatory clothing or hairstyle rules, a forced change or non-recognition of a change of one's name, religion or gender (for instance, a State's refusal to alter the birth registration of a transsexual) or any form of indoctrination ("brainwashing") or forced personality change interfere with the right to privacy. The intimacy of a person must be protected by respecting generally acknowledged obligations of confidentiality (for instance, those of physicians and priests) and guarantees of secrecy (for instance, in voting), and by enacting appropriate data protection laws with enforceable rights to information, correction and deletion of personal data.

Protection of individual autonomy

The extent to which the sphere of autonomy is protected by the right to privacy is a highly controversial issue. Individual autonomy — i.e., the area of private life in which human beings strive to achieve self-realization through action that does not interfere with the rights of others — is central to the liberal concept of privacy. In principle, autonomy gives rise to a right to one's own body, which also comprises a right to act in a manner injurious to one's health, including committing suicide. Nevertheless, societies have consistently deemed such behaviour to be harmful to the common good and morals, and have often prohibited and penalized its manifestations (for instance, suicide, passive euthanasia and drug, alcohol and nicotine consumption). Whether the right of a woman over her own body gives rise to

a right to abortion is a disputed question to which different answers have been provided
by various supreme courts and constitutional courts. The right to privacy also implies an individual's right to communication with others, including the right to develop emotional
relationships. The right to sexual autonomy and sexual relations is especially important, and Governments must be particularly careful when interfering with sexual matters. 103

Protection of the family

Protection of the family is essential to the right to privacy. Institutional guarantees for the
family (i.e., its legal recognition and specific benefits deriving from that status, and the regulation of the legal relationship between spouses, partners, parents and children, etc.)
is intended to protect the social order from trends towards disintegration and to preserve
specific family functions (such as reproduction or bringing up children) — considered indispensable to a society's survival — rather than condone their transfer to other social institutions or the State. The human rights to *marry and found a family, including reproductive*
rights, to equality of spouses, to protection of motherhood and the special rights
of children as laid down in CRC are directly linked to the institutional guarantee of the family. The right of children not to be separated from their parents, the common responsibilities
of both parents for the upbringing and development of the child and the rights to family reunification, foster placement and adoption are particularly important.

The right to privacy entails the protection of family life against arbitrary or unlawful interference, above all by State authorities. One typical interference is the mandatory separation
of children from their parents on grounds of gross disregard of parental duties and the placement of the children under the guardianship of the State. Having heard a number
of cases, the European Court of Human Rights developed certain minimum guarantees for
the parents and children concerned, such as participation in the respective administrative
proceedings, judicial review and regular contact between parents and children during the
time of their placement in foster homes in order to allow family reunification. In the same
vein, after a divorce, both spouses retain the right of access to their children.

Protection of the home

The protection of the home is another important aspect of privacy, since the home conveys a feeling of familiarity, shelter and security, and therefore symbolizes a place of refuge from

What does "family" mean in international human rights law?

In addition to support under the Universal Declaration of Human Rights, the institution of the
family, as the "natural and fundamental group unit of society", enjoys special protection under
article 23 of CCPR, article 10 of CESCR, article 16 of the European Social Charter, article 8 of
ECHR, article 17 of ACHR and article 18 of African Charter on Human and Peoples' Rights.
Th is broad range indicates that the meaning of the term "family" transcends the concept of
a nuclear family prevalent in highly industrialized countries, and encompasses much larger
units, such as the extended family, for example in African societies. In addition to blood relations
and statutory ties (marriage, adoption, registration of homosexual partnerships, etc.),
cohabitation, an economic relationship and the specifi c social and cultural values in a given
society are the key criteria used to determine whether a group with a given type of relationship
between human beings constitutes a family.

Box 62

104

public life where one can best shape one's life according to one's own wishes without fear of
disturbance. In practice, "home" does not apply only to actual dwellings, but also to various
houses or apartments, regardless of legal title (ownership, rental, occupancy, and even
illegal use) or nature of use (as main domicile, weekend house or even business premises).

Every invasion of that sphere — described under the term "home" — that occurs without
the consent of the individuals concerned represents an interference. Th e classic form of
interference is a police search for locating and arresting someone or fi nding evidence to be
used in criminal proceedings. But it is not the only type of interference. Th e violent destruction
of homes by security forces, forced evictions, the use of hidden television cameras or
listening devices, electronic surveillance practices or extreme forms of environmental pollution
(such as noise or noxious fumes) may constitute interference with the right to protection

of the home. Such interference is permissible only if it complies with domestic law and is not arbitrary, i.e., if it occurs for a specific purpose and in accordance with the principle of proportionality. Police searches, seizure and surveillance are usually permissible only on the basis of a written warrant issued by a court, and must not be misused or create disturbance beyond the pursuit of a specific purpose, such as securing evidence.

Protection of private correspondence

Although the term "correspondence" was initially applied to written letters, it now covers all forms of communication at a distance: by telephone, cable, telex, facsimile, electronic mail or other mechanical or electronic means. Protection of correspondence means respect for the secrecy of such communication. Any withholding, censorship, inspection,

Limits on State interference with family life in relation to immigration, expulsion, deportation and extradition laws and policies

Although there is no general right of aliens to enter and reside in a country, arbitrary and discriminatory immigration policies violate the right to family protection and reunification. The longer an alien has lived in a country, especially after marrying and establishing a family there, the stronger the arguments of the Governments must be to justify the person's expulsion and deportation. For instance, in the case of *Berrehab v. the Netherlands* (1988), the European Court of Human Rights held that the mere fact of divorce from his Dutch wife could not justify the expulsion of a Moroccan man who had maintained close ties with his daughter in the Netherlands. On the other hand, if an alien's right to family life must be weighed against such legitimate State interests as the prevention of disorder or crime, then serious criminal conduct by the person in question would usually justify the break-up of a family, even after a long term of residence. Only in exceptional cases of second-generation immigrants with no real attachment to their country of origin or of persons with serious disabilities or diseases has the European Court found that there was a violation of the right to family life. In other words, States enjoy a wide margin of discretion in implementing policies regarding aliens, but must try to strike a balance between legitimate

public interests and the requirement to protect family life and other private circumstances, such
as a regular occupation or property or homeownership in the country of residence.

Box 63

interception or publication of private correspondence constitutes interference. The most
common forms of such interference are surveillance measures secretly taken by State
agencies (opening letters, monitoring telephone conversations and intercepting faxes and
e-mails, etc.) for the purpose of administering justice, preventing crime (e.g., through censorship
of detainees' correspondence) or combating terrorism. As is the case for house
searches, interference with correspondence must comply with domestic law (i.e., as a rule,
it requires a court order) and with the principle of proportionality.

Freedom of movement

Article 13 of UDHR

"1. Everyone has the right to freedom of movement and residence within the borders of each State.
2. Everyone has the right to leave any country, including his own, and to return to his country."

Article 12 of CCPR

"1. Everyone lawfully within the territory of a State shall, within that territory, have the right to liberty of movement and freedom to choose his residence.
2. Everyone shall be free to leave any country, including his own.
3. The above-mentioned rights shall not be subject to any restrictions except those which
are provided by law, are necessary to protect national security, public order, public health
or morals or the rights and freedoms of others, and are consistent with the other rights recognized in the present Covenant.
4. No one shall be arbitrarily deprived of the right to enter his own country."

The right to privacy and the fight against terrorism

The right to privacy has been particularly affected by laws enacted recently in a number of
countries to broaden police and intelligence service powers to combat terrorism. In addition
to the extension of traditional police functions such as search, seizure and surveillance (often
without prior authorization by a court), typical examples include electronically supported
surveillance of "sleeper units" and other potential terrorists by means of screening, scanning,

processing, combining, matching, storing and monitoring huge amounts of private data, and
such methods as the automatic taking of fingerprints and blood and DNA samples of target
groups, which are often selected through racial profiling.

In this area (as in connection with other human rights, such as the rights to personal liberty and
fair trial), *members of parliament bear a key responsibility:* they must ensure that any extension
of police and intelligence powers, if necessary at all, takes place:

1. Transparently and democratically;
2. With due respect for international human rights standards;
3. Without undermining the precious values of a free and democratic society: individual liberty, privacy and the rule of law.

Box 64

Article 13 of CCPR

"An alien lawfully in the territory of a State Party to the present Covenant may be expelled
therefrom only in pursuance of a decision reached in accordance with law and shall,
except where compelling reasons of national security otherwise require, be allowed
to submit the reasons against his expulsion and to have his case reviewed by, and
be represented for the purpose before, the competent authority or a person
or persons especially designated by the competent authority."

The Universal Declaration of Human Rights and CCPR protect the right of every person sojourning lawfully in a country to move freely and choose a place of residence anywhere
on the territory of that country. This right should be protected from both public and private
interference.

THE FREEDOM OF MOVEMENT OF ALIENS WITHIN A STATE

Since this right relates only to persons who are lawfully in the territory of a State, Governments
may impose restrictions on the entry of aliens, screening those who seek entry.
Whether an alien is "lawfully" in the territory of a State should be determined according to domestic law, which may specify entry restrictions, provided that they meet the State's
international obligations.

Aliens who enter a country illegally but whose status is subsequently regularized must be considered to be in the territory lawfully. If a person is lawfully in a country, any restriction
imposed on that person or any treatment of that person other than the treatment reserved to nationals must be justified under article 12 (3) of CCPR.

A good example of restrictions imposed on an alien and admissible under that article is provided by the case of *Celepli v. Sweden* before the Human Rights Committee (1994). Mr. Celepli, a Turkish citizen of Kurdish origin living in Sweden, was ordered to leave the country on grounds of suspected involvement in terrorist activities. That order was not enforced, and he was allowed to stay on, in a municipality where he had to report regularly to the police. The Human Rights Committee found that these restrictions were in conformity with the provisions of article 12 (3) of CCPR, and were therefore legal.

FREEDOM TO LEAVE A COUNTRY

Article 12 (2) of CCPR stipulates that all persons (citizens and aliens, and even persons sojourning in a country illegally) are free to leave the territory of a State. This right applies to short and long visits abroad and to (permanent or semi-permanent) emigration. Enjoyment of this right should not depend on the purpose or duration of travel abroad. This right imposes obligations on both the State of residence and the State of nationality.

For instance, the State of nationality must issue travel documents or passports to all citizens both within and outside the national territory. If a State refuses to issue a passport or requires its citizens to obtain exit visas in order to leave, there is interference, which is difficult to justify. Moreover, the Human Rights Committee has condemned a national

law which restricted the right of women to leave the country by requiring their husbands' consent.

LIMITATIONS

Freedom of movement must not be restricted except where such restrictions are provided for by law and where they are necessary on grounds of national security, public order, public health or morals or the rights and freedoms of others (article 12 (3) of CCPR). According to the Human Rights Committee, these requirements would not be met, for instance, "if an individual were prevented from leaving a country merely on the grounds that he or she is the holder of 'State secrets', or if an individual were prevented from travelling internally without a specific permit". Likewise, preventing women from moving freely or from leaving the country without the consent or the escort of a male person constitutes a violation of article 12 of CCPR. On the other hand, restrictions on access to military zones on national security grounds or limitations on the freedom to settle in areas inhabited by indigenous or minority communities may constitute permissible restrictions.

Barriers to freedom of movement: examples

Freedom of movement is often subjected to the unnecessary barriers listed below, which make
travelling within or between countries diffi cult or impossible. Parliamentarians may wish to
oppose such measures.

Movement within the country
- Obligation to obtain a permit for internal travel
- Obligation to apply for permission to change residence
- Obligation to seek approval by the local authorities of the place of destination
- Administrative delays in processing written applications

Movement to another country
- Lack of access to the authorities or to information regarding requirements
- Requirement to apply for special forms in order to obtain the actual application forms for
the issuance of a passport
- Requirement to produce statements of support by employers or relatives
- Requirement to submit an exact description of the travel route
- High fees for the issuance of a passport
- Unreasonable delays in the issuance of travel documents
- Restrictions on family members travelling together
- Requirement to make a repatriation deposit or have a return ticket
- Requirement to produce an invitation from the State of destination
- Harassment of applicants

Box 65

108

THE RIGHT TO ENTER ONE'S OWN COUNTRY

Article 12 (4) of CCPR implies that one has the right to remain in one's own country and to return to it after having left it, and it may entitle a person to enter a country for the fi rst
time (if he or she is a national of that country but was born abroad). Th e right to return is
particularly important for refugees seeking voluntary repatriation.

Th e wording "one's own country" refers primarily to citizens of that country. In exceptional
cases, persons who have resided for a very long period in a country as aliens, or who were born there as second-generation immigrants, may consider their country of residence
as their "own" country.

Freedom of thought, conscience and religion

Article 18 of UDHR

"Everyone has the right to freedom of thought, conscience and religion; this right includes
freedom to change his religion or belief, and freedom, either alone or in community with
others and in public or private, to manifest his religion or belief in teaching, practice,

worship and observance."
Article 18 of CCPR
"1. Everyone shall have the right to freedom of thought, conscience and religion. This right
shall include freedom to have or to adopt a religion or belief of his choice, and freedom, either individually or in community with others and in public or private, to manifest his religion or belief in worship, observance, practice and teaching.

Enacting limitations and overseeing their implementation
Drawing up legislation
In adopting laws that provide for restrictions under article 12 (3) of CCPR, parliaments should
always be guided by the principle that the restrictions must not defeat the purpose of the right.
The laws must stipulate precise criteria for the restrictions — which should be implemented
objectively — and respect the principle of proportionality; the restrictions should be appropriate,
should be the least intrusive possible, and should be proportionate to the interest to be protected.

Implementation
If a State decides to impose restrictions, they should be specified in a law. Restrictions not
provided for by law and not in conformity with article 12 (3) of CCPR directly violate freedom
of movement. Actual implementation of any restrictions should meet the requirements of necessity and proportionality, as explained above. Furthermore, the restrictions must be
consistent with other rights provided for under CCPR and with the principles of equality and
non-discrimination.

Box 66

109

2. No one shall be subject to coercion which would impair his freedom to have or to adopt
a religion or belief of his choice.
3. Freedom to manifest one's religion or beliefs may be subject only to such limitations as
are prescribed by law and are necessary to protect public safety, order, health, or morals or
the fundamental rights and freedoms of others.
4. The States Parties to the present Covenant undertake to have respect for the liberty of
parents and, when applicable, legal guardians to ensure the religious and moral education

of their children in conformity with their own convictions."

The right to freedom of thought, conscience and religion is so essential that it is not subject to derogation, even in a state of emergency. What is known as the *forum internum*, i.e., the right to form one's own thoughts, opinions, conscience, convictions and beliefs, is an absolute right protected against any form of State interference, such as indoctrination ("brainwashing"). However, the public manifestation of religion or belief may be restricted on legitimate grounds.

The terms "religion" and "belief" should be interpreted broadly, to include traditional as well as non-traditional beliefs and religions, whether theistic, non-theistic or atheist. The freedom to have or to adopt a religion or belief includes the freedom to choose, which may entail replacing a previously held religion or belief with another, or to adopt atheist views, or to retain one's religion or belief.

PROHIBITION OF COERCION

Under no circumstances may a person be coerced by the use or threat of physical force or penal sanctions to adopt, adhere to or recant a specific religion or belief. The prohibition also applies to policies or measures that have the same effect. For instance, membership per se in a religious group may not disqualify a person from public service positions.

MANIFESTING A RELIGION OR BELIEF

The meaning of "manifestation" is very broad. It encompasses:
- Worship: performing ritual and ceremonial acts, building places of worship, using ritual formulae and objects, displaying symbols, and observing holidays and days of rest;
- Observance: performing ceremonial acts, applying dietary regulations, wearing distinctive clothing or headgear, and using a specific language;
- Practice and teaching: choosing religious leaders, priests and teachers, setting up seminaries or religious schools, and producing or distributing religious texts or publications.

Since the manifestation of one's religion or belief is necessarily active, it may affect the enjoyment of some rights by other persons, and in extreme cases even endanger society.

Under article 18 (3) of CCPR, therefore, it can be subject to specific limitations.

LIMITATIONS ON THE MANIFESTATION OF ONE'S RELIGION OR BELIEF

Limitations on the freedom to *manifest* one's religion or beliefs are subject to strictly specifi
ed conditions, and are allowed only if they are:
• Prescribed by law; and
• Necessary for protecting public safety, order, health, or morals or the fundamental rights and freedoms of others.
One example of permissible grounds for a limitation of the freedom to manifest one's religion or belief is when such manifestations amount to propaganda for war or advocacy
of national, racial or religious hatred that constitutes incitement to discrimination, hostility
or violence. All too often, religious intolerance is the source of violent confl icts between ethnic and religious groups.

RELIGIOUS AND MORAL EDUCATION
Article 18 (4) of CCPR requires States to respect the freedom of parents and legal guardians
to bring up their children in accordance with their own religious and moral convictions. Compulsory religious or moral education in public schools is not incompatible with that provision, if religion is taught in an objective and pluralistic manner (for instance, as part of a course on the general history of religion and ethics). If one religion is taught in a public
school, provisions should be made for non-discriminatory exemptions or alternatives, accommodating
the wishes of all parents or legal guardians.

Freedom of opinion and expression
Article 19 of UDHR
"Everyone has the right to freedom of opinion and expression; this right includes freedom
to hold opinions without interference and to seek, receive and impart information and ideas through any media and regardless of frontiers."

The ban on overt religious symbols in French schools
Controversy over a French law enacted in 2004 shows how sensitive the issue of placing limits
on manifestations of religion or belief can be. A bill was passed by a massive majority of members
of parliament, banning overt religious symbols from French State schools. Th e law has been widely seen as targeting the Islamic headscarf, although the ban includes Jewish skullcaps
and large Christian crosses.
While the French parliament and Government justify the law by invoking the principle of secularity
(strict separation of State and religion) and the need to protect Muslim girls against gender-

specific discrimination, many human rights groups have argued that the ban violates the
right to freedom of religion or belief and that it constitutes coercion, expressly forbidden under
article 18 (2) of CCPR.

Box 67
111
Article 19 of CCPR
"1. Everyone shall have the right to hold opinions without interference.
2. Everyone shall have the right to freedom of expression; this right shall include freedom to
seek, receive and impart information and ideas of all kinds, regardless of frontiers, either
orally, in writing or in print, in the form of art, or through any other media of his choice.
3. The exercise of the rights provided for in paragraph 2
of this article carries with it special duties and responsibilities.
It may therefore be subject to certain restrictions,
but these shall only be such as are provided by law and are necessary:
(a) For respect of the rights or reputations of others;
(b) For the protection of national security or of public order, or of public health or morals."

Two main elements can be distinguished in the above provisions:
- Freedom of opinion; and
- Freedom of expression.

FREEDOM OF OPINION

The right to hold opinions is by nature passive and forms an absolute freedom. CCPR allows
for no exceptions or restrictions in the enjoyment of that freedom — whose absolute
nature, however, vanishes as soon as the holder of an opinion manifests it, as that aspect
is related to the freedom of expression. As we shall see, the latter can and even must be
restricted under some circumstances.

FREEDOM OF EXPRESSION

Freedom of expression, along with freedom of assembly and association, is a cornerstone
of democratic society. Democracy cannot be realized without a free flow of ideas and information,
and the possibility for people to gather, to discuss and voice ideas, criticism
and demands, to defend their interests and rights and to set up organizations for that purpose,
such as trade unions and political parties. The United Nations Special Rapporteur
on freedom of expression has described that right as "an essential test right, the enjoyment
of which illustrates the degree of enjoyment of all human rights enshrined in the International

Bill of Human Rights, and that respect for this right reflects a country's standards of fair play, justice and integrity." 33

All regional and international monitoring bodies have underlined the paramount importance of this right for democracy. The African Commission on Human and Peoples' Rights did so by adopting the Declaration of Principles on Freedom of Expression in Africa in October 2002.

33 UN Commission on Human Rights, *Report of the Special Rapporteur on the promotion and protection of the right to freedom of opinion and expression* (E/CN.4/2002/75), January 2002.

Freedom of expression comprises not only the right of individuals to express their own thoughts, but also the right to seek, receive and impart information and ideas of all kinds.

It has therefore an individual and social dimension: it is a right that belongs to individuals, and also implies the collective right to receive any information whatsoever and to have access to the thoughts expressed by others.

Freedom of expression – a broad right

In the case of *Handyside v. the United Kingdom* (1976), a publishing firm put out "the Little Red Book", intended for — and made available to — schoolchildren aged 12 or more. The book contained chapters on sex and addresses for help and advice on sexual matters. As a result of a number of complaints received by the authorities, the applicant's premises were searched, copies of the book were seized, and the applicant was found guilty of having in his possession obscene books for publication for gain. He was fined and ordered to pay costs. The conviction was upheld on appeal, and the books that had been seized were destroyed. A revised edition was later issued. The European Court of Human Rights ruled that there had been no violation of the right to freedom of expression, since the authorities had limited themselves to what was strictly necessary in a democratic society. However, it stressed that the utmost attention should be paid to the principles characterizing a democratic society. It held that freedom of expression

constituted one of the essential foundations of such a society, and was a basic condition for its
progress and for the development of every individual. Subject to legitimate restrictions, it was
applicable "not only to information or ideas that are favourably received or regarded as inoffensive
or as a matter of indifference, but also to those that offend, shock or disturb the State or any
sector of the population. Such are the demands of pluralism, tolerance and broad-mindedness
without which there is no democratic society".

In the case of *Feldek v. Slovakia* (2001), in which the applicant had been found guilty of defamation
for accusing a newly appointed minister of having a fascist past, the European Court
reaffirmed that freedom of expression was of the highest importance in the context of political
debate, and considered that very strong reasons were required to justify restrictions on
political speech. It held that the applicant's statement was a value judgement, the truthfulness
of which was not susceptible to proof, and stated that the "requirement to prove the truth of a
value judgement is impossible to fulfil and infringes freedom of opinion itself". Elaborating on
the extent to which a value judgement had to be linked to facts, the Court concluded that the
applicant's freedom of expression had been violated, because the domestic courts had failed
to establish any pressing social need for protecting the personal rights of the minister which
would have been stronger than the applicant's right to freedom of expression and the general
interest in promoting freedoms on issues of public interest.

In the *Jersild case* (1994), a reporter had been sentenced for incitement to discrimination after
he had interviewed skinheads who had expressed radical racist and anti-foreign statements. The
European Court found that the sentence violated freedom of expression, especially because the
programme, on the whole, was critical of skinheads and their ideology, and therefore did not
constitute incitement to discrimination.

Box 68

"Freedom of expression is a cornerstone upon which the very existence of a

democratic society rests. It is indispensable for the formation of public opinion. It is also a conditio sine qua non for the development of political parties, trade unions, scientific and cultural societies and, in general, those who wish to influence the public. It represents, in short, the means that enable the community, when exercising its options, to be sufficiently informed. Consequently, it can be said that a society that is not well informed is not a society that is truly free."
Inter-American Court of Human Rights,
Advisory Opinion OC-5/85, paragraph 70.

Freedom to impart information and ideas

This aspect of the freedom of expression is of particular importance to parliamentarians, because it entails the freedom to express oneself politically. In the case of *Kivenmaa v. Finland* (1994) concerning a demonstration to denounce the human rights record of a foreign head of State who was on an official visit to Finland, the Human Rights Committee found that "the right for an individual to express his political opinions, including obviously his opinions on the question of human rights, forms part of the freedom of expression guaranteed by article 19 of the Covenant". It is, as the European Court of Human Rights has consistently stated, "not only applicable to 'information' or 'ideas' that are favourably received or regarded as inoffensive or as a matter of indifference, but also to those that offend, shock or disturb" (see Box 68).

Freedom to seek and receive information

"Public bodies hold information not for themselves but as custodians of the public good and everyone has a right to access this information, subject to clearly defined rules established by law."
Declaration of Principles on Freedom of Expression in Africa, article IV.

Without freedom to seek and receive information, the media, members of parliament and others would be unable to expose cases of possible corruption, mismanagement or inefficiency and to ensure transparent and accountable government. In his 1995 report to the United Nations Commission on Human Rights, the Special Rapporteur on freedom of opinion and expression stressed that "freedom will be bereft of all effectiveness if the people have no access to information. Access to information is basic to the democratic way of life. The tendency to withhold information from the people at large is therefore strongly to be checked." 34

34 E/CN.4/1995/32, paragraph 35.

Media freedom

A crucial aspect of freedom of expression is freedom of the press and other media. The Human Rights Committee stated in its general comment No. 10 that "… because of the development of modern mass media, effective measures are necessary to prevent such control
of the media as would interfere with the right of everyone to freedom of expression in a way that is not provided for …".

Restrictions

Article 19 (3) of CCPR underscores that the exercise of the right to freedom of expression
carries with it special duties and responsibilities, and that this justifies some restrictions on that right.

Any restriction on the right to freedom of expression must, however, meet the following strict tests of justification:

• The restriction must be *provided by law* (legislation enacted by parliament, common law articulated by the courts or professional rules). The restriction must be precise and meet the criteria of legal certainty and predictability: it must be accessible to the individual concerned and its consequences for him or her must be foreseeable. Laws that are too vague or allow for excessive discretion in their application fail to protect individuals against arbitrary interference and do not constitute adequate safeguards against abuse;

Laws on access to information

Many countries have adopted access-to-information laws. Such laws have proved instrumental
in exposing human rights violations and fighting impunity. In her study on impunity prepared
for the United Nations Commission on Human Rights in 2004, the Independent Expert (to
update the set of principles for the protection and the promotion of human rights through action
to combat impunity) provided a number of examples in which such laws enabled victims of human rights violations to know the truth. For instance, "the South African History Archive
of the University of Witwatersrand has utilized South Africa's Promotion of Access to Information
Act, which was adopted in 2000, to pursue 'missing' records and expose the degree to which some files were concealed from the country's truth commission." The expert recommended
that, "in view of their potential for enhancing citizens' access to the truth concerning human rights violations, States that have not already done so adopt legislation enabling citizens
to obtain access to Government documents, including those disclosing information concerning
human rights violations." She cited as model in this regard Mexico's Federal Access to Information

Act (*Ley Federal de Acceso a la Información*), enacted in 2002, "which bars the withholding
of documents that describe 'grave violations' of human rights". 35

Box 69

35 E/CN.4/2004/88, paragraph 20.

115

- The restriction must be *necessary* for:

respecting the rights or reputations of others;

protecting national security, public order, public health or morals.

The latter criterion can be met only if the restriction addresses a pressing social need and is proportional to the legitimate aim pursued, so that the harm to freedom of expression
does not outweigh the benefits.

Restriction on grounds of national security and public order

In the case of *Mukong v. Cameroon* (1994), a journalist claimed that his right to freedom of expression and opinion had been violated, and that he had been repeatedly arrested and
some of his books had been banned by the State because of his activities as an advocate of
multiparty democracy. The State invoked national security and public order under article
19 (3) of CCPR. The Human Rights Committee concluded that the measures taken by the
State were not necessary, and considered that "the legitimate objective of safeguarding and indeed strengthening national unity under difficult political circumstances cannot be
achieved by attempting to muzzle advocacy of multiparty democracy, democratic tenets and human rights".

Safeguarding freedom of the media

Parliament may take a number of steps that can contribute to ensuring that there are free and
independent media, including the following measures:

- Revising media laws and amending them, if necessary, to bring them into conformity with
article 19 of CCPR, in particular, as recommended by the United Nations Special Rapporteur
on the freedom of opinion and expression, abolishing any laws that punish press offences with imprisonment, except in cases involving racist or discriminatory comments
or calls to violence, and ensuring that any fines for offences such as libel, defamation and
insults, etc., are not out of proportion with the harm suffered by the victims;
- Encouraging plurality and independence of newspapers;

- Ensuring that broadcasters are protected against political and commercial influence, including
through the appointment of an independent governing board and respect for editorial independence;
- Ensuring that an independent broadcasting licensing authority is set up;
- Establishing clear criteria for payment and withdrawal of Government subsidies to the press, in order to avoid the use of subsidies for stifling criticism of the authorities;
- Avoiding excessive concentration of media control; implementing measures ensuring impartial
allocation of resources and equitable access to the media; and adopting antitrust legislation regarding the media;
- Promoting universal access to the Internet.

Box 70

Restriction on grounds of public morals

In the case of *Open Door Counselling and Dublin Woman Well Centre and Others v. Ireland*
(1992), two corporate applicants had engaged in non-directive counselling of pregnant women in Ireland, concerning the possibility of obtaining abortions in clinics in
Great Britain. A perpetual injunction had been issued to restrain them from that activity on the grounds that abortion was illegal under the Irish Constitution. The European Court
of Human Rights, while stating that a State's discretion in the area of protection of morals
was not unfettered and unreviewable, stressed that the national authorities enjoyed a wide margin of appreciation in matters of morals and reiterated its position that it was not
possible to find among the legal and social orders of the States parties a uniform European
concept of morals. However, it considered that the injunction imposed was too broad and
disproportionate. It held therefore that it constituted a violation of the applicants' right both to disseminate information and to receive such information.

Restriction on the ground of respect for the rights and reputation of others

In the case of *Krone Verlag GmbH & Co. KG v. Austria* (2002) concerning the prevention of a newspaper from publishing the picture of a politician in conjunction with allegations

Freedom of expression and parliamentarians: closer scrutiny of any interference with their freedom of expression, but also greater tolerance of criticism

Freedom of expression is the parliamentarians' main working tool. The IPU Committee on the
Human Rights of Parliamentarians has consistently stressed that, in accordance with their representative
mandates, parliamentarians must be able to express themselves freely as defenders of the rights of the citizens who elect them.

In the important case of *Castells v. Spain* (1992), which involved a member of parliament who had been convicted for publishing an article accusing the Government of complicity in several attacks and murders, the European Court of Human Rights stated that "while freedom of expression is important for everybody, it is especially so for an elected representative of the people. He represents his electorate, draws attention to their preoccupations and defends their interests. Accordingly, interferences with the freedom of expression of an opposition member of parliament ... call for the closest scrutiny on the part of the Court...". It also affirmed that "the limits of permissible criticism are wider with regard to the Government than in relation to a private citizen, or even a politician. In a democratic system the actions or omissions of the Government must be subject to the close scrutiny not only of the legislative and judicial authorities but also of the press and public opinion. Furthermore, the dominant position which the Government occupies makes it necessary for it to display restraint in resorting to criminal proceedings, particularly where other means are available for replying to the unjustified attacks and criticisms of its adversaries or the media ...". In many instances, the European Court has ruled that in order to protect freedom of expression, people should be allowed to criticize politicians more harshly than those who had not chosen to be public figures (see, for instance, the cases of *Lingens v. Austria* (1986) and *Dichand and Others v. Austria* (2002).

Box 71

about his financial situation, the European Court of Human Rights found that the interference by the authorities was prescribed by law and pursued the legitimate aim of protecting the privacy of a person, but did not meet the test of necessity in a democratic society. It found that the issue raised was of public interest, that it concerned a public figure and that the publication of the picture in itself did not disclose any details of the politician's private life. Consequently, the interference did not address a pressing social need, and constituted a violation of freedom of expression.

Mandatory limitations on freedom of expression
Article 20 of CCPR lists mandatory limitations to article 19 in relation to propaganda for war and advocacy of national, racial or religious hatred that constitutes incitement to
discrimination, hostility or violence. The Human Rights Committee has stated that "for article 20 to become fully effective, there *ought to be a law* making it clear that propaganda
and advocacy as described therein are contrary to public policy, and providing for an appropriate
sanction in case of violation" (general comment No. 11).
The Human Rights Committee has encouraged Governments to take legal measures to restrict the publication or dissemination of obscene and pornographic material portraying
women and girls as objects of violence or degrading or inhuman treatment (general comment
No. 28).

Freedom of peaceful assembly and association
Article 20 of UDHR
"1. Everyone has the right to freedom of peaceful assembly and association.
2. No one may be compelled to belong to an association."

The case of *Faurisson v. France* (Human Rights Committee, 1996)
Mr. Faurisson was a professor of literature at the University of the Sorbonne in Paris until
1973 and at the University of Lyons until 1991, when he was removed from his chair for having
questioned the existence of extermination gas chambers in Nazi concentration camps. In 1990,
the French legislature passed the Gayssot Act, which amended the 1881 law on the freedom
of the press by making it an offence to contest the existence of the category of crimes against
humanity defined in the London Charter of 8 August 1945, on the basis of which the Nazi leaders
were tried and convicted by the Nuremberg Tribunal in 1945-1946. In 1991, the author was
convicted of repeating the same views in a published interview.
The author submitted a communication to the Human Rights Committee, contending that the
Gayssot Act violated his right to freedom of expression and academic freedom. The Human
Rights Committee found that the restriction of Mr. Faurisson's freedom of expression was permissible
under article 19 (3) of CCPR, because that restriction served the aspirations of the

Jewish community to live free from fear of an atmosphere of anti-Semitism. The Human Rights
Committee also found that the restriction was necessary to fight racism and anti-Semitism.

Box 72

118

Article 21 of CCPR

"The right of peaceful assembly shall be recognized. No restrictions may be placed on the
exercise of this right other than those imposed in conformity with the law and which are
necessary in a democratic society in the interests of national security or public safety,
public order, the protection of public health or morals or the protection of the rights and
freedoms of others."

Article 22 (1) and (2) of CCPR

"1. Everyone shall have the right to freedom of association with others, including the right
to form and join trade unions for the protection of his interests.
2. No restrictions may be placed on the exercise of this right other than those which are
prescribed by law and which are necessary in a democratic society in the interests of
national security or public safety, public order, the protection of public health or morals
or the protection of the rights and freedoms of others. This article shall not prevent the
imposition of lawful restrictions on members of the armed forces and of the police in their
exercise of this right."

Freedom of peaceful assembly and of association are, together with freedom of expression,
key rights in a democratic society, since they enable the people to participate in the democratic process. As is the case for freedom of expression, they too are subject to certain
limitations.

FREEDOM OF ASSEMBLY

Scope

Protecting freedom of assembly guarantees the right to hold meetings aimed at discussing
information or ideas publicly or at disseminating them. However, assemblies are protected
only if they are "peaceful" — a term that must be interpreted broadly. For instance, States
parties must prevent a peaceful assembly from leading to a riot as a result of provocation
or the use of force by security forces or private parties, such as counter-demonstrators or
agents provocateurs.

States are under an obligation to take positive measures to guarantee this right and

protect it against interference by State agencies and private parties alike. To that end, the
authorities must take measures to ensure the smooth functioning of gatherings and demonstrations.
Accordingly, they should be informed of the location and time of a planned
assembly with sufficient advance notice, and should be granted access to it.

Limitations

Th e right to assemble peacefully is subject to restrictions, which must be:

• In conformity with the law: interference with the freedom of assembly can be
undertaken independently by administrative authorities, particularly the police, on
the basis of a general statutory authorization;

• Necessary in a democratic society: for instance, they must be proportional and
compatible with the basic democratic values of pluralism, tolerance, broad-mindedness
and people's sovereignty; accordingly, breaking up an assembly forcefully is permissible
only if all other milder means have failed;

• Aimed at a legitimate purpose, such as national security, public safety (an assembly
may be broken up if it constitutes a specific threat to persons or passers-by), public
order, public health and public morals and the rights and freedoms of others.

FREEDOM OF ASSOCIATION

Scope

Protecting freedom of association guarantees the right of anyone to found an association
with like-minded persons or to join an existing association. Th us, a strict one-party system
that precludes the formation and activities of other political parties violates freedom of association.

Th e formation of and membership in an association must be voluntary; nobody
may be forced — directly or indirectly — by the State or by private parties to join a political
party, a religious society, a commercial undertaking or a sports club. States are under an
obligation to provide the legal framework for setting up associations and to protect this
right against interference by private parties.

Freedom of association includes the right to form and join trade unions to protect one's
interests. Trade union rights are more specifically laid down in article 8 of CESCR.

The case of *Socialist Party of Turkey (STP) and Others v. Turkey*
(European Court of Human Rights, 2003)

STP was formed on 6 November 1992, but on 30 November 1993 the Constitutional Court of
Turkey ordered its dissolution on the grounds that its programme was liable to undermine the
territorial integrity of the State and the unity of the nation. It found that STP had called for a

right of self-determination for the Kurds and supported the right to "wage a war of independence",
and likened its views to those of terrorist groups. The applicants alleged, inter alia, that the party's dissolution had infringed their rights, as guaranteed under article 11 of ECHR on
freedom of association.

The European Court of Human Rights found that the dissolution of STP amounted to an interference
with the applicants' right to freedom of association. There could be no justification for hindering a political group merely because it sought to debate in public the situation of part of
the State's population and to participate in the nation's political life in order to find, by democratic
means, solutions capable of satisfying every group concerned. Moreover, since the Constitutional
Court had ruled even before STP had begun its activities, the European Court found that there was no evidence before it to support the allegation that STP had any responsibility for
the problems posed by terrorism in Turkey. According to the European Court, the dissolution
was therefore disproportionate and unnecessary in a democratic society.

Box 73

120

Limitations

Freedom of association is subject to the same restrictions as freedom of assembly: any limitations must be provided for by law, necessary in a democratic society and serve one of
the purposes justifying interference, namely protection of national security, public safety,
public order, public health or morals and the interests and freedoms of others. Associations
that advocate national, racial or religious hatred should be banned in the interest of others, pursuant to article 20 (2) of CCPR, which prohibits any advocacy of national, racial
or religious hatred.

The right to participate in government

Article 21 of UDHR

"1. Everyone has the right to take part in the government of his country, directly or through freely chosen representatives.

2. Everyone has the right to equal access to public service in his country.

3. The will of the people shall be the basis of the authority of government; this will shall be
expressed in periodic and genuine elections which shall be by universal and equal suffrage

and shall be held by secret vote or by equivalent free voting procedures."
Article 25 of CCPR
"Every citizen shall have the right and the opportunity:
(a) To take part in the conduct of public affairs, directly or through freely chosen representatives;
(b) To vote and to be elected at genuine periodic elections, which shall be by universal and equal suffrage and shall be held by secret ballot, guaranteeing the free expression of the will of the electors;
(c) To have access, on general terms of equality, to public service in his country."

The right to take part in government is a cornerstone of modern democracy and therefore crucial for parliament. The correct implementation of this right has direct implications for the democratic nature of parliament, and ultimately for the legitimacy of the Government and its policies.

The right in fact has three components, which are explained below:
- The general right to public participation;
- The right to vote and be elected;
- Equal access to public service.

THE GENERAL RIGHT TO PUBLIC PARTICIPATION

The right to public participation consists of (a) indirect participation in public affairs through elected representatives, and (b) direct participation in public affairs.

Indirect participation

It is mainly through elections and the constitution of representative bodies — particularly a national parliament — that the people participate in the conduct of public affairs, express their will and hold the Government to account. The Human Rights Committee has stated that the powers of representative bodies should be legally enforceable and should not be restricted to advisory functions, and that the representatives should exercise only the powers given to them in accordance with constitutional provisions (general comment No. 25). For parliaments truly to reflect the will of the people, elections must be genuine, free and fair and held at not unduly long intervals. In 1994, IPU adopted the Declaration on Criteria for Free and Fair Elections, which specifies criteria for voting and election rights; candidature, party and campaign rights and responsibilities; and the rights and responsibilities of States. The United Nations — as part of its electoral assistance and electoral observation activities — has also established clear criteria for what should be common elements of electoral laws and procedures.

Direct participation

Direct participation means that not only elected representatives, but citizens too are able to
participate directly in public affairs, either through public debate and dialogue with elected
representatives, referendums and popular initiatives, or through self-organization, guaranteed
under the freedoms of expression, assembly and association. In the case of *Marshall v. Canada* (1991), however, the Human Rights Committee recognized a broad margin of discretion of States with regard to granting direct rights of political participation:
"It must be beyond dispute that the conduct of public affairs in a democratic State is the task of representatives of the people, elected for that purpose, and public officials appointed
in accordance with the law. Invariably, the conduct of public affairs affects the

The IPU Declaration on Criteria for Free and Fair Elections (1994)

The authority of parliament derives largely from its capacity to reflect faithfully the diversity of
all components of society, and this in turn depends on the way elections are organized. IPU has
therefore put considerable effort into the formulation of election criteria. An important outcome
of that work is the Declaration on Criteria for Free and Fair Elections, which was adopted
in 1994. It is mainly based on a study of the content and rules of international law and State
practice in respect of elections, covering the entire electoral process, from the electoral law to
balloting, monitoring the poll, counting ballots, proclaiming the results, examining complaints
and resolving disputes. The Declaration also addresses the issues of voting and election rights;
candidature, party and campaign rights and responsibilities; and the rights and responsibilities
of the State. The first such document to express a worldwide political consensus on the subject,
the Declaration has been used as a guideline for elections in many countries.

Box 74

interests of large segments of the population or even the population as a whole, while in
other instances it affects more directly the interests of more specific groups of society. Although prior consultations, such as public hearings or consultations with the most interested
groups, may often be envisaged by law or have evolved as public policy in the

conduct of public affairs, article 25 (a) of the Covenant cannot be understood as meaning
that any directly affected group, large or small, has the unconditional right to choose
the modalities of participation in the conduct of public affairs. That, in fact, would be an
extrapolation of the right to direct participation by the citizens, far beyond the scope of article 25 (a)."

THE RIGHT TO VOTE AND BE ELECTED

The right to vote and be elected is crucial for parliament as a democratic institution, for members of parliament, and for democracy as a whole. Its proper implementation and realization has a direct impact on the way voters perceive their elected representatives, on
the legitimacy of the legislation that parliament enacts and on the decisions it takes. It is therefore directly related to the essence of parliament and the idea of popular rule through
representatives. Any breach of this right has direct consequences for parliament's legitimacy
and even an impact — in the most serious cases — on law and order and on stability in a country. Moreover, parliamentarians are guardians of the proper exercise of the right
to vote and to stand for election.

For elections to be free and fair, they must take place in an atmosphere free from intimidation
and respectful of fundamental human rights, particularly with respect for freedom of expression, of assembly and of association, with independent judicial procedures and with protection from discrimination. Elections must be organized in a way ensuring that the will of the people is freely and effectively expressed and the electorate is offered an
actual choice.

The right to vote and be elected should be established by law on the basis of non-discrimination
and equal access of all persons to the election process. Although participation in elections may be limited to the citizens of a State, no restriction on unreasonable grounds, such as physical disability, illiteracy, educational background, party membership
or property requirements, is permitted.

The right to vote

Persons entitled to vote should be able to register, and any manipulation of registration and
the voting itself, such as intimidation or coercion, should be prohibited by law. The elections
should be based on the principle of "one person, one vote". The drawing of electoral boundaries and the methods of vote allocation should not distort the distribution of voters

or discriminate against any social groups.
Positive measures should be taken to solve diffi culties such as illiteracy, language barriers
(information should also be made available in minority languages), poverty or obstacles to freedom of movement.

Citizens should be protected from coercion or from attempts to compel them to reveal their voting intentions or preferences, and the principle of the secret ballot must be upheld.

The right to be elected
Th e right to stand for election may be subject to restrictions, such as minimum age, but they must be justifi able and reasonable. As said, physical disability, illiteracy, educational
background, party membership or property requirements should never apply as restrictive
conditions.
Furthermore, conditions relating to nomination dates, fees or deposits should be reasonable
and not discriminatory. Th e Human Rights Committee has expressed concern
over the fi nancial costs involved in seeking election to public offi ce in the United States of
America, and considered that they adversely aff ect the right to stand for election.

Voting procedures
Elections should be free and fair, and periodic. Voters should be free to support or oppose
the Government, and form opinions independently. Elections must be held by secret ballot,
ensuring that the will of the electors is expressed freely.
Measures should be adopted to guarantee genuine, free, fair and periodic elections, and laws and procedures should be introduced ensuring that the right to vote can actually be
freely exercised by all citizens.
One such crucial measure is the establishment of an independent authority to supervise the electoral process. It is important to ensure the security of ballot boxes during voting. After the voting, ballots should be counted in the presence of (international) observers, candidates or their agents.

EQUAL ACCESS TO PUBLIC SERVICE
As regards public service positions, the basic principle of equality must govern the appointment
criteria and processes, promotion, suspension and dismissal, which should be objective and reasonable.
In their oversight functions, parliamentarians should pay particular attention to conditions
for access, existing restrictions, the processes for appointment, promotion, suspension

and dismissal or removal from office, and the judicial or other review mechanisms available with regard to these processes.

MEDIA AND POLITICAL PARTIES

Lastly, it is essential that citizens, candidates and elected representatives be able freely to discuss and communicate information and ideas on political affairs, hold peaceful demonstrations and meetings, publish political material and campaign for election. An independent press and free media — key elements of such an environment — and respect for freedom of association, ensuring the possibility to form and join political parties, are crucial for a well-functioning democracy.

CHAPTER 13:
WHAT PARLIAMENTARIANS SHOULD KNOW ABOUT THE ECONOMIC, SOCIAL AND CULTURAL RIGHTS CONTAINED IN THE UNIVERSAL DECLARATION OF HUMAN RIGHTS

The most serious violations of economic, social and cultural rights today are attributable to poverty. Accordingly, addressing poverty is key to the prevention of human rights violations and the promotion and protection of human rights. A discussion of the main economic, social and cultural rights should therefore be preceded by an examination of the social and economic trends that currently have an impact on their enjoyment by all.

Social and economic trends and developments

Rapid globalization affects the enjoyment of human rights considerably. Both its positive and negative effects in that area are well known. At the World Summit for Social Development held in Copenhagen in 1995, it was underscored that while the enhanced mobility and communications, the increased trade and capital flows and the technological advances generated by globalization had opened new opportunities for sustained economic growth and development worldwide and for a creative sharing of experiences, ideals, values and aspirations, globalization had also been "accompanied by intensified poverty, unemployment and social disintegration".36

In many countries, deregulation, liberalization, privatization and similar trends towards a reduction of the role of the State and a transfer of traditional governmental functions to market forces have negatively affected the enjoyment of the rights to education, health care and water and of labour rights — especially in the case of vulnerable groups. The following sections, which set out international standards in the area of economic and social rights, show that there is a significant and possibly widening gap between State obligations and the ability or willingness of States to fulfil them. Moreover, globalization has led to a "privatization of human rights abuses". In many countries (not only the so-called "failed States"), such non-State actors as intergovernmental organizations, transnational corporations, private security companies, paramilitary and guerrilla forces, organized crime and terrorist groups are responsible for more serious and widespread human rights abuses than Governments (see Box 57 on the privatization of prisons).

The gap between rich and poor countries, and within the same society between rich and poor people, has continued to widen. Roughly one billion people live in conditions of ex-

36 World Summit for Social Development, *Copenhagen Declaration on Social Development*, paragraph 14.

126

Globalization and human rights

In 2000, the United Nations Commission on Human Rights designated two Special Rapporteurs to study globalization and its impact on the full enjoyment of human rights. Their 2001 progress report contained the following statements:

"In reviewing the global communications and technological developments heralded by those who can only see the bright side of globalization, it is also essential to remain cognizant of the fact that they are taking place in what can only be described as a sea of stark disparity. The persistence (and growth) of the problems of fatal disease, hunger, inadequate clothing, insuffi cient shelter, labour dislocation and the lack of food in many parts of the world is an increasing cause for concern. The growing competition for and exploitation of mineral and other natural resources are heightening tensions and conflicts....

It is of considerable concern that the processes of globalization are taking place within a context of increased social tension and political discordance…. Viewed from a human rights perspective, the organization and operation of these (anti-globalization) movements and the retaliation against them raise numerous questions concerning the rights to free expression, assembly and association. Ultimately, they also raise questions about participation, exclusion and discrimination – features of the human rights regime that lie at the core of the many instruments that make up the human rights corpus.... Globalization is therefore not simply an issue of economics; it is very much a political phenomenon... Coming to grips with the politics of globalization is thus an essential prerequisite to the design of alternative structures of international economy and governance."

In the opinion of the Special Rapporteurs, "globalization is not divinely ordained" but "rather... the product of human society". "As such, it is motivated by specific ideologies, interests and institutions. We must ask ourselves what the possibilities and limitations presented by globalization are, and how we can strategically and creatively engage them. Most importantly, how do we ensure that in the discussion about globalization and its impact on human rights, we adhere to the principles of meaningful participation and inclusion in the decision-making processes?" 37

Box 75

37 J. Olaka-Onyango and Deepika Udagama, Special Rapporteurs of the United Nations Sub-Commission on the Promotion and Protection of Human Rights, *Progress report on globalization and its impact on the full enjoyment of human rights,* E/CN.4/Sub.2/2001/10, paragraphs 7, 10, 11 and 12.

treme poverty worldwide, without adequate food, shelter, education and health care. At the same time, globalization helps to provide accurate information on living conditions in any part of the world, to make rich and poor societies ever more interdependent and to develop advanced scientific means and technology to combat poverty. In our "global village", it is therefore inadmissible that such a significant part of humanity is destitute.

THE ERADICATION OF POVERTY

"Eradicating poverty must be our first goal in this new millennium. Governments have committed themselves to taking action through strategies and programmes, which aim to reduce poverty and eliminate extreme poverty. The denial of human rights is inherent in poverty."

Mary Robinson, former United Nations High Commissioner for Human Rights, Preface in Draft Guidelines:
A Human Rights Approach to Poverty Reduction Strategies, OHCHR, Geneva, September 2002.

In the light of the preceding considerations, poverty eradication has in the past decade emerged as the overarching objective of development. At the same time, the definition of poverty has gradually been broadened. While for a long time the poor had been described only in material terms (such as "those living on less than a dollar a day"), it is in fact the non-material dimensions of poverty that shock. Those characteristics are increasingly used in statistics to describe the phenomenon of poverty. Worldwide, roughly one billion people lack adequate shelter, sufficient food, literacy and access to safe drinking water and to basic health services. Every day, 34,000 children under five die from hunger and preventable diseases.

These facts are not new, and yet as stated above, the gap between the rich and the poor is widening, making the failure effectively to address poverty in the face of rapid globalization increasingly indefensible. In that context, in September 2000 the United Nations General Assembly adopted several Millennium Development Goals, including the goal to halve the number of people living in extreme poverty by 2015, and by the same year to achieve a number of ambitious targets, such as universal primary education, reduction of under-five child mortality by two thirds and maternal mortality by three quarters, and a halving of the proportion of people who suffer from hunger and lack access to safe drinking water. Since poverty constitutes a denial of several human rights, a human rights approach is needed to strengthen poverty reduction strategies. In response to a request made by the CESCR Committee in July 2001, Ms. Mary Robinson, the United Nations High Commissioner for Human Rights at that time, developed, with the assistance of three experts, Draft Guidelines: A Human Rights Approach to Poverty Reduction Strategies (published in September 2002). In defining poverty, they adopt the widely accepted view, first advocated by Amartya Sen, that a poor person is an individual deprived of basic capabilities, such as the capability to be free from hunger, live in good health and be literate. Examples of human rights with

constitutive relevance to poverty are the rights to food, shelter, health and education. Other

human rights have instrumental relevance to poverty; their enjoyment helps to enjoy the

constitutively relevant ones. For instance, enjoyment of the right to work is conducive to the

enjoyment of such other human rights as the rights to food, health and housing. Such civil

and political rights as the rights to personal security, equal access to justice and political rights and freedoms also have instrumental relevance to the fight against poverty.

INTERNATIONAL FINANCIAL INSTITUTIONS AND THE FIGHT AGAINST POVERTY

Since 1996, the international financial institutions have started to recognize the importance

of poverty reduction. In their Comprehensive Development Programme, the World Bank Group and the International Monetary Fund (IMF), also known as the Bretton

United Nations Millennium Development Goals

1. Eradicate extreme poverty and hunger
Target for 2015: Halve the proportion of people living on less than a dollar a day and those

who suffer from hunger.

2. Achieve universal primary education
Target for 2015: Ensure that all boys and girls complete primary school.

3. Promote gender equality and empower women
Targets for 2005 and 2015: Eliminate gender disparities in primary and secondary education preferably by 2005, and at all levels by 2015.

4. Reduce child mortality
Target for 2015: Reduce by two thirds the mortality rate among children under five.

5. Improve maternal health
Target for 2015: Reduce by three quarters the ratio of women dying in childbirth.

6. Combat HIV/AIDS, malaria and other diseases
Target for 2015: Halt and begin to reverse the spread of HIV/AIDS and the incidence of malaria and other major diseases.

7. Ensure environmental sustainability
Integrate the principles of sustainable development into country policies and programmes

and reverse the loss of environmental resources.
By 2015, reduce by half the proportion of people without access to safe drinking water.
By 2020, achieve significant improvement in the lives of at least 100 million slum-dwellers.

8. Develop a global partnership for development, with targets for aid, trade and debt relief

*Develop further an open trading and financial system that includes a commitment to good
governance, development and poverty reduction – nationally and internationally.
Address the least developed countries' special needs, and the special needs of landlocked and small island developing States.
Deal comprehensively with developing countries' debt problems.
Develop decent and productive work for youth.
In cooperation with pharmaceutical companies, provide access to affordable essential drugs
in developing countries.
In cooperation with the private sector, make available the benefits of new technologies
— especially information and communications technologies.*

Box 76

129

Woods Institutions, make poverty reduction a basis for a new strategy of debt relief and development cooperation. Highly indebted and other poor countries are encouraged to develop, in a participatory process, poverty reduction strategy papers (PRSPs) specifying poverty reduction and eradication targets and benchmarks in various areas, such as food
production, health, education, labour, justice, good governance and democratization. Still,
such programmes have been criticized by many, including the United Nations Special Rapporteurs
on globalization and human rights (see Box 75), for insisting on macroeconomic discipline and effectively negating the claims of local ownership and participation.38 A survey conducted for the United Nations Population Fund (UNFPA) examined the extent to which PRSPs covered seven thematic population and development issues, including human
rights, in 44 developing countries up until 2001. It revealed that human rights issues linked explicitly to international treaties were the theme least covered, and that most countries did not mention human rights at all.39
Although human rights have not yet played a major role in PRSP development and implementation,
the general United Nations policy of human rights integration will lead to a

Added value of a human-rights-based approach

Responding to the question about the added value of a human-rights-based approach to poverty
reduction, and to development in general, the Draft Guidelines provide a convincing answer:
empowerment.
A human-rights-based approach offers an explicit and compelling normative framework for the
formulation of poverty-reduction strategies because effective poverty reduction is not possible

without empowerment of the poor. The norms and values of international human rights law
have the potential to achieve such empowerment. Once such an approach is adopted, poverty
reduction no longer means merely satisfying the needs of the poor. It also means recognizing
that the poor have rights, and that there are concomitant legal obligations for others. Poverty
reduction then becomes more than charity, more than a moral obligation; it becomes a legal
obligation, which implies that the entities bound by duty, including States, intergovernmental
organizations and global actors, should be held accountable.
In addition to the concepts of legality, accountability and empowerment, other distinguishing
features of a human rights approach include the principles of universality, non-discrimination
and equality, participation and the recognition of the interdependence of all human rights.
Several United Nations institutions and programmes, in particular UNDP and OHCHR, have
adopted a rights-based approach to human development, defining the objectives of development
in terms of legally enforceable entitlements. The approach aims to heighten the level of
accountability in the development process by identifying rights holders (and their entitlements)
and corresponding duty bearers (and their obligations) and by translating universal standards
into locally defined targets for measuring progress.

Box 77

38 Oloka-Onyango and Udagama, op. cit, paragraph 53.
39 Coverage of population and development themes in poverty reduction strategy papers, challenges and opportunities for
UNFPA, 11 March 2002.

human rights approach to poverty reduction strategies in the activities of UNDP, the Bretton
Woods Institutions and other multilateral and bilateral donor agencies.
This chapter's remaining sections — largely based on the general comments of the
CESCR Committee — focus on economic, social and cultural rights guaranteed under
the Universal Declaration of Human Rights and CESCR, and highlight related practical
issues.

The right to social security
Article 22 of UDHR

"Everyone, as a member of society, has the right to social security and is entitled to realization, through national effort and international cooperation and in accordance with the organization and resources of each State, of the economic, social and cultural rights indispensable for his dignity and the free development of his personality."
Article 25 of UDHR

"1. Everyone has the right to a standard of living adequate for the health and well-being of himself and of his family, including food, clothing, housing and medical care and necessary social services, and the right to security in the event of unemployment, sickness, disability, widowhood, old age or other lack of livelihood in circumstances beyond his control.
2. Motherhood and childhood are entitled to special care and assistance. All children, whether born in or out of wedlock, shall enjoy the same social protection."
Article 9 of CESCR

"The States Parties to the present Covenant recognize the right of everyone to social security, including social insurance."

WHAT IS A SOCIAL SECURITY SYSTEM?

Ideally, a social security system should aim to provide comprehensive coverage against all situations that may threaten a person's ability to earn an income and maintain an adequate standard of living. Social security areas are summed up in the Social Security (Minimum Standards) Convention, 1952 (No. 102). They are:

- Medical care;
- Sickness benefits;
- Unemployment benefits;
- Old-age benefits;
- Employment injury benefits;
- Family and maternity benefits;
- Invalidity benefits;
- Survivors' benefits.

In a social security system, a distinction is drawn between social insurance programmes — which provide for benefits tied to the interruption of employment earnings — and social assistance programmes — which provide for benefits that supplement insufficient incomes of members of vulnerable groups. Both types of programmes are intended to guarantee the material conditions required for an adequate standard of living and to offer protection from the effects of poverty and material insecurity.

As regards the developing world, the following observations on social security are in

order:
- Few countries have set up comprehensive social security schemes providing universal coverage;
- Social security schemes tend to target special groups (such as children or pregnant women);
- Social security schemes are often emergency relief programmes providing support in the event of calamities.

Obstacles frequently encountered by developing countries in trying to establish a social security system include poverty, administrative incapacity, debt and the structural adjustment policies imposed by international financial institutions.

KEY FACTORS TO BE CONSIDERED IN RELATION TO THE RIGHT TO SOCIAL SECURITY

In their efforts to ensure the exercise of the right to social security, States and particularly
parliaments should keep in mind the following recommendations:
- A national plan of action — including goals, measurable progress indicators and clear time frames — should be drawn up; and mechanisms should be set up to monitor advancement in realizing the right;
- Relevant legislative measures should provide for the progressive realization of the right
and be non-discriminatory;
- During the progressive realization of the right, a minimum level of social security should be guaranteed to the most vulnerable social groups (such as the elderly, children in poor families, sick and disabled persons);

Social security for the elderly: CESCR general comment No. 6

"The International Covenant on Economic, Social and Cultural Rights does not contain any
explicit reference to the rights of older persons, although article 9, dealing with 'the right
of everyone to social security, including social insurance', implicitly recognizes the right to
old-age benefits. Nevertheless, in view of the fact that the Covenant's provisions apply fully to
all members of society, it is clear that older persons are entitled to enjoy the full range of rights
recognized in the Covenant."

Box 78

132

- The adoption of social security measures should be monitored; and retrogressive measures (reducing social security benefits or coverage) should be avoided;
- Administrative and judicial procedures should be made available to enable potential beneficiaries to seek redress;
- Provisions should be drawn up to implement measures to avoid corruption and fraud with regard to social security benefits.

The right to work and rights at work

Article 23 (1) of UDHR
"Everyone has the right to work, to free choice of employment, to just and favourable conditions of work and to protection against unemployment."
Article 6 of CESCR
*"1. Th e States Parties to the present Covenant recognize the right to work, which includes
the right of everyone to the opportunity to gain his living by work which he freely chooses or
accepts, and will take appropriate steps to safeguard this right.
2. Th e steps to be taken by a State Party to the present Covenant to achieve the full realization of this right shall include technical and vocational guidance and training programmes, policies and techniques to achieve steady economic, social and cultural development and full and productive employment under conditions safeguarding fundamental political and economic freedoms to the individual."*
Article 7 of CESCR
*"Th e States Parties to the present Covenant recognize the right of everyone to the enjoyment of just and favourable conditions of work which ensure, in particular:
(a) Remuneration which provides all workers, as a minimum, with:
(i) Fair wages and equal remuneration for work of equal value without distinction of any kind, in particular women being guaranteed conditions of work not inferior to those enjoyed by men, with equal pay for equal work;
(ii) A decent living for themselves and their families in accordance with the provisions of the present Covenant;
(b) Safe and healthy working conditions;
(c) Equal opportunity for everyone to be promoted in his employment to an appropriate higher level, subject to no considerations other than those of seniority and competence;
(d) Rest, leisure and reasonable limitation of working hours and periodic holidays with pay, as well as remuneration for public holidays."*

THE RIGHT TO WORK

Th e right to work primarily protects individuals against exclusion from the economy, and
also the unemployed against social isolation.

Free choice, provided for in article 6 (1) of CESCR, should be stressed: work and access to resources should be distributed in a way ensuring that anyone who wishes to work can
do so and freely choose or accept a job, for the purpose of, inter alia, earning one's living
with that job.

In the context of human rights, "work" means more than mere "wage labour". But whether it is more integrated into other activities and aspects of life (for instance, among
indigenous peoples) or less (for instance, in the case of wage labourers), work always signifi

es performance of activities that meet needs and provide services to the group or society,
and are therefore accepted and rewarded.
When legislation is being drafted on the right to work and its implementation through policies or programmes, particular attention should be paid to prohibiting discrimination with regard to access to work. Legislation should also aim at facilitating the entry of specifi
c groups — such as women, the elderly and the disabled — into the labour market, and in general at protecting and upholding a worker's right to earn his or her living by taking up a freely chosen occupation.
Th e main goal of employment policies should be the attainment of full employment as quickly as possible, in accordance with a nation's resources. Over and above social benefi ts,
those policies should address the concerns of the long-term unemployed and low-income
earners through the development of public work programmes.
Th e State should ensure that generally accessible and free or reasonably priced technical
and vocational guidance and training programmes are established, and that free employment
services for all workers are put in place.

RIGHTS AT WORK

Article 7 of CESCR guarantees the right of every person to just and favourable conditions of work. Th ese conditions include:
• A remuneration which provides all workers, as a minimum, with:

Work-related duties of States under article 1 of the European Social Charter
• To accept as one of their primary aims and responsibilities the achievement and maintenance
of as high and stable a level of employment as possible, with a view to the attainment of full employment.
• To protect eff ectively the right of the worker to earn his or her living in an occupation chosen freely.
• To establish and maintain free employment services for all workers.
• To provide or promote appropriate vocational guidance, training and rehabilitation.
Box 79

- Fair wages and equal payment for work of equal value, without any discrimination (particularly against women);
- A decent living for the workers and their families;
• Safe and healthy working conditions;
• Equal opportunities for promotion on the basis of seniority and competence;
• Reasonable working hours, rest, leisure, periodic paid holidays and remunerated public
holidays.

Therefore, parliamentarians should ensure that the following key elements are stipulated
in legislation and implemented in practice:
- A minimum wage, enough for decent living conditions for the workers and their families, and prohibition of forced labour;
- Standards for safe, healthy and systematically monitored working conditions;
- The right to form and join trade unions, which should be able to function autonomously
at the national and international levels;
- Non-discrimination in the workplace (against inter alia women, minorities, disabled persons and religious groups) in respect of:
- Wages: pay should always be equal for equal work;
- Opportunities for promotion: these should be equal and based on seniority and performance.

The right to an adequate standard of living

Article 25 of UDHR

"1. Everyone has the right to a standard of living adequate for the health and wellbeing of himself and his family, including food, clothing, housing and medical care and necessary social services, and the right to security in the event of unemployment, sickness, disability, widowhood, old age or other lack of livelihood in circumstances beyond his control.

2. Motherhood and childhood are entitled to special care and assistance. All children, whether born in or out of wedlock, shall enjoy the same social protection."

Article 11 of CESCR

"1. The States Parties to the present Covenant recognize the right of everyone to an adequate standard of living for himself and his family, including adequate food, clothing and housing, and to the continuous improvement of living conditions. The States Parties will take appropriate steps to ensure the realization of this right, recognizing to this effect
the essential importance of international cooperation based on free consent.

2. The States Parties to the present Covenant, recognizing the fundamental right of everyone to be free from hunger, shall take, individually and through international cooperation, the measures, including specific programmes, which are needed:

(a) To improve methods of production, conservation and distribution of food by making full use of technical and scientific knowledge, by disseminating knowledge of the principles
of nutrition and by developing or reforming agrarian systems in such a way as to achieve the most efficient development and utilization of natural resources;

(b) Taking into account the problems of both food-importing and food-exporting countries,
to ensure an equitable distribution of world food supplies in relation to need."

Article 12 of CESCR

"1. The States Parties to the present Covenant recognize the right of everyone to the

enjoyment of the highest attainable standard of physical and mental health.
2. The steps to be taken by the States Parties to the present Covenant to achieve the full realization of this right shall include those necessary for:
(a) The provision for the reduction of the stillbirth-rate and of infant mortality and for the
healthy development of the child;
(b) The improvement of all aspects of environmental and industrial hygiene;
(c) The prevention, treatment and control of epidemic, endemic, occupational and other diseases;
(d) The creation of conditions which would assure to all medical service and medical attention in the event of sickness."

Article 25 of UDHR guarantees a social right that — in a way — is an umbrella entitlement:
the right to an adequate standard of living. In addition to the right to social security dealt
with above, this right also comprises the following rights:
- The right to adequate food;
- The right to adequate clothing;
- The right to housing;
- The right to health.

Article 11 of CESCR covers the core of the right to an adequate standard of living (food, clothing and housing) and recognizes the right to continuous improvement of living conditions.

States parties to the Covenant commit themselves to "take appropriate steps to ensure the realization of this right, recognizing to this effect the essential importance of international cooperation based on free consent". Under article 11 of CESCR, the CESCR Committee has also derived the right to water.

Hunger and poverty in the world fly in the face of the right to an adequate standard of living. This right should therefore form the basis of all national and international hungerand
poverty-reduction plans and strategies.

THE RIGHT TO FOOD

Although the international community has often reaffirmed the importance of respecting
fully the right to adequate food, there are still considerable gaps in this area between international
law standards and the situation actually prevailing in many parts of the world.

More than 840 million people throughout the world are chronically hungry, and millions of people suffer from famine caused by natural disasters, civil strife, wars and the use of
food as a political weapon. Moreover, the CESCR Committee has observed that "malnutrition
and undernutrition and other problems which relate to the right to adequate food and

the right to freedom from hunger also exist in some of the most economically developed
countries".40 The problem is therefore global, and needs the international community's full
attention.

In 1996, the World Food Summit set the goal of halving the number of undernourished people by 2015; and the first Millennium Development Goal consists in halving both the proportion of people living on less than a dollar a day and those who suffer from hunger
by the same year.

While some developing countries have succeeded in reducing hunger steadily, the overall
picture remains grim. According to FAO estimates, although the proportion of people who are chronically undernourished continued to fall slowly between 1995-1997 and 2000-2002, the number of undernourished people actually increased by 18 million. In the
period 2000-2002, it was estimated that some 852 million people were undernourished worldwide (9 million in industrialized countries, 28 million in countries in transition and 815 million in developing countries).41

In countries that have succeeded in reducing hunger, GDP per capita has increased more than five times faster (at 2.6 per cent per annum.) than in countries where undernourishment
has risen (0.5 per cent per annum). The most successful countries also display faster agricultural growth, lower rates of HIV/AIDS infection and slower population growth.42

How can the right to food be realized?

"Hunger and malnutrition are by no means dictated by fate or a curse of nature; they are man-made"

Jean Ziegler, United Nations Special Rapporteur on the right to food,
Report on the right to food (E/CN.4/2001/53), 2001, paragraph 6.

The right to adequate food is inseparable from the inherent dignity of the person and indispensable
to the enjoyment of other human rights.

The right to food is realized when every woman, man and child, alone or in community with others, has physical and economic access at all times to adequate food or to means for its procurement. It does not mean that a Government must hand out free food for all,
but it entails a Government duty to respect, to protect, to fulfil and, under certain circumstances,
to provide for that right.

40 CESCR, general comment No. 12 (1999).
41 Food and Agriculture Organization of the United Nations, The State of Food Insecurity in the World 2004, Rome, 2004.
42 Ibid.

Specific examples of measures to take and activities to carry out follow.

A framework law should be adopted as a key instrument for drawing up and implementing national strategies on food and food security for all.

In reviewing the constitution and national laws, and in aligning them with international human rights law on the right to food, particular attention should be paid to the need to *prevent discrimination* in relation to the access to food or to related resources. The following measures are called for:

1. Guaranteeing *access to food*, both economically and physically, to the members of all groups, including the poor and segments of society that are vulnerable or suffer from discrimination.

No acts should disrupt access to adequate food (for instance, evicting people from their land arbitrarily, introducing toxic substances into the food chain knowingly, or, in situations of armed conflict, destroying productive resources and blocking the provision of relief food supplies to the civilian population).

Measures should be adopted to prevent enterprises or individuals from impairing people's access to adequate food. The obligation to protect entails enactment of consumer protection laws and action if, for instance, a company pollutes water supplies or if monopolies distort food markets or the seed supply.

2. Guaranteeing that all, and particularly women, have full and equal *access to economic resources,* including the right to inherit and own land and other property, and access to credit, natural resources and appropriate technology.

A framework law on food

While under CESCR States have an obligation to ensure the exercise of the right to food and must legislate to that effect, hungry citizens may seek redress only if the Covenant can be directly invoked before the national courts — which is rarely the case — or has been incorporated into the national laws. Therefore, the Committee which monitors implementation of the Covenant has insisted that countries should pass laws protecting the right to food, and has recommended in particular that States consider the *adoption of a framework law* ensuring, inter alia, that redress is provided for violations of the right to food.

CESCR general comment No. 12 states: "The framework law should include provisions on its purpose; the targets or goals to be achieved and the time frame to be set for the achievement of those targets; the means by which the purpose could be achieved described in broad terms, in particular the intended collaboration with civil society and the private sector and

with international organizations; institutional responsibility for the process; and the national
mechanisms for its monitoring, as well as possible recourse procedures. In developing the
benchmarks and framework legislation, States parties should actively involve civil society organizations."

Box 80
138
To guarantee and strengthen people's access to and use of resources and means of livelihood, measures should be taken to ensure that:
- People have adequate wages or access to land, respectively to buy or produce food;
- Vulnerable groups are identified and policies are implemented to provide them with access to adequate food by enhancing their ability to feed themselves (for instance, through improved employment prospects, an agrarian reform programme for landless groups or the provision of free milk in schools to improve child nutrition).
3. Measures should be taken to respect and protect self-employment and remunerated work that ensures decent living conditions for workers and their families, and to prevent denial of access to jobs on the basis of gender, race or other discriminatory criteria, since such discrimination would affect the ability of workers to feed themselves.
4. Maintaining land registries.
The Government should devise adequate farmer-support programmes with particular emphasis on those most in need, for example by securing indigenous peoples' rights to their ancestral lands, empowering women and supporting small-scale producers and peasants
in remote locations (such as mountains or deserts).
Food should be provided whenever individuals or groups are unable to feed themselves for reasons beyond their control, including natural or other disasters (forms of support might include direct food distributions, cash transfers or food-for-work programmes).

Must action be taken immediately?
Like other economic, social and cultural rights, the obligation of States to fulfil and protect
the right to adequate food is subject to progressive realization, which means that States are
not required to achieve its full realization immediately, but must take measures to achieve
it progressively *by maximum use of available resources*. However, the following obligations
are not subject to progressive realization, and States have a duty to take immediate action
in respect of them:
• Refraining from any discrimination in relation to access to food and to means and entitlements for its procurement;
• Providing basic minimum subsistence (thereby ensuring freedom from hunger);
• Avoiding retrogressive measures.

THE RIGHT TO CLOTHING

The right to adequate clothing is the third explicitly stated component of the right to an adequate standard of living (after the right to social security and the right to food). Governments
must respect the way people, particularly members of minorities and indigenous
people, dress, and must protect them against arbitrary or discriminatory dress codes, harassment
and similar interferences by State and non-State actors. Moreover, Governments
must make adequate clothing available to those in need, including the poor, detainees, refugees and internally displaced persons. The type of clothing depends on local — cultural,
social and climatic — conditions. At the very least, poor people are entitled to clothing that
enable them to appear in public without shame.

THE RIGHT TO HOUSING

The right to adequate housing should not be understood narrowly as the right to have a roof over one's head, but should rather be seen as the right to live somewhere in security,
peace and dignity.
Homelessness is the extreme form of denial of the right to housing and is constitutive of poverty. But the precarious situation of millions of slum-dwellers and inhabitants of remote
rural areas, who face problems of overcrowding, lack of sewage treatment, pollution, seasonal exposure to the worst conditions and lack of access to drinking water and other
infrastructure, also constitutes a serious denial of the right to adequate housing. The Millennium
Development Goals include a specific goal in this area: "to achieve a significant improvement in the lives of at least 100 million slum-dwellers by 2020".

The right to housing: realization of its elements

CESCR general comment No. 4 on the right to adequate housing defines that right as comprising
the following specific concerns.

a. Legal security of tenure

All persons should possess a degree of security of tenure guaranteeing legal protection against
forced eviction, harassment and other threats. Governments should consequently take immediate
measures aimed at conferring legal security of tenure on households that have none. Such steps should be taken in consultation with the affected persons and groups.

b. Availability of services, materials and infrastructure

All beneficiaries of the right to adequate housing should have sustainable access to natural

and common resources: clean drinking water, energy for cooking, heating and lighting, sanitation and washing facilities, food storage facilities, refuse disposal, site drainage and
emergency services.

c. Affordable housing

Personal or household costs associated with housing should be such that they do not compromise
or threaten the satisfaction of other basic needs. Housing subsidies should be available for those unable to obtain affordable housing, and tenants should be protected
from unreasonable rent levels or rent increases. Plans of action must be drawn up, including
public expenditure programmes for low-income housing and housing subsidies, giving priority to the most vulnerable groups, such as persons with disabilities, the elderly, minorities,
indigenous peoples, refugees and internally displaced persons.
In societies where the main housing construction materials are natural, steps should be taken by the authorities to ensure the availability of such materials.

d. Habitable housing

To be adequate, housing must provide the occupants with adequate space and protect them
from cold, damp, heat, rain, wind or other threats to health, structural hazards and disease
vectors. The physical safety of the occupants must be guaranteed.

e. Accessible housing

To be adequate, housing must be accessible to those entitled to it. Disadvantaged groups
must be provided with full and sustainable access to adequate housing resources. Accordingly,
such groups as the elderly, children, disabled people, the terminally ill, HIV-positive individuals, persons with persistent medical problems, mentally ill persons, victims of natural disasters, and people living in disaster-prone areas should enjoy priority in respect
of housing. Housing laws and policy should take into account the special housing needs of
these and other vulnerable groups.

f. Fitting location

To be adequate, housing must be located so as to allow access to employment, health-care
services, schools, childcare centres and other social facilities; it should not be built on polluted
sites or in immediate proximity to pollution sources infringing on the occupants' right to health.

g. Culturally adequate housing
Housing construction, the building materials used and the underlying policies must preserve
cultural identity and diversity. The cultural dimensions of housing should not be
sacrificed to facilitate housing development or modernization projects.

The list of these extensive rights highlights some of the complexities associated with the right to adequate housing, and reveals the many areas that a State must consider in fulfilling its legal obligation to satisfy the housing needs of the population. Any persons, families, households, groups or communities living in conditions below the level of these entitlements may reasonably claim that they do not enjoy the right to adequate housing as
enshrined in international human rights law.

Furthermore, it is necessary to:
• Ensure that this right is protected from:
• Arbitrary demolitions;
• Forced or arbitrary evictions;
• Ethnic and religious segregation and displacement;
• Discrimination;
• Harassment and similar interferences;
• Take positive measures to reduce the number of homeless people and to provide them
with adequate living space, protected from harsh weather and health hazards;
• Set up judicial, quasi-judicial, administrative or political enforcement mechanisms capable of providing redress to victims of any alleged infringement of the right to adequate housing.

THE RIGHT TO HEALTH
Article 25 (1) of the Universal Declaration of Human Rights, which provides for health and
well-being guarantees, lays down the basis for an international legal framework ensuring
the right to health. Article 12 of CESCR further elaborates that right and outlines relevant
State obligations.

According to WHO, health is "a state of complete physical, mental and social wellbeing and not merely the absence of disease or infirmity".44 The right to health is therefore an inclusive right that not only relates to personal physical health, but also overlaps with many other human rights and various human rights issues. In 1997, the States, NGOs and
private actors participating in the Fourth International Conference on Health Promotion adopted the Jakarta Declaration on Leading Health Promotion into the 21st Century. The
Declaration reflects the inclusive character of the right to health and defines the requirements

for policies aimed at its enjoyment: "peace, shelter, education, social security, social

The Villa la Dulce case: including the excluded in social housing plans by means of judicial action[43]

In October 2000, a group of families that had been living in precarious housing conditions occupied a building in Buenos Aires, the Villa la Dulce, which had been vacant for more than 10 years. In July 2001, a judge ordered the immediate eviction of the 180 people then living in the house. They obeyed the judicial order but, as they had nowhere else to go, built shacks on the paths and streets around the building. With the support of several officials, negotiations were opened with the local authorities and an agreement was signed in November 2001 under which the Government would provide the evicted people with shelter within 60 days. That did not happen.

With a local NGO's support, the evicted people brought legal action to have their right to adequate housing, guaranteed in the Argentine Constitution, enforced. Following an on-site visit, the judge hearing the case issued a temporary order sequestrating US$ 500,000 out of the municipal budget's funds for the construction of adequate housing. In order to solve the immediate housing problem, the judge also negotiated a judicial agreement to move the families to city hotels. Owing to problems regarding the construction of the houses, the Government renegotiated with the evicted families, and a final agreement incorporating international standards applicable to the right to adequate housing was signed in December 2003. The agreement provided for the construction of 91 homes. It gave preference to builders who had homeless workers representing at least 20 per cent of their staff, and involved leases with viable purchase options and special funding facilities enabling the beneficiaries to own their homes.

This case shows that using judicial strategies and litigation to enforce constitutionally guaranteed social rights can influence housing policy decisions.

Box 81

[43] See *Housing and ESC Rights Law Quarterly*, Vol.1-No.1, pages 1-4.
[44] Constitution of the World Health Organization, Principles, 1946.

relations, food, income, the empowerment of women, a stable ecosystem, sustainable resource
use, social justice, respect for human rights, and equity. Above all, poverty is the greatest threat to health".

This section does not address the extended meaning of the right to health and the relations
between health and the rights to food, housing and life, which are discussed elsewhere in this handbook.

The narrower definition of the right to health

Taking a focused approach, one may break down the right to health into its application in
four separate areas:
1. Maternal, child and reproductive health;
2. Healthy workplaces and natural environments;
3. Prevention, treatment and control of diseases, including access to essential medicines and basic medical services;
4. Access to safe drinking water.

Various measures can be taken to ensure that the right to health is implemented. By bringing their own functions and powers to bear, parliaments can play a decisive role in that process.

Generally speaking, enjoyment of the right to health implies primary health care for all, without discrimination; a national public health strategy and plan of action; and the establishment
of national health indicators, benchmarks and monitoring mechanisms.

Health and poverty

In the developing countries and in the West, there is a pronounced correlation between health
problems and poverty. Poor people — with relatively limited access to health care and social
protection — are in general less healthy, die younger and have higher child and maternal mortality.

At the same time, illness aggravates poverty — through income loss and health-care costs
— transforming the poverty cycle into a downward spiral. Therefore, improving the health of
the poor is a crucial development objective.

Of the eight Millennium Development Goals, three call for specific health improvements by
2015: reducing child mortality, reducing maternal mortality and checking the spread of HIV/
AIDS, malaria and tuberculosis. Health is also a key factor in respect of the first Millennium
Development Goal (eradication of poverty and extreme hunger).

Good health contributes to development and poverty reduction in several ways. It raises labour
productivity, thereby encouraging domestic and foreign investment, improves human capital,
and increases the rate of national savings. Investment in health is therefore a sustainable measure
ensuring many positive external benefits.

Box 82

Health insurance mechanisms and educational programmes on health problems and
prevention are necessary, and members of parliament should ensure that sufficient funding
is made available for such efforts and for health-related research and development.

Groups in need of special attention

Health issues specific to particular groups such as persons with physical or mental disabilities,
the poor, women, children and people living with HIV/AIDS require special attention.
Targeted policies and sufficient health budgets geared to the needs of these groups are necessary.

Regarding the poor, key health issues include the enhancement of access to health services,
the introduction of appropriate immunization programmes and the implementation
of basic environmental measures (especially waste disposal). Members of parliament can
be highly instrumental in drafting relevant laws, ensuring their implementation and raising
public awareness of the situation of the poor.

Women's access to health, medical care and family planning services requires special
attention. Parliamentarians should ensure enactment of laws that prohibit and eradicate
FGM.45

Laws ensuring the provision to all children of necessary medical assistance and health
care should be enacted and implemented. It is essential to launch programmes designed to
reduce infant and child mortality and to conduct information programmes on children's
health and nutrition, the advantages of breastfeeding, the importance of hygiene and environmental
sanitation and accident prevention.

Disabled children should have access to and receive education, training and health-care
services, and should benefit from rehabilitation services, preparation for employment and
recreation opportunities, with a view to ensuring maximum social integration and individual
development.

Lastly, people living with HIV/AIDS — in December 2004 they were close to 40 million worldwide46 - should be protected against all forms of discrimination. Th e costs of their medical examinations should be covered, and drugs should be provided to them on
a regular basis.47

THE RIGHT TO WATER

In addition to the rights to food, housing and clothing (provided for explicitly under article
25 of the Universal Declaration of Human Rights and article 11 of CESCR), the right to an

45 In September 2001, IPU launched a parliamentary campaign to stop violence against women, focused on the eradication of
FGM. Further information may be found on the IPU website http://www.ipu.org/wmn-e/fgm.htm.
46 Dr. Peter Piot, Executive Director of UNAIDS, Message on the occasion of World AIDS Day, 1 December 2004.
47 For detailed information on this subject, see Handbook for Legislators on HIV/AIDS, Law and Human Rights, UNAIDS/IPU,
Geneva 1999.

144

adequate standard of living may comprise other basic needs. General comment No. 15 of
the CESCR Committee, adopted in November 2002, identifi es the "human right to water"
as an essential component of that umbrella right, stating that it "clearly falls within the category of guarantees essential for securing an adequate standard of living, particularly since it is one of the most fundamental conditions for survival". Th e right to water is also
referred to in article 14 (2) of CEDAW and article 24 (2) of CRC.

What is the right to water?

Th e right to water entitles all human beings to suffi cient, safe, acceptable, physically accessible
and aff ordable water for personal and domestic uses. It is essential for the realization of many other rights, such as the right to life, health and food. Although what constitutes
water adequacy varies depending on conditions, the following factors apply in all circumstances:

Availability: A regular water supply must be available to every person in a quantity suffi cient for personal and domestic uses. Th ese uses ordinarily include drinking, personal hygiene, laundering, food preparation, sanitation and household cleanliness. Th e volume of water available for each person should meet WHO guidelines. Some individuals and groups may need additional water because of particular health, climate and work conditions;

Quality: Th e water available for personal and domestic use must be safe, i.e., free from micro-organisms, chemical substances and radiation detrimental to health. Its colour,

odour and taste should be appropriate for the various personal and domestic uses;
Accessibility: Water and water facilities and services must be accessible to *all* persons living in the territory of a State, without discrimination. Accessibility has four overlapping dimensions:
Physical access: For all population groups, water and adequate water facilities and services must physically be within safe reach. Enough, safe and acceptable water must be accessible in every household, educational institution, health-care establishment and workplace, or in their immediate vicinity. The quality of all water facilities and services must be sufficiently good and culturally appropriate, and must meet gender, life-cycle and privacy requirements. The physical security of persons accessing water facilities and services must be guaranteed;
Economic access: Water and water facilities and services must be universally affordable. The direct and indirect costs and charges associated with securing water must be reasonable and not compromise or threaten the enjoyment of other rights guaranteed under CESCR;
Non-discriminatory access: By law and in practice, water and water facilities and services must be accessible to all, including the most vulnerable or marginalized population groups, without discrimination on any grounds;
Information access: Accessibility includes the right to seek, receive and impart information concerning water issues.

Water and the right to life
- Every year, 2.2 million people die of diarrhoea.
- Millions more suffer nutritional, educational and economic loss through diarrhoeal disease
that improvements in water supply and sanitation could prevent.
- Nearly 3.4 million people die annually from water-related diseases.
- At any one time 1.5 billion people — one in every four people worldwide — suffer from parasitic
worm infections, stemming from human excreta and solid wastes in the environment.48

Box 83
Types of violations of the right to water
Violations of the obligation to respect the right to water:
- Arbitrary or unjustified disconnection or exclusion from water services or facilities;
- Discriminatory or unaffordable increases in the price of water;
- Pollution and diminution of water resources, affecting human health.

Violations of the obligation to protect the right to water:
- Failure to enact or enforce laws to prevent the contamination and inequitable extraction
of water;
- Failure to effectively regulate and control private water-service providers;
- Failure to protect water distribution systems (e.g., piped networks and wells) from interference, damage and destruction.

Violations of the obligation to fulfil the right to water:

- Failure to adopt or implement a national water policy designed to ensure the right to water
for everyone;
- Insufficient expenditure or misallocation of public resources, resulting in the nonenjoyment
of the right to water by individuals or groups, particularly vulnerable or marginalized groups;
- Failure to monitor the realization of the right to water at the national level inter alia by using right-to-water indicators and benchmarks;
- Failure to take measures to reduce the inequitable distribution of water facilities and services;
- Failure to adopt mechanisms for emergency relief;
- Failure to ensure that everyone enjoys the right at a minimum essential level;
- Failure of a State to take into account its international legal obligations regarding the right to water when entering into agreements with other States or with international organizations.

Box 84

48 Global Water Supply and Sanitation Assessment 2000 Report, Summary of the Report.

What activities can contribute to ensuring the enjoyment of the right to water?

First, Governments should provide for the availability, adequate quality and accessibility of water, as outlined above. Progressive implementation of all of the measures described
above will eventually lead to full realization of the right to water. Parliaments can monitor
and promote the following specific Government measures:

- If necessary, Governments should adopt a national water strategy and plan of action to ensure a water supply and management system that provides all inhabitants with a sufficient amount of clean and safe water for their personal and domestic use. The strategy and plan of action should include tools — such as right-to-water indicators and benchmarks — for monitoring progress closely, and should specifically target all disadvantaged or marginalized groups;
- Governments should take effective measures to prevent third parties, including transnational corporations, from obstructing equal access to clean water, polluting water resources and engaging in inequitable water extraction practices;
- Governments should take measures to prevent, treat and control water-related diseases
and, in particular, ensure access to adequate sanitation.

The right to education

Article 26 (1) of UDHR

"Everyone has the right to education. Education shall be free, at least in the elementary and fundamental stages. Elementary education shall be compulsory. Technical and professional education shall be made generally available and higher education shall be

equally accessible to all on the basis of merit."

Article 13 of CESCR

"1. The States Parties to the present Covenant recognize the right of everyone to education.

[...]

2. The States Parties to the present Covenant recognize that, with a view to achieving the full realization of this right:

(a) Primary education shall be compulsory and available free to all;

(b) Secondary education in its different forms, including technical and vocational secondary education, shall be made generally available and accessible to all by every appropriate means, and in particular by the progressive introduction of free education;

(c) Higher education shall be made equally accessible to all, on the basis of capacity, by every appropriate means, and in particular by the progressive introduction of free education;

(d) Fundamental education shall be encouraged or intensified as far as possible for those persons who have not received or completed the whole period of their primary education;

(e) The development of a system of schools at all levels shall be actively pursued, an adequate fellowship system shall be established, and the material conditions of teaching staff shall be continuously improved.

3. The States Parties to the present Covenant undertake to have respect for the liberty of parents and, when applicable, legal guardians to choose for their children schools, other than those established by the public authorities, which conform to such minimum educational standards as may be laid down or approved by the State and to ensure the religious and moral education of their children in conformity with their own convictions.

4. No part of this article shall be construed so as to interfere with the liberty of individuals and bodies to establish and direct educational institutions, subject always to the observance of the principles set forth in paragraph 1 of this article and to the requirement that the education given in such institutions shall conform to such minimum standards as may be laid down by the State."

Article 14 of CESCR

"Each State Party to the present Covenant which, at the time of becoming a Party, has not been able to secure in its metropolitan territory or other territories under its jurisdiction compulsory primary education, free of charge, undertakes, within two years, to work out and adopt a detailed plan of action for the progressive implementation, within a reasonable number of years, to be fixed in the plan, of the principle of compulsory education free of charge for all."

In addition to being enshrined and outlined in international law and core treaties as shown
above, the right to education is also referred to in articles 28 and 29 of CRC, and the second
and third Millennium Development Goals, which lay down important standards and goals
concerning its enjoyment. The right is inextricably linked to the dignity of the human being,
and its realization is conducive to the development of the individual and of society as
a whole. It empowers economically and socially marginalized people, is crucial in the *fight
against poverty,* safeguards children from exploitation and has a limiting effect on population
growth. It is therefore key to the realization of many other human rights.

*"A sustained state of democracy thus requires a democratic climate and culture
constantly nurtured and reinforced by education and other vehicles of culture and
information. Hence, a democratic society must be committed to education in the
broadest sense of the term, and more particularly civic education and the shaping
of a responsible citizenry.*
Inter-Parliamentary Union, Universal Declaration on Democracy,
Cairo, September 1997, paragraph 19.

The above provisions of the Universal Declaration of Human Rights and CESCR set
clear goals that States parties should aim to meet in order to ensure the realization of the
human right to education. But what are the *practical* implications of those provisions for
States, and in particular for parliaments? To provide an answer, the right to education may
be broken down into the following two components:
1. Enhancement of access to education;
2. Freedom to choose the type and content of education.

148

49 Data based on "People, Poverty, Possibilities", State of the World Population 2002, United Nations Population Fund.

Poverty and education[49]

Globally, 113 million children, two thirds of whom are girls, do not attend school. Moreover,
improving the quality of education, expanding basic education towards international universal
primary education targets, and reducing disparities in access and coverage present major
challenges. There is long-standing international agreement that primary education should be
universal in the early twenty-first century. The gaps in educational attendance and attainment

according to wealth imply that the poor are much farther away from achieving this goal than
others. But why are enrolment rates lower and educational outcomes worse among the poor?

The supply

First, it is harder for poor children to reach a school. Schools tend to be concentrated in wealthier
cities and areas. In Guinea, for instance, the average travel time required to reach the nearest
primary school is 47 minutes in rural areas, but only 19 minutes in urban areas.

In most countries, however, the physical accessibility of schools is not the central issue. Expenditure
on education has in many places increased over the past few decades, but spending
increases that are not accompanied by special attention to the needs of the poor can reinforce
wealth-related disparities rather than reduce them.

Evidence from a range of developing countries suggests that Government activities that benefit
the wealthy absorb a larger share of public spending on education. In Latin America, disparities
in scholastic achievement have been attributed to the ineffectiveness of publicly run schools,
mainly attended by the poor, and primary and secondary education — the level of schooling
that most benefits the poor — receives a relatively small share of total education expenditures.

Even when Governments allocate sufficient resources to the aim of enhancing the accessibility
and quality of education available to the poor, the administrative capacity may be insufficient
for delivering the services.

The quality of education, including curricula, textbooks, teaching methods, teacher training,
pupil-teacher ratios and parental participation, determines the outcomes (such as retention
rates, attainment levels and test scores).

The demand

Demand for education depends on perceived returns to the family. This mainly includes expected
income, but also involves better health and lower fertility rates. According to one study,
average earnings may increase by 10 per cent for each additional year of schooling, provided
that opportunities for educated workers are available.

In some countries, demand for education is lower because expected returns on education are
reduced inter alia by the cost of education, the low quality of public schooling and discrimination
against ethnic or linguistic groups and against women in the labour market.

School fees

Recent research, including research based on State reports submitted to the CRC and CESCR
Committees, shows that (even compulsory) basic education is not always free. School fees have a
direct impact on the accessibility of the educational system, and place the poor at a disadvantage.

Box 85

These two components can be further subdivided into four areas of obligation: availability,
accessibility, acceptability and adaptability, as stipulated in general comment No. 13 of the CESCR Committee. These concepts comprise the following practical measures:

Availability of functioning educational institutions and programmes
- Obligatory and free primary education for all (to protect children from child labour);
- Teacher training programmes;
- Adequate working conditions for teachers, including the right to form unions and bargain collectively.

Accessibility of education to everyone
- Economically affordable secondary and higher education;
- Non-discriminatory access to education;
- Adequate education-grant system for disadvantaged groups;
- Adequate funding for education in rural areas;
- Mechanisms for monitoring policies, institutions, programmes, spending patterns and other practices in the education sector.

Acceptability of form and substance
- Legislation guaranteeing the quality of curricula and teaching methods;
- Minimum educational standards (on admission, curricula, recognition of certificates, etc.) and related monitoring mechanisms;
- Guarantee of the right to establish private institutions.

Adaptability of curricula
- Curriculum design and education funding in conformity with the pupils' and students' actual needs.

Plans of action

State efforts to realize the right to education should be progressive. They should be effective
and expeditious to a warranted degree. State obligations are not of equal urgency in all areas (basic, primary, secondary and higher education): Governments are expected to give

priority to the introduction of compulsory and free primary education while taking steps for the realization of the right to education at other levels.

States that at the time of becoming a party to CESCR have not been able to secure compulsory and free primary education should adopt and implement a national educational plan, as laid down in article 14 of the Covenant. The plan should be drawn up and adopted within two years for the progressive implementation, within a reasonable number of years to be fixed in that plan, of the principle of compulsory education free of charge for all. The two-year specification does not absolve a State party from this obligation in case it fails to act within that period.

150
The 105th Inter-Parliamentary Conference "asserts that education is a prerequisite for promoting sustainable development, securing a healthy environment, ensuring peace and democracy and achieving the objectives of combating poverty, slowing population growth, and creating equality between the sexes; culture is a fundamental component of the development process".
Resolution on "Education and culture as essential factors in promoting the participation of men and women in political life and as prerequisites for the development of peoples", Havana, April 2001, paragraph 1

Concluding remark

Human rights are an evolving concept. Their evolution is a process in which members of parliament and parliamentary bodies can play a leading role. This role can be instrumental in all phases of the process: initiating and promoting a national or international dialogue, supporting standard-setting bodies, participating in drawing up legal instruments, ensuring the adoption and ratification of international treaties, following up on them and monitoring their implementation. That way, parliamentarians can be essential partners in remoulding the world on the basis of fairness, equality and human rights.

151
List of abbreviations
ACHR American Convention on Human Rights, also known as
≪Pact of San Jose, Costa Rica≫
AU African Union
CAT Convention against Torture and Other Cruel, Inhuman or Degrading Treatment or Punishment
CCPR International Covenant on Civil and Political Rights

CEDAW Convention on the Elimination of All Forms of Discrimination against Women
CERD International Convention on the Elimination of All Forms of Racial Discrimination
CESCR International Covenant on Economic, Social and Cultural Rights
CMW International Convention on the Protection of the Rights of All Migrant Workers and Members of Their Families
CRC Convention on the Rights of the Child
DAW Division for the Advancement of Women
DESA United Nations Department of Economic and Social Affairs
ECHR European Convention for the Protection of Human Rights and Fundamental Freedoms
ECOSOC Economic and Social Council
FAO Food and Agriculture Organization of the United Nations
FGM Female genital mutilation
GATS General Agreement on Trade in Services
IACHR Inter-American Commission on Human Rights
ICC International Criminal Court
ICTR International Criminal Tribunal for Rwanda
ICTY International Criminal Tribunal for the former Yugoslavia
ILO International Labour Organization
IMF International Monetary Fund
INSTRAW United Nations International Research and Training Institute for the Advancement of Women
IPU Inter-Parliamentary Union
NGO Non-governmental organization
NHRI National human rights institution
OAS Organization of American States
OHCHR Office of the United Nations High Commissioner for Human Rights
OP Optional Protocol
PRSP Poverty reduction strategy paper
TRIPS Agreement on Trade-Related Aspects of Intellectual Property Rights
UDHR Universal Declaration of Human Rights
UNDP United Nations Development Programme
UNESCO United Nations Educational, Scientific and Cultural Organization
UNFPA United Nations Population Fund
UN-HABITAT United Nations Human Settlement Programme
UNHCR United Nations High Commissioner for Refugees
UNICEF United Nations Children's Fund
UNIFEM United Nations Development Fund for Women
UNITAR United Nations Institute for Training and Research

UNRISD United Nations Research Institute for Social Development
UNRWA United Nations Relief and Works Agency for Palestine Refugees in the Near East
UNU United Nations University
WFP World Food Programme
WHO World Health Organization
WTO World Trade Organization

Annex 1
Universal Declaration of Human Rights
Preamble

Whereas recognition of the inherent dignity and of the equal and inalienable rights of all members of the human family is the foundation of freedom, justice and peace in the world,

Whereas disregard and contempt for human rights have resulted in barbarous acts which have outraged the conscience of mankind, and the advent of a world in which human beings shall enjoy freedom of speech and belief and freedom from fear and want has been proclaimed as the highest aspiration of the common people,

Whereas it is essential, if man is not to be compelled to have recourse, as a last resort, to rebellion against tyranny and oppression, that human rights should be protected by the rule of law,

Whereas it is essential to promote the development of friendly relations between nations,

Whereas the peoples of the United Nations have in the Charter reaffi rmed their faith in fundamental human rights, in the dignity and worth of the human person and in the equal rights of men and women and have determined to promote social progress and better standards of life in larger freedom,

Whereas Member States have pledged themselves to achieve, in cooperation with the United Nations, the promotion of universal respect for and observance of human rights and fundamental freedoms,

Whereas a common understanding of these rights and freedoms is of the greatest importance for the full realization of this pledge,

Now, therefore,

Th e General Assembly,

Proclaims this Universal Declaration of Human Rights as a common standard of achievement for all peoples and all nations, to the end that every individual and every organ of

society, keeping this Declaration constantly in mind, shall strive by teaching and education
to promote respect for these rights and freedoms and by progressive measures, national and international, to secure their universal and effective recognition and observance, both
among the peoples of Member States themselves and among the peoples of territories under
their jurisdiction.

Article 1
All human beings are born free and equal in dignity and rights. They are endowed with reason and conscience and should act towards one another in a spirit of brotherhood.

Article 2
Everyone is entitled to all the rights and freedoms set forth in this Declaration, without distinction of any kind, such as race, colour, sex, language, religion, political or other opinion,
national or social origin, property, birth or other status.
Furthermore, no distinction shall be made on the basis of the political, jurisdictional or international status of the country or territory to which a person belongs, whether it be
independent, trust, non-self-governing or under any other limitation of sovereignty.

Article 3
Everyone has the right to life, liberty and security of person.

Article 4
No one shall be held in slavery or servitude; slavery and the slave trade shall be prohibited
in all their forms.

Article 5
No one shall be subjected to torture or to cruel, inhuman or degrading treatment or punishment.

Article 6
Everyone has the right to recognition everywhere as a person before the law.

Article 7
All are equal before the law and are entitled without any discrimination to equal protection
of the law. All are entitled to equal protection against any discrimination in violation of this Declaration and against any incitement to such discrimination.

Article 8
Everyone has the right to an effective remedy by the competent national tribunals for acts violating the fundamental rights granted him by the constitution or by law.

Article 9
No one shall be subjected to arbitrary arrest, detention or exile.

Article 10
Everyone is entitled in full equality to a fair and public hearing by an independent and

impartial tribunal, in the determination of his rights and obligations and of any criminal charge against him.
Article 11
1. Everyone charged with a penal off ence has the right to be presumed innocent until proved guilty according to law in a public trial at which he has had all the guarantees necessary for his defence.

2. No one shall be held guilty of any penal off ence on account of any act or omission which did not constitute a penal off ence, under national or international law, at the time when it was committed. Nor shall a heavier penalty be imposed than the one that was applicable at the time the penal off ence was committed.
Article 12
No one shall be subjected to arbitrary interference with his privacy, family, home or correspondence,
nor to attacks upon his honour and reputation. Everyone has the right to the protection of the law against such interference or attacks.
Article 13
1. Everyone has the right to freedom of movement and residence within the borders of each State.
2. Everyone has the right to leave any country, including his own, and to return to his country.
Article 14
1. Everyone has the right to seek and to enjoy in other countries asylum from persecution.
2. Th is right may not be invoked in the case of prosecutions genuinely arising from nonpolitical
crimes or from acts contrary to the purposes and principles of the United Nations.
Article 15
1. Everyone has the right to a nationality.
2. No one shall be arbitrarily deprived of his nationality nor denied the right to change his nationality.
Article 16
1. Men and women of full age, without any limitation due to race, nationality or religion, have the right to marry and to found a family. Th ey are entitled to equal rights as to marriage, during marriage and at its dissolution.
2. Marriage shall be entered into only with the free and full consent of the intending spouses.
3. Th e family is the natural and fundamental group unit of society and is entitled to protection by society and the State.
Article 17
1. Everyone has the right to own property alone as well as in association with others.
2. No one shall be arbitrarily deprived of his property.
Article 18

Everyone has the right to freedom of thought, conscience and religion; this right includes
freedom to change his religion or belief, and freedom, either alone or in community
with others and in public or private, to manifest his religion or belief in teaching, practice,
worship and observance.

Article 19
Everyone has the right to freedom of opinion and expression; this right includes freedom
to hold opinions without interference and to seek, receive and impart information
and ideas through any media and regardless of frontiers.

Article 20
1. Everyone has the right to freedom of peaceful assembly and association.
2. No one may be compelled to belong to an association.

Article 21
1. Everyone has the right to take part in the government of his country, directly or through freely chosen representatives.
2. Everyone has the right to equal access to public service in his country.
3. Th e will of the people shall be the basis of the authority of government; this will shall be expressed in periodic and genuine elections which shall be by universal and equal suff rage and shall be held by secret vote or by equivalent free voting procedures.

Article 22
Everyone, as a member of society, has the right to social security and is entitled to realization,
through national eff ort and international cooperation and in accordance with
the organization and resources of each State, of the economic, social and cultural rights indispensable for his dignity and the free development of his personality.

Article 23
1. Everyone has the right to work, to free choice of employment, to just and favourable conditions of work and to protection against unemployment.
2. Everyone, without any discrimination, has the right to equal pay for equal work.
3. Everyone who works has the right to just and favourable remuneration ensuring for himself and his family an existence worthy of human dignity, and supplemented, if necessary, by other means of social protection.
4. Everyone has the right to form and to join trade unions for the protection of his interests.

Article 24
Everyone has the right to rest and leisure, including reasonable limitation of working hours and periodic holidays with pay.

Article 25
1. Everyone has the right to a standard of living adequate for the health and well-being of himself and of his family, including food, clothing, housing and medical care and

necessary social services, and the right to security in the event of unemployment, sickness, disability, widowhood, old age or other lack of livelihood in circumstances beyond his control.

2. Motherhood and childhood are entitled to special care and assistance. All children, whether born in or out of wedlock, shall enjoy the same social protection.

Article 26

1. Everyone has the right to education. Education shall be free, at least in the elementary and fundamental stages. Elementary education shall be compulsory. Technical and professional education shall be made generally available and higher education shall be equally accessible to all on the basis of merit.

2. Education shall be directed to the full development of the human personality and to the strengthening of respect for human rights and fundamental freedoms. It shall promote understanding, tolerance and friendship among all nations, racial or religious groups, and shall further the activities of the United Nations for the maintenance of peace.

3. Parents have a prior right to choose the kind of education that shall be given to their children.

Article 27

1. Everyone has the right freely to participate in the cultural life of the community, to enjoy the arts and to share in scientific advancement and its benefits.

2. Everyone has the right to the protection of the moral and material interests resulting from any scientific, literary or artistic production of which he is the author.

Article 28

Everyone is entitled to a social and international order in which the rights and freedoms set forth in this Declaration can be fully realized.

Article 29

1. Everyone has duties to the community in which alone the free and full development of his personality is possible.

2. In the exercise of his rights and freedoms, everyone shall be subject only to such limitations as are determined by law solely for the purpose of securing due recognition and respect for the rights and freedoms of others and of meeting the just requirements of morality, public order and the general welfare in a democratic society.

3. These rights and freedoms may in no case be exercised contrary to the purposes and principles of the United Nations.

Article 30

Nothing in this Declaration may be interpreted as implying for any State, group or person any right to engage in any activity or to perform any act aimed at the destruction of any of the rights and freedoms set forth herein.

Annex 2
International Covenant on Civil and Political Rights

Preamble

The States Parties to the present Covenant,

Considering that, in accordance with the principles proclaimed in the Charter of the United
Nations, recognition of the inherent dignity and of the equal and inalienable rights of all members of the human family is the foundation of freedom, justice and peace in the world,

Recognizing that these rights derive from the inherent dignity of the human person,

Recognizing that, in accordance with the Universal Declaration of Human Rights, the ideal
of free human beings enjoying civil and political freedom and freedom from fear and want
can only be achieved if conditions are created whereby everyone may enjoy his civil and political rights, as well as his economic, social and cultural rights,

Considering the obligation of States under the Charter of the United Nations to promote universal respect for, and observance of, human rights and freedoms,

Realizing that the individual, having duties to other individuals and to the community to which he belongs, is under a responsibility to strive for the promotion and observance of
the rights recognized in the present Covenant,

Agree upon the following articles:

PART I

Article 1

1. All peoples have the right of self-determination. By virtue of that right they freely determine their political status and freely pursue their economic, social and cultural development.
2. All peoples may, for their own ends, freely dispose of their natural wealth and resources
without prejudice to any obligations arising out of international economic cooperation, based upon the principle of mutual benefit, and international law. In no case may a people be deprived of its own means of subsistence.
3. The States Parties to the present Covenant, including those having responsibility for the administration of Non-Self-Governing and Trust Territories, shall promote the realization of the right of self-determination, and shall respect that right, in conformity with the provisions of the Charter of the United Nations.

PART II

Article 2

1. Each State Party to the present Covenant undertakes to respect and to ensure to all individuals within its territory and subject to its jurisdiction the rights recognized in the present Covenant, without distinction of any kind, such as race, colour, sex, language, religion, political or other opinion, national or social origin, property, birth or other status.
2. Where not already provided for by existing legislative or other measures, each State

Party to the present Covenant undertakes to take the necessary steps, in accordance with its constitutional processes and with the provisions of the present Covenant, to adopt such laws or other measures as may be necessary to give effect to the rights recognized in the present Covenant.
3. Each State Party to the present Covenant undertakes:
(a) To ensure that any person whose rights or freedoms as herein recognized are violated
shall have an effective remedy, notwithstanding that the violation has been committed by persons acting in an official capacity;
(b) To ensure that any person claiming such a remedy shall have his right thereto determined by competent judicial, administrative or legislative authorities, or by any other competent authority provided for by the legal system of the State, and to develop the possibilities of judicial remedy;
(c) To ensure that the competent authorities shall enforce such remedies when granted.

Article 3

The States Parties to the present Covenant undertake to ensure the equal right of men and women to the enjoyment of all civil and political rights set forth in the present Covenant.

Article 4

1. In time of public emergency which threatens the life of the nation and the existence of which is officially proclaimed, the States Parties to the present Covenant may take measures derogating from their obligations under the present Covenant to the extent strictly required by the exigencies of the situation, provided that such measures are not inconsistent with their other obligations under international law and do not involve discrimination solely on the ground of race, colour, sex, language, religion or social origin.
2. No derogation from articles 6, 7, 8 (paragraphs 1 and 2), 11, 15, 16 and 18 may be made
under this provision.
3. Any State Party to the present Covenant availing itself of the right of derogation shall immediately inform the other States Parties to the present Covenant, through the intermediary of the Secretary-General of the United Nations, of the provisions from
160
which it has derogated and of the reasons by which it was actuated. A further communication
shall be made, through the same intermediary, on the date on which it terminates such derogation.

Article 5

1. Nothing in the present Covenant may be interpreted as implying for any State, group or person any right to engage in any activity or perform any act aimed at the destruction of any of the rights and freedoms recognized herein or at their limitation to a greater extent than is provided for in the present Covenant.
2. There shall be no restriction upon or derogation from any of the fundamental human rights recognized or existing in any State Party to the present Covenant pursuant

to law, conventions, regulations or custom on the pretext that the present Covenant does not recognize such rights or that it recognizes them to a lesser extent.

PART III

Article 6

1. Every human being has the inherent right to life. This right shall be protected by law. No one shall be arbitrarily deprived of his life.
2. In countries which have not abolished the death penalty, sentence of death may be imposed only for the most serious crimes in accordance with the law in force at the time of the commission of the crime and not contrary to the provisions of the present Covenant and to the Convention on the Prevention and Punishment of the Crime of Genocide. This penalty can only be carried out pursuant to a final judgement rendered by a competent court.
3. When deprivation of life constitutes the crime of genocide, it is understood that nothing
in this article shall authorize any State Party to the present Covenant to derogate in any way from any obligation assumed under the provisions of the Convention on the Prevention and Punishment of the Crime of Genocide.
4. Anyone sentenced to death shall have the right to seek pardon or commutation of the sentence. Amnesty, pardon or commutation of the sentence of death may be granted in all cases.
5. Sentence of death shall not be imposed for crimes committed by persons below eighteen
years of age and shall not be carried out on pregnant women.
6. Nothing in this article shall be invoked to delay or to prevent the abolition of capital punishment by any State Party to the present Covenant.

Article 7

No one shall be subjected to torture or to cruel, inhuman or degrading treatment or punishment. In particular, no one shall be subjected without his free consent to medical or scientific experimentation.

Article 8

1. No one shall be held in slavery; slavery and the slave-trade in all their forms shall be prohibited.
2. No one shall be held in servitude.
3. (a) No one shall be required to perform forced or compulsory labour;
(b) Paragraph 3 (a) shall not be held to preclude, in countries where imprisonment with hard labour may be imposed as a punishment for a crime, the performance of hard labour in pursuance of a sentence to such punishment by a competent court;
(c) For the purpose of this paragraph the term "forced or compulsory labour" shall not include:
(i) Any work or service, not referred to in subparagraph (b), normally required of a person who is under detention in consequence of a lawful order of a court, or of a person during conditional release from such detention;
(ii) Any service of a military character and, in countries where conscientious

objection is recognized, any national service required by law of conscientious objectors;
(iii) Any service exacted in cases of emergency or calamity threatening the life or well-being of the community;
(iv) Any work or service which forms part of normal civil obligations.

Article 9
1. Everyone has the right to liberty and security of person. No one shall be subjected to arbitrary arrest or detention. No one shall be deprived of his liberty except on such grounds and in accordance with such procedure as are established by law.
2. Anyone who is arrested shall be informed, at the time of arrest, of the reasons for his arrest and shall be promptly informed of any charges against him.
3. Anyone arrested or detained on a criminal charge shall be brought promptly before a judge or other offi cer authorized by law to exercise judicial power and shall be entitled
to trial within a reasonable time or to release. It shall not be the general rule that persons awaiting trial shall be detained in custody, but release may be subject to guarantees to appear for trial, at any other stage of the judicial proceedings, and, should occasion arise, for execution of the judgement.
4. Anyone who is deprived of his liberty by arrest or detention shall be entitled to take proceedings before a court, in order that that court may decide without delay on the lawfulness of his detention and order his release if the detention is not lawful.
5. Anyone who has been the victim of unlawful arrest or detention shall have an enforceable
right to compensation.

Article 10
1. All persons deprived of their liberty shall be treated with humanity and with respect for the inherent dignity of the human person.

2. (a) Accused persons shall, save in exceptional circumstances, be segregated from convicted
persons and shall be subject to separate treatment appropriate to their status as unconvicted persons;
(b) Accused juvenile persons shall be separated from adults and brought as speedily as possible for adjudication.
3. Th e penitentiary system shall comprise treatment of prisoners the essential aim of which shall be their reformation and social rehabilitation. Juvenile off enders shall be segregated from adults and be accorded treatment appropriate to their age and legal status.

Article 11
No one shall be imprisoned merely on the ground of inability to fulfi l a contractual obligation.

Article 12
1. Everyone lawfully within the territory of a State shall, within that territory, have the right to liberty of movement and freedom to choose his residence.

2. Everyone shall be free to leave any country, including his own.
3. The above-mentioned rights shall not be subject to any restrictions except those which are provided by law, are necessary to protect national security, public order (ordre public), public health or morals or the rights and freedoms of others, and are consistent with the other rights recognized in the present Covenant.
4. No one shall be arbitrarily deprived of the right to enter his own country.

Article 13

An alien lawfully in the territory of a State Party to the present Covenant may be expelled
therefrom only in pursuance of a decision reached in accordance with law and shall, except where compelling reasons of national security otherwise require, be allowed to submit
the reasons against his expulsion and to have his case reviewed by, and be represented for the purpose before, the competent authority or a person or persons especially designated
by the competent authority.

Article 14

1. All persons shall be equal before the courts and tribunals. In the determination of any criminal charge against him, or of his rights and obligations in a suit at law, everyone shall be entitled to a fair and public hearing by a competent, independent and impartial tribunal established by law. The press and the public may be excluded from all or part of a trial for reasons of morals, public order (ordre public) or national security in a democratic society, or when the interest of the private lives of the parties so requires, or to the extent strictly necessary in the opinion of the court in special circumstances where publicity would prejudice the interests of justice; but any judgement rendered in a criminal case or in a suit at law shall be made public except where the interest of juvenile persons otherwise requires or the proceedings concern matrimonial disputes or the guardianship of children.
2. Everyone charged with a criminal offence shall have the right to be presumed innocent
until proved guilty according to law.
3. In the determination of any criminal charge against him, everyone shall be entitled to the following minimum guarantees, in full equality:
(a) To be informed promptly and in detail in a language which he understands of the nature and cause of the charge against him;
(b) To have adequate time and facilities for the preparation of his defence and to communicate
with counsel of his own choosing;
(c) To be tried without undue delay;
(d) To be tried in his presence, and to defend himself in person or through legal assistance
of his own choosing; to be informed, if he does not have legal assistance, of this

right; and to have legal assistance assigned to him, in any case where the interests of justice so require, and without payment by him in any such case if he does not have sufficient means to pay for it;
(e) To examine, or have examined, the witnesses against him and to obtain the attendance
and examination of witnesses on his behalf under the same conditions as witnesses against him;
(f) To have the free assistance of an interpreter if he cannot understand or speak the language used in court;
(g) Not to be compelled to testify against himself or to confess guilt.
4. In the case of juvenile persons, the procedure shall be such as will take account of their age and the desirability of promoting their rehabilitation.
5. Everyone convicted of a crime shall have the right to his conviction and sentence being
reviewed by a higher tribunal according to law.
6. When a person has by a final decision been convicted of a criminal offence and when subsequently his conviction has been reversed or he has been pardoned on the ground that a new or newly discovered fact shows conclusively that there has been a miscarriage
of justice, the person who has suffered punishment as a result of such conviction shall be compensated according to law, unless it is proved that the non-disclosure of the unknown fact in time is wholly or partly attributable to him.
7. No one shall be liable to be tried or punished again for an offence for which he has already been finally convicted or acquitted in accordance with the law and penal procedure
of each country.

Article 15

1. No one shall be held guilty of any criminal offence on account of any act or omission which did not constitute a criminal offence, under national or international law, at the time when it was committed. Nor shall a heavier penalty be imposed than the one that was applicable at the time when the criminal offence was committed. If, subse164 quent to the commission of the offence, provision is made by law for the imposition of the lighter penalty, the offender shall benefit thereby.
2. Nothing in this article shall prejudice the trial and punishment of any person for any act or omission which, at the time when it was committed, was criminal according to the general principles of law recognized by the community of nations.

Article 16

Everyone shall have the right to recognition everywhere as a person before the law.

Article 17

1. No one shall be subjected to arbitrary or unlawful interference with his privacy, family,
home or correspondence, nor to unlawful attacks on his honour and reputation.
2. Everyone has the right to the protection of the law against such interference or attacks.

Article 18
1. Everyone shall have the right to freedom of thought, conscience and religion. This right shall include freedom to have or to adopt a religion or belief of his choice, and freedom, either individually or in community with others and in public or private, to manifest his religion or belief in worship, observance, practice and teaching.
2. No one shall be subject to coercion which would impair his freedom to have or to adopt a religion or belief of his choice.
3. Freedom to manifest one's religion or beliefs may be subject only to such limitations as are prescribed by law and are necessary to protect public safety, order, health, or morals or the fundamental rights and freedoms of others.
4. The States Parties to the present Covenant undertake to have respect for the liberty of parents and, when applicable, legal guardians to ensure the religious and moral education of their children in conformity with their own convictions.

Article 19
1. Everyone shall have the right to hold opinions without interference.
2. Everyone shall have the right to freedom of expression; this right shall include freedom
to seek, receive and impart information and ideas of all kinds, regardless of frontiers, either orally, in writing or in print, in the form of art, or through any other
media of his choice.
3. The exercise of the rights provided for in paragraph 2 of this article carries with it special duties and responsibilities. It may therefore be subject to certain restrictions, but these shall only be such as are provided by law and are necessary:
(a) For respect of the rights or reputations of others;
(b) For the protection of national security or of public order *(ordre public)*, or of public health or morals.

Article 20
1. Any propaganda for war shall be prohibited by law.
2. Any advocacy of national, racial or religious hatred that constitutes incitement to discrimination, hostility or violence shall be prohibited by law.

Article 21
The right of peaceful assembly shall be recognized. No restrictions may be placed on the exercise of this right other than those imposed in conformity with the law and which are necessary in a democratic society in the interests of national security or public safety,
public order *(ordre public)*, the protection of public health or morals or the protection of the rights and freedoms of others.

Article 22
1. Everyone shall have the right to freedom of association with others, including the right to form and join trade unions for the protection of his interests.
2. No restrictions may be placed on the exercise of this right other than those which are prescribed by law and which are necessary in a democratic society in the interests of national security or public safety, public order *(ordre public)*, the protection of public

health or morals or the protection of the rights and freedoms of others. This article shall not prevent the imposition of lawful restrictions on members of the armed forces and of the police in their exercise of this right.

3. Nothing in this article shall authorize States Parties to the International Labour Organization
Convention of 1948 concerning Freedom of Association and Protection
of the Right to Organize to take legislative measures which would prejudice, or to apply the law in such a manner as to prejudice, the guarantees provided for in that Convention.

Article 23

1. The family is the natural and fundamental group unit of society and is entitled to protection by society and the State.
2. The right of men and women of marriageable age to marry and to found a family shall
be recognized.
3. No marriage shall be entered into without the free and full consent of the intending spouses.
4. States Parties to the present Covenant shall take appropriate steps to ensure equality of rights and responsibilities of spouses as to marriage, during marriage and at
its dissolution. In the case of dissolution, provision shall be made for the necessary protection of any children.

Article 24

1. Every child shall have, without any discrimination as to race, colour, sex, language, religion, national or social origin, property or birth, the right to such measures of
protection as are required by his status as a minor, on the part of his family, society and the State.
2. Every child shall be registered immediately after birth and shall have a name.
3. Every child has the right to acquire a nationality.

Article 25

Every citizen shall have the right and the opportunity, without any of the distinctions mentioned in article 2 and without unreasonable restrictions:
(a) To take part in the conduct of public affairs, directly or through freely chosen representatives;
(b) To vote and to be elected at genuine periodic elections which shall be by universal and equal suffrage and shall be held by secret ballot, guaranteeing the free expression of the will of the electors;
(c) To have access, on general terms of equality, to public service in his country.

Article 26

All persons are equal before the law and are entitled without any discrimination to the equal protection of the law. In this respect, the law shall prohibit any discrimination and guarantee to all persons equal and effective protection against discrimination on any

ground such as race, colour, sex, language, religion, political or other opinion, national or
social origin, property, birth or other status.

Article 27
In those States in which ethnic, religious or linguistic minorities exist, persons belonging to such minorities shall not be denied the right, in community with the other members of their group, to enjoy their own culture, to profess and practise their own religion, or to
use their own language.

PART IV
Article 28
1. The re shall be established a Human Rights Committee (hereafter referred to in the present Covenant as the Committee). It shall consist of eighteen members and shall carry out the functions hereinafter provided.
2. The Committee shall be composed of nationals of the States Parties to the present Covenant who shall be persons of high moral character and recognized competence in the fi eld of human rights, consideration being given to the usefulness of the participation
of some persons having legal experience.
3. The members of the Committee shall be elected and shall serve in their personal capacity.

Article 29
1. The members of the Committee shall be elected by secret ballot from a list of persons
possessing the qualifi cations prescribed in article 28 and nominated for the purpose by the States Parties to the present Covenant.
2. Each State Party to the present Covenant may nominate not more than two persons. These persons shall be nationals of the nominating State.
3. A person shall be eligible for renomination.

Article 30
1. The initial election shall be held no later than six months after the date of the entry into force of the present Covenant.
2. At least four months before the date of each election to the Committee, other than an
election to fi ll a vacancy declared in accordance with article 34, the Secretary-General of the United Nations shall address a written invitation to the States Parties to the present Covenant to submit their nominations for membership of the Committee within three months.
3. The Secretary-General of the United Nations shall prepare a list in alphabetical order of all the persons thus nominated, with an indication of the States Parties which have nominated them, and shall submit it to the States Parties to the present Covenant no later than one month before the date of each election.
4. Elections of the members of the Committee shall be held at a meeting of the States

Parties to the present Covenant convened by the Secretary General of the United Nations at the Headquarters of the United Nations. At that meeting, for which two thirds of the States Parties to the present Covenant shall constitute a quorum, the persons elected to the Committee shall be those nominees who obtain the largest number of votes and an absolute majority of the votes of the representatives of States Parties present and voting.

Article 31
1. Th e Committee may not include more than one national of the same State.
2. In the election of the Committee, consideration shall be given to equitable geographical
distribution of membership and to the representation of the diff erent forms of civilization and of the principal legal systems.

Article 32
1. Th e members of the Committee shall be elected for a term of four years. Th ey shall be eligible for re-election if renominated. However, the terms of nine of the members elected at the fi rst election shall expire at the end of two years; immediately after the fi rst election, the names of these nine members shall be chosen by lot by the Chairman of the meeting referred to in article 30, paragraph 4.
2. Elections at the expiry of offi ce shall be held in accordance with the preceding articles
of this part of the present Covenant.

Article 33
1. If, in the unanimous opinion of the other members, a member of the Committee has ceased to carry out his functions for any cause other than absence of a temporary character, the Chairman of the Committee shall notify the Secretary-General of the United Nations, who shall then declare the seat of that member to be vacant.
2. In the event of the death or the resignation of a member of the Committee, the Chairman
shall immediately notify the Secretary-General of the United Nations, who shall declare the seat vacant from the date of death or the date on which the resignation takes eff ect.

Article 34
1. When a vacancy is declared in accordance with article 33 and if the term of offi ce of the member to be replaced does not expire within six months of the declaration of the vacancy, the Secretary-General of the United Nations shall notify each of the States Parties to the present Covenant, which may within two months submit nominations in accordance with article 29 for the purpose of fi lling the vacancy.
2. Th e Secretary-General of the United Nations shall prepare a list in alphabetical order of the persons thus nominated and shall submit it to the States Parties to the present Covenant. Th e election to fi ll the vacancy shall then take place in accordance with the relevant provisions of this part of the present Covenant.
3. A member of the Committee elected to fi ll a vacancy declared in accordance with article 33 shall hold offi ce for the remainder of the term of the member who vacated

the seat on the Committee under the provisions of that article.

Article 35
The members of the Committee shall, with the approval of the General Assembly of the United Nations, receive emoluments from United Nations resources on such terms and conditions as the General Assembly may decide, having regard to the importance of the Committee's responsibilities.

Article 36
The Secretary-General of the United Nations shall provide the necessary staff and facilities
for the effective performance of the functions of the Committee under the present Covenant.

Article 37
1. The Secretary-General of the United Nations shall convene the initial meeting of the Committee at the Headquarters of the United Nations.
2. After its initial meeting, the Committee shall meet at such times as shall be provided in its rules of procedure.
3. The Committee shall normally meet at the Headquarters of the United Nations or at the United Nations Office at Geneva.

Article 38
Every member of the Committee shall, before taking up his duties, make a solemn declaration
in open committee that he will perform his functions impartially and conscientiously.

Article 39
1. The Committee shall elect its officers for a term of two years. They may be reelected.
2. The Committee shall establish its own rules of procedure, but these rules shall provide,
inter alia, that:
(a) Twelve members shall constitute a quorum;
(b) Decisions of the Committee shall be made by a majority vote of the members present.

Article 40
1. The States Parties to the present Covenant undertake to submit reports on the measures
they have adopted which give effect to the rights recognized herein and on the progress made in the enjoyment of those rights:
(a) Within one year of the entry into force of the present Covenant for the States Parties concerned;
(b) Thereafter whenever the Committee so requests.
2. All reports shall be submitted to the Secretary-General of the United Nations, who shall transmit them to the Committee for consideration. Reports shall indicate the factors and difficulties, if any, affecting the implementation of the present Covenant.

3. The Secretary-General of the United Nations may, after consultation with the Committee,
transmit to the specialized agencies concerned copies of such parts of the
reports as may fall within their field of competence.
4. The Committee shall study the reports submitted by the States Parties to the present Covenant. It shall transmit its reports, and such general comments as it may consider appropriate, to the States Parties. The Committee may also transmit to the Economic and Social Council these comments along with the copies of the reports it has received from States Parties to the present Covenant.
5. The States Parties to the present Covenant may submit to the Committee observations
on any comments that may be made in accordance with paragraph 4 of this article.

Article 41
1. A State Party to the present Covenant may at any time declare under this article that it recognizes the competence of the Committee to receive and consider communications
to the effect that a State Party claims that another State Party is not fulfilling its obligations under the present Covenant. Communications under this article may be received and considered only if submitted by a State Party which has made a declaration recognizing in regard to itself the competence of the Committee. No communication
shall be received by the Committee if it concerns a State Party which has not made such a declaration. Communications received under this article shall be dealt with in accordance with the following procedure:
(a) If a State Party to the present Covenant considers that another State Party is not giving effect to the provisions of the present Covenant, it may, by written communication,
bring the matter to the attention of that State Party. Within three months after the receipt of the communication the receiving State shall afford the State which sent the communication an explanation, or any other statement in writing clarifying the matter which should include, to the extent possible and pertinent, reference to domestic procedures and remedies taken, pending, or available in the matter;
(b) If the matter is not adjusted to the satisfaction of both States Parties concerned within six months after the receipt by the receiving State of the initial communication, either State shall have the right to refer the matter to the Committee, by notice given to the Committee and to the other State;
(c) The Committee shall deal with a matter referred to it only after it has ascertained that all available domestic remedies have been invoked and exhausted in the matter, in conformity with the generally recognized principles of international law. This shall not be the rule where the application of the remedies is unreasonably prolonged;
(d) The Committee shall hold closed meetings when examining communications under this article;
(e) Subject to the provisions of subparagraph (c), the Committee shall make available

its good offi ces to the States Parties concerned with a view to a friendly solution of the matter on the basis of respect for human rights and fundamental freedoms as recognized in the present Covenant;
(f) In any matter referred to it, the Committee may call upon the States Parties concerned,
referred to in subparagraph (b), to supply any relevant information;
(g) Th e States Parties concerned, referred to in subparagraph (b), shall have the right to be represented when the matter is being considered in the Committee and to make submissions orally and/or in writing;
(h) Th e Committee shall, within twelve months after the date of receipt of notice under subparagraph (b), submit a report:
(i) If a solution within the terms of subparagraph (e) is reached, the Committee shall confi ne its report to a brief statement of the facts and of the solution reached;
(ii) If a solution within the terms of subparagraph (e) is not reached, the Committee shall confi ne its report to a brief statement of the facts; the written submissions and record of the oral submissions made by the States Parties concerned shall be attached to the report.
In every matter, the report shall be communicated to the States Parties concerned.
2. Th e provisions of this article shall come into force when ten States Parties to the present Covenant have made declarations under paragraph 1 of this article. Such dec171
larations shall be deposited by the States Parties with the Secretary-General of the United Nations, who shall transmit copies thereof to the other States Parties. A declaration
may be withdrawn at any time by notifi cation to the Secretary-General. Such a withdrawal shall not prejudice the consideration of any matter which is the subject of a communication already transmitted under this article; no further communication by any State Party shall be received after the notifi cation of withdrawal of the declaration
has been received by the Secretary-General, unless the State Party concerned has made a new declaration.

Article 42

1. (a) If a matter referred to the Committee in accordance with article 41 is not resolved to the satisfaction of the States Parties concerned, the Committee may, with the prior consent of the States Parties concerned, appoint an ad hoc Conciliation Commission (hereinafter referred to as the Commission). Th e good offi ces of the Commission shall be made available to the States Parties concerned with a view to an amicable solution of the matter on the basis of respect for the present Covenant;
(b) Th e Commission shall consist of fi ve persons acceptable to the States Parties concerned.
If the States Parties concerned fail to reach agreement within three months on all or part of the composition of the Commission, the members of the Commission concerning whom no agreement has been reached shall be elected by secret ballot by a two-thirds majority vote of the Committee from among its members.

2. The members of the Commission shall serve in their personal capacity. They shall not be nationals of the States Parties concerned, or of a State not Party to the present Covenant, or of a State Party which has not made a declaration under article 41.
3. The Commission shall elect its own Chairman and adopt its own rules of procedure.
4. The meetings of the Commission shall normally be held at the Headquarters of the United Nations or at the United Nations Office at Geneva. However, they may be held at such other convenient places as the Commission may determine in consultation
with the Secretary-General of the United Nations and the States Parties concerned.
5. The secretariat provided in accordance with article 36 shall also service the commissions
appointed under this article.
6. The information received and collated by the Committee shall be made available to the Commission and the Commission may call upon the States Parties concerned to supply any other relevant information.
7. When the Commission has fully considered the matter, but in any event not later than twelve months after having been seized of the matter, it shall submit to the Chairman of the Committee a report for communication to the States Parties concerned:
(a) If the Commission is unable to complete its consideration of the matter within twelve months, it shall confine its report to a brief statement of the status of its consideration
of the matter;
172
(b) If an amicable solution to the matter on the basis of respect for human rights as recognized in the present Covenant is reached, the Commission shall confine its report to a brief statement of the facts and of the solution reached;
(c) If a solution within the terms of subparagraph (b) is not reached, the Commission's report shall embody its findings on all questions of fact relevant to the issues between the States Parties concerned, and its views on the possibilities of an amicable solution of the matter. This report shall also contain the written submissions and a record of the oral submissions made by the States Parties concerned;
(d) If the Commission's report is submitted under subparagraph (c), the States Parties concerned shall, within three months of the receipt of the report, notify the Chairman of the Committee whether or not they accept the contents of the report of the Commission.
8. The provisions of this article are without prejudice to the responsibilities of the Committee under article 41.
9. The States Parties concerned shall share equally all the expenses of the members of the Commission in accordance with estimates to be provided by the Secretary-General of the United Nations.
10. The Secretary-General of the United Nations shall be empowered to pay the expenses

of the members of the Commission, if necessary, before reimbursement by
the States Parties concerned, in accordance with paragraph 9 of this article.

Article 43

The members of the Committee, and of the ad hoc conciliation commissions which may
be appointed under article 42, shall be entitled to the facilities, privileges and immunities
of experts on mission for the United Nations as laid down in the relevant sections of the
Convention on the Privileges and Immunities of the United Nations.

Article 44

The provisions for the implementation of the present Covenant shall apply without prejudice
to the procedures prescribed in the field of human rights by or under the constituent
instruments and the conventions of the United Nations and of the specialized agencies
and shall not prevent the States Parties to the present Covenant from having recourse to
other procedures for settling a dispute in accordance with general or special international
agreements in force between them.

Article 45

The Committee shall submit to the General Assembly of the United Nations, through
the Economic and Social Council, an annual report on its activities.

PART V

Article 46

Nothing in the present Covenant shall be interpreted as impairing the provisions of the
Charter of the United Nations and of the constitutions of the specialized agencies which
define the respective responsibilities of the various organs of the United Nations and of the
specialized agencies in regard to the matters dealt with in the present Covenant.

Article 47

Nothing in the present Covenant shall be interpreted as impairing the inherent right of
all peoples to enjoy and utilize fully and freely their natural wealth and resources.

PART VI

Article 48

1. The present Covenant is open for signature by any State Member of the United Nations
or member of any of its specialized agencies, by any State Party to the Statute of the
International Court of Justice, and by any other State which has been invited by the
General Assembly of the United Nations to become a Party to the present Covenant.

2. The present Covenant is subject to ratification. Instruments of ratification shall be
deposited with the Secretary-General of the United Nations.

3. The present Covenant shall be open to accession by any State referred to in paragraph
1 of this article.

4. Accession shall be effected by the deposit of an instrument of accession with the Secretary-
General of the United Nations.
5. The Secretary-General of the United Nations shall inform all States which have signed this Covenant or acceded to it of the deposit of each instrument of ratification or accession.

Article 49
1. The present Covenant shall enter into force three months after the date of the deposit
with the Secretary-General of the United Nations of the thirty-fifth instrument of ratification or instrument of accession.
2. For each State ratifying the present Covenant or acceding to it after the deposit of the thirty-fifth instrument of ratification or instrument of accession, the present Covenant shall enter into force three months after the date of the deposit of its own instrument of ratification or instrument of accession.

Article 50
The provisions of the present Covenant shall extend to all parts of federal States without
any limitations or exceptions.

Article 51
1. Any State Party to the present Covenant may propose an amendment and file it with the Secretary-General of the United Nations. The Secretary-General of the United Nations shall thereupon communicate any proposed amendments to the States Parties to the present Covenant with a request that they notify him whether they favour a conference of States Parties for the purpose of considering and voting upon the proposals. In the event that at least one third of the States Parties favours such a conference, the Secretary-General shall convene the conference under the auspices of the United Nations. Any amendment adopted by a majority of the States Parties present and voting at the conference shall be submitted to the General Assembly of the United Nations for approval.
2. Amendments shall come into force when they have been approved by the General Assembly
of the United Nations and accepted by a two-thirds majority of the States Parties to the present Covenant in accordance with their respective constitutional processes.
3. When amendments come into force, they shall be binding on those States Parties which have accepted them, other States Parties still being bound by the provisions of the present Covenant and any earlier amendment which they have accepted.

Article 52
Irrespective of the notifications made under article 48, paragraph 5, the Secretary-General of the United Nations shall inform all States referred to in paragraph 1 of the same
article of the following particulars:
(a) Signatures, ratifications and accessions under article 48;

(b) The date of the entry into force of the present Covenant under article 49 and the date of the entry into force of any amendments under article 51.

Article 53

1. The present Covenant, of which the Chinese, English, French, Russian and Spanish texts are equally authentic, shall be deposited in the archives of the United Nations.
2. The Secretary-General of the United Nations shall transmit certified copies of the present Covenant to all States referred to in article 48.

Annex 3

International Covenant on Economic, Social and Cultural Rights

Preamble

The States Parties to the present Covenant,

Considering that, in accordance with the principles proclaimed in the Charter of the United
Nations, recognition of the inherent dignity and of the equal and inalienable rights of all members of the human family is the foundation of freedom, justice and peace in the world,

Recognizing that these rights derive from the inherent dignity of the human person,

Recognizing that, in accordance with the Universal Declaration of Human Rights, the ideal
of free human beings enjoying freedom from fear and want can only be achieved if conditions
are created whereby everyone may enjoy his economic, social and cultural rights, as well as his civil and political rights,

Considering the obligation of States under the Charter of the United Nations to promote universal respect for, and observance of, human rights and freedoms,

Realizing that the individual, having duties to other individuals and to the community to which he belongs, is under a responsibility to strive for the promotion and observance of
the rights recognized in the present Covenant,

Agree upon the following articles:

PART I

Article 1

1. All peoples have the right of self-determination. By virtue of that right they freely determine their political status and freely pursue their economic, social and cultural development.
2. All peoples may, for their own ends, freely dispose of their natural wealth and resources
without prejudice to any obligations arising out of international economic cooperation, based upon the principle of mutual benefit, and international law. In no case may a people be deprived of its own means of subsistence.
3. The States Parties to the present Covenant, including those having responsibility for the administration of Non-Self-Governing and Trust Territories, shall promote the

realization of the right of self-determination, and shall respect that right, in conformity with the provisions of the Charter of the United Nations.

PART II
Article 2

1. Each State Party to the present Covenant undertakes to take steps, individually and through international assistance and cooperation, especially economic and technical, to the maximum of its available resources, with a view to achieving progressively the full realization of the rights recognized in the present Covenant by all appropriate means, including particularly the adoption of legislative measures.
2. Th e States Parties to the present Covenant undertake to guarantee that the rights enunciated in the present Covenant will be exercised without discrimination of any kind as to race, colour, sex, language, religion, political or other opinion, national or social origin, property, birth or other status.
3. Developing countries, with due regard to human rights and their national economy, may determine to what extent they would guarantee the economic rights recognized in the present Covenant to non-nationals.

Article 3
Th e States Parties to the present Covenant undertake to ensure the equal right of men and women to the enjoyment of all economic, social and cultural rights set forth in the present Covenant.

Article 4
Th e States Parties to the present Covenant recognize that, in the enjoyment of those rights provided by the State in conformity with the present Covenant, the State may subject
such rights only to such limitations as are determined by law only in so far as this may be compatible with the nature of these rights and solely for the purpose of promoting the
general welfare in a democratic society.

Article 5
1. Nothing in the present Covenant may be interpreted as implying for any State, group or person any right to engage in any activity or to perform any act aimed at the destruction
of any of the rights or freedoms recognized herein, or at their limitation to
a greater extent than is provided for in the present Covenant.
2. No restriction upon or derogation from any of the fundamental human rights recognized
or existing in any country in virtue of law, conventions, regulations or custom
shall be admitted on the pretext that the present Covenant does not recognize such rights or that it recognizes them to a lesser extent.

PART III
Article 6

1. The States Parties to the present Covenant recognize the right to work, which includes the right of everyone to the opportunity to gain his living by work which he freely chooses or accepts, and will take appropriate steps to safeguard this right.
2. The steps to be taken by a State Party to the present Covenant to achieve the full realization of this right shall include technical and vocational guidance and training programmes, policies and techniques to achieve steady economic, social and cultural development and full and productive employment under conditions safeguarding fundamental political and economic freedoms to the individual.

Article 7

The States Parties to the present Covenant recognize the right of everyone to the enjoyment
of just and favourable conditions of work which ensure, in particular:
(a) Remuneration which provides all workers, as a minimum, with:
(i) Fair wages and equal remuneration for work of equal value without distinction of any kind, in particular women being guaranteed conditions of work not inferior to those enjoyed by men, with equal pay for equal work;
(ii) A decent living for themselves and their families in accordance with the provisions of the present Covenant;
(b) Safe and healthy working conditions;
(c) Equal opportunity for everyone to be promoted in his employment to an appropriate higher level, subject to no considerations other than those of seniority and competence;
(d) Rest, leisure and reasonable limitation of working hours and periodic holidays with pay, as well as remuneration for public holidays.

Article 8

1. The States Parties to the present Covenant undertake to ensure:
(a) The right of everyone to form trade unions and join the trade union of his choice, subject only to the rules of the organization concerned, for the promotion and protection
of his economic and social interests. No restrictions may be placed on the exercise of this right other than those prescribed by law and which are necessary in a democratic society in the interests of national security or public order or for the protection of the rights and freedoms of others;
(b) The right of trade unions to establish national federations or confederations and the right of the latter to form or join international trade-union organizations;
(c) The right of trade unions to function freely subject to no limitations other than those prescribed by law and which are necessary in a democratic society in the interests of national security or public order or for the protection of the rights and freedoms of others;
(d) The right to strike, provided that it is exercised in conformity with the laws of the particular country.
2. This article shall not prevent the imposition of lawful restrictions on the exercise of these rights by members of the armed forces or of the police or of the administration of the State.

3. Nothing in this article shall authorize States Parties to the International Labour Organisation
Convention of 1948 concerning Freedom of Association and Protection of the
Right to Organize to take legislative measures which would prejudice, or apply the law
in such a manner as would prejudice, the guarantees provided for in that Convention.

Article 9
The States Parties to the present Covenant recognize the right of everyone to social security, including social insurance.

Article 10
The States Parties to the present Covenant recognize that:
1. The widest possible protection and assistance should be accorded to the family, which
is the natural and fundamental group unit of society, particularly for its establishment
and while it is responsible for the care and education of dependent children.
Marriage must be entered into with the free consent of the intending spouses.
2. Special protection should be accorded to mothers during a reasonable period before
and after childbirth. During such period working mothers should be accorded paid
leave or leave with adequate social security benefits.
3. Special measures of protection and assistance should be taken on behalf of all children
and young persons without any discrimination for reasons of parentage or other
conditions. Children and young persons should be protected from economic and social
exploitation. Their employment in work harmful to their morals or health or dangerous
to life or likely to hamper their normal development should be punishable by
law. States should also set age limits below which the paid employment of child labour
should be prohibited and punishable by law.

Article 11
1. The States Parties to the present Covenant recognize the right of everyone to an adequate
standard of living for himself and his family, including adequate food, clothing
and housing, and to the continuous improvement of living conditions. The States
Parties will take appropriate steps to ensure the realization of this right, recognizing
to this effect the essential importance of international cooperation based on free
consent.
2. The States Parties to the present Covenant, recognizing the fundamental right of
everyone to be free from hunger, shall take, individually and through international
cooperation, the measures, including specific programmes, which are needed:

(a) To improve methods of production, conservation and distribution of food by making
full use of technical and scientific knowledge, by disseminating knowledge of the
principles of nutrition and by developing or reforming agrarian systems in such a way
as to achieve the most efficient development and utilization of natural resources;
(b) Taking into account the problems of both food-importing and food-exporting
countries, to ensure an equitable distribution of world food supplies in relation to

need.

Article 12

1. The States Parties to the present Covenant recognize the right of everyone to the enjoyment
of the highest attainable standard of physical and mental health.
2. The steps to be taken by the States Parties to the present Covenant to achieve the full
realization of this right shall include those necessary for:
(a) The provision for the reduction of the stillbirth-rate and of infant mortality and for the healthy development of the child;
(b) The improvement of all aspects of environmental and industrial hygiene;
(c) The prevention, treatment and control of epidemic, endemic, occupational and other diseases;
(d) The creation of conditions which would assure to all medical service and medical attention in the event of sickness.

Article 13

1. The States Parties to the present Covenant recognize the right of everyone to education.
They agree that education shall be directed to the full development of the human personality and the sense of its dignity, and shall strengthen the respect for human rights and fundamental freedoms. They further agree that education shall enable all persons to participate effectively in a free society, promote understanding, tolerance and friendship among all nations and all racial, ethnic or religious groups, and further the activities of the United Nations for the maintenance of peace.
2. The States Parties to the present Covenant recognize that, with a view to achieving the full realization of this right:
(a) Primary education shall be compulsory and available free to all;
(b) Secondary education in its different forms, including technical and vocational secondary
education, shall be made generally available and accessible to all by every appropriate means, and in particular by the progressive introduction of free education;
(c) Higher education shall be made equally accessible to all, on the basis of capacity, by every appropriate means, and in particular by the progressive introduction of free education;
(d) Fundamental education shall be encouraged or intensified as far as possible for those persons who have not received or completed the whole period of their primary education;

(e) The development of a system of schools at all levels shall be actively pursued, an adequate fellowship system shall be established, and the material conditions of teaching staff shall be continuously improved.
3. The States Parties to the present Covenant undertake to have respect for the liberty of parents and, when applicable, legal guardians to choose for their children schools, other than those established by the public authorities, which conform to such minimum

educational standards as may be laid down or approved by the State and to ensure the religious and moral education of their children in conformity with their own convictions.

4. No part of this article shall be construed so as to interfere with the liberty of individuals and bodies to establish and direct educational institutions, subject always to the observance of the principles set forth in paragraph 1 of this article and to the requirement that the education given in such institutions shall conform to such minimum standards as may be laid down by the State.

Article 14

Each State Party to the present Covenant which, at the time of becoming a Party, has not been able to secure in its metropolitan territory or other territories under its jurisdiction compulsory primary education, free of charge, undertakes, within two years, to work out and adopt a detailed plan of action for the progressive implementation, within a reasonable number of years, to be fixed in the plan, of the principle of compulsory education free of charge for all.

Article 15

1. The States Parties to the present Covenant recognize the right of everyone:
(a) To take part in cultural life;
(b) To enjoy the benefits of scientific progress and its applications;
(c) To benefit from the protection of the moral and material interests resulting from any scientific, literary or artistic production of which he is the author.

2. The steps to be taken by the States Parties to the present Covenant to achieve the full realization of this right shall include those necessary for the conservation, the development and the diffusion of science and culture.

3. The States Parties to the present Covenant undertake to respect the freedom indispensable for scientific research and creative activity.

4. The States Parties to the present Covenant recognize the benefits to be derived from the encouragement and development of international contacts and cooperation in the scientific and cultural fields.

PART IV

Article 16

1. The States Parties to the present Covenant undertake to submit in conformity with this part of the Covenant reports on the measures which they have adopted and the progress made in achieving the observance of the rights recognized herein.

2. (a) All reports shall be submitted to the Secretary-General of the United Nations, who shall transmit copies to the Economic and Social Council for consideration in accordance with the provisions of the present Covenant;
(b) The Secretary-General of the United Nations shall also transmit to the specialized agencies copies of the reports, or any relevant parts therefrom, from States Parties to the present Covenant which are also members of these specialized agencies in so far as these reports, or parts therefrom, relate to any matters which fall within the responsibilities
of the said agencies in accordance with their constitutional instruments.

Article 17
1. The States Parties to the present Covenant shall furnish their reports in stages, in accordance with a programme to be established by the Economic and Social Council within one year of the entry into force of the present Covenant after consultation with the States Parties and the specialized agencies concerned.
2. Reports may indicate factors and difficulties affecting the degree of fulfilment of obligations
under the present Covenant.
3. Where relevant information has previously been furnished to the United Nations or to any specialized agency by any State Party to the present Covenant, it will not be necessary to reproduce that information, but a precise reference to the information so furnished will suffice.

Article 18
Pursuant to its responsibilities under the Charter of the United Nations in the field of human rights and fundamental freedoms, the Economic and Social Council may make arrangements
with the specialized agencies in respect of their reporting to it on the progress made in achieving the observance of the provisions of the present Covenant falling within
the scope of their activities. These reports may include particulars of decisions and recommendations
on such implementation adopted by their competent organs.

Article 19
The Economic and Social Council may transmit to the Commission on Human Rights for study and general recommendation or, as appropriate, for information the reports concerning
human rights submitted by States in accordance with articles 16 and 17, and those concerning human rights submitted by the specialized agencies in accordance with article
18.
182

Article 20
The States Parties to the present Covenant and the specialized agencies concerned may submit comments to the Economic and Social Council on any general recommendation

under article 19 or reference to such general recommendation in any report of the Commission
on Human Rights or any documentation referred to therein.

Article 21
The Economic and Social Council may submit from time to time to the General Assembly
reports with recommendations of a general nature and a summary of the information received from the States Parties to the present Covenant and the specialized agencies on
the measures taken and the progress made in achieving general observance of the rights recognized in the present Covenant.

Article 22
The Economic and Social Council may bring to the attention of other organs of the United Nations, their subsidiary organs and specialized agencies concerned with furnishing
technical assistance any matters arising out of the reports referred to in this part of the present Covenant which may assist such bodies in deciding, each within its field of competence,
on the advisability of international measures likely to contribute to the effective progressive implementation of the present Covenant.

Article 23
The States Parties to the present Covenant agree that international action for the achievement of the rights recognized in the present Covenant includes such methods as the conclusion of conventions, the adoption of recommendations, the furnishing of technical
assistance and the holding of regional meetings and technical meetings for the purpose of consultation and study organized in conjunction with the Governments concerned.

Article 24
Nothing in the present Covenant shall be interpreted as impairing the provisions of the Charter of the United Nations and of the constitutions of the specialized agencies which define the respective responsibilities of the various organs of the United Nations and of the
specialized agencies in regard to the matters dealt with in the present Covenant.

Article 25
Nothing in the present Covenant shall be interpreted as impairing the inherent right of all peoples to enjoy and utilize fully and freely their natural wealth and resources.

PART V

Article 26
1. The present Covenant is open for signature by any State Member of the United Nations
or member of any of its specialized agencies, by any State Party to the Statute of the International Court of Justice, and by any other State which has been invited by the General Assembly of the United Nations to become a party to the present

Covenant.

2. The present Covenant is subject to ratification. Instruments of ratification shall be deposited with the Secretary-General of the United Nations.

3. The present Covenant shall be open to accession by any State referred to in paragraph 1 of this article.

4. Accession shall be effected by the deposit of an instrument of accession with the Secretary-General of the United Nations.

5. The Secretary-General of the United Nations shall inform all States which have signed the present Covenant or acceded to it of the deposit of each instrument of ratification or accession.

Article 27

1. The present Covenant shall enter into force three months after the date of the deposit with the Secretary-General of the United Nations of the thirty-fifth instrument of ratification or instrument of accession.

2. For each State ratifying the present Covenant or acceding to it after the deposit of the thirty-fifth instrument of ratification or instrument of accession, the present Covenant shall enter into force three months after the date of the deposit of its own instrument of ratification or instrument of accession.

Article 28

The provisions of the present Covenant shall extend to all parts of federal States without any limitations or exceptions.

Article 29

1. Any State Party to the present Covenant may propose an amendment and file it with the Secretary-General of the United Nations. The Secretary-General shall thereupon communicate any proposed amendments to the States Parties to the present Covenant with a request that they notify him whether they favour a conference of States Parties for the purpose of considering and voting upon the proposals. In the event that at least one third of the States Parties favours such a conference, the Secretary-General shall convene the conference under the auspices of the United Nations. Any amendment adopted by a majority of the States Parties present and voting at the conference shall be submitted to the General Assembly of the United Nations for approval.

2. Amendments shall come into force when they have been approved by the General Assembly of the United Nations and accepted by a two-thirds majority of the States Parties to the present Covenant in accordance with their respective constitutional processes.

3. When amendments come into force they shall be binding on those States Parties which have accepted them, other States Parties still being bound by the provisions of the present Covenant and any earlier amendment which they have accepted.

Article 30
Irrespective of the notifications made under article 26, paragraph 5, the Secretary-General of the United Nations shall inform all States referred to in paragraph 1 of the same
article of the following particulars:
(a) Signatures, ratifications and accessions under article 26;
(b) The date of the entry into force of the present Covenant under article 27 and the date of the entry into force of any amendments under article 29.

Article 31
1. The present Covenant, of which the Chinese, English, French, Russian and Spanish texts are equally authentic, shall be deposited in the archives of the United Nations.
2. The Secretary-General of the United Nations shall transmit certified copies of the present Covenant to all States referred to in article 26.

Annex 4
INTERNATIONAL INSTRUMENTS ON THE INTERNET
The following texts can be accessed through the OHCHR web page:
http://www.ohchr.org/english/law/index.htm

THE INTERNATIONAL BILL OF HUMAN RIGHTS
- Universal Declaration of Human Rights
- International Covenant on Economic, Social and Cultural Rights
- International Covenant on Civil and Political Rights
- Optional Protocol to the International Covenant on Civil and Political Rights
- Second Optional Protocol to the International Covenant on Civil and Political Rights, aiming at the abolition of the death penalty

WORLD CONFERENCE ON HUMAN RIGHTS AND MILLENNIUM ASSEMBLY
- Vienna Declaration and Programme of Action
- United Nations Millennium Declaration

THE RIGHT OF SELF-DETERMINATION
- United Nations Declaration on the Granting of Independence to Colonial Countries and Peoples
- General Assembly resolution 1803 (XVII) of 14 December 1962: "Permanent sovereignty over natural resources"
- International Convention against the Recruitment, Use, Financing and Training of Mercenaries

RIGHTS OF INDIGENOUS PEOPLES AND MINORITIES
- Indigenous and Tribal Peoples Convention, 1989 (ILO Convention No. 169)
- Declaration on the Rights of Persons Belonging to National or Ethnic, Religious and Linguistic Minorities

PREVENTION OF DISCRIMINATION
- ILO Convention No. 100 concerning equal remuneration
- ILO Convention No. 111 concerning discrimination in respect of employment and occupation

- International Convention on the Elimination of all Forms of Racial Discrimination
- Declaration on Race and Racial Prejudice

c INTER-PARLIAMENTARY UNION AND OFFICE OF THE
UNITED NATIONS HIGH COMMISSIONER FOR HUMAN RIGHTS
2005

All rights reserved. No part of this publication may be reproduced, stored in a retrieval system, or transmitted in any form or by any means, electronic, mechanical, photocopying, recording, or otherwise, without the prior permission of the Inter-Parliamentary Union and the Offi ce of the United Nations High Commissioner for Human Rights

Th is Handbook is distributed on condition that it be neither lent nor otherwise distributed, including by commercial means, without the prior permission of the publishers, in any form other than the original and on condition that the next publisher meets the same requirements.

ISBN 92-9142-266-5

Inter-Parliamentary Union
Chemin du Pommier 5
CH - 1218 Le Grand-Saconnex
Tel. +4122 919 41 50
Fax +4122 919 41 60
E-mail: postbox@mail.ipu.org
Web site: www.ipu.org

Offi ce of the United Nations High Commissioner for Human Rights
OHCHR
Palais des Nations
Avenue de la Paix 8-14
CH - 1211 Geneva 10
Tel. +4122 917 90 00
Fax +4122 917 01 23
E-mail: publications@ohchr.org
Web site: www.ohchr.org

This publication is intended for parliamentarians who want to familiarize themselves with the framework that has been set up since 1945 by the United Nations and regional organizations to protect and promote human rights. It presents the notion of human rights and the meaning of the rights enshrined in the Universal Declaration of Human Rights.

It specifies the State's obligations to protect and promote human rights, and contains suggestions as to action parliaments and their members may take to contribute to their implementation.

CHapter -3

Understanding Human Rights

Making sense of human rights
A short introduction

Introduction

This guide is designed for officials in public authorities to assist them in working with the Human Rights Act 1998 – which has been described as the most important piece of constitutional legislation passed in the United Kingdom sinthe achievement of universal suffrage in 1918. It tells you (at pages 6 to 9) what rights are contained in thHuman Rights Act. It explains at page 3 how, in certain circumstances, rights can be refused or restricted – in particular where there is a real and serious danger to public safety. This guide is short and simple. It gives you a brief introduction to human rights for use in straightforward situations. More detailed guidance can be found in the human rights handbook for public officials, *Human Rights and Human Lives*, produced by the Ministry of Justice. **If you are unsure about anything, seek legal advice.**

ce e

1 Making sense of human rights: a short intr oduction

What are human rights?

Human rights are rights and freedoms that belong to all individuals regardless of their nationality and citizenship. They are fundamentally important in maintaining a fair and civilised society.

What is the European Convention on Human Rights?

The European Convention on Human Rights (ECHR) was drafted by the nations of the Council of Europe (including the UK) in the aftermath of World War II. The Council of Europe was founded to defend human rights, parliamentary democracy and the rule of law, and to ensure that the atrocities and cruelties committed during the war would never be repeated.

What is the Human Rights Act?

In October 2000, The Human Rights Act came into effect in the UK. This meant that people in the UK could take cases about their human rights into a UK court. Previously they had to take complaints about their human rights to the European Court of Human Rights in Strasbourg, France. The rights contained in the Convention are included at Schedule 1 of the Human Rights Act. For the purposes of the Human Rights Act they are known as 'the Convention Rights'.

What are the Convention rights? There are 16 basic rights in the Human Rights Act – all taken from the European Convention on Human Rights. As you would expect, they concern matters of life and death, like freedom from torture and being killed, but they also cover rights in everyday life, such as what a person can say and do, their beliefs, their right to a fair trial and many other similar basic entitlements. They are listed at pages 6 to 9. Can I ever refuse or restrict a right that someone is claiming? Sometimes – especially if there is a real and serious danger to public safety. Not all Convention rights carry the same weight. They can be grouped into three broad types: •
Absolute rights – such as the right to protection from torture and inhuman and degrading treatment (Article 3). The state can never withhold or take away these rights. • Limited rights – such as the right to liberty (Article 5). These rights may be limited under explicit and finite circumstances. **If in doubt, seek legal advice.** • Qualified rights – rights which require a balance between the rights of the individual and the needs of the wider community or state interest. These include: the right to respect for private and family life (Article 8); the right to manifest one's religion or beliefs (Article 9); freedom of expression (Article 10); freedom of assembly and association (Article 11); the right to peaceful enjoyment of property (Protocol 1, Article 1); and, to some extent, the right to education (Protocol 1, Article 2).

Interference with qualified rights is permissible only if: • there is a clear legal basis for the interference with the qualified right that people can find out about and understand, and • the action/interference seeks to achieve a legitimate aim. Legitimate aims are set out in each article containing a qualified right and they vary from article to article. They include, for example, the interests of national security, the prevention of disorder or crime, and public safety. Any interference with one of the rights contained in Articles 8–11 must fall under one of the permitted aims set out in the relevant article, and • the action is necessary in a democratic society. This means that the action or interference must be in response to 'a pressing social need', and must be no greater than that necessary to address the social need. **If you have any doubts about whether a right can be refused or restricted, seek legal advice without delay.**

How do I know that I am respecting human rights?

The flowchart in this booklet's centre spread gives you broad guidance on reaching a decision that might restrict someone's rights, and is designed to help you in applying human rights in the workplace. It will be particularly relevant when you have to consider balancing one right against another, or one person's rights against the interests of society.

The flowchart is fairly selfexplanatory. However, if you would like to understand it in greater detail, you can find a full explanation at page 56 of the human rights handbook *Human rights: human lives*.

The Convention rights

(Article 1 is introductory and is not incorporated into the Human Rights Act.)

Article 2: Right to life

A person has the right to have their life protected by law. There are only certain very limited circumstances where it is acceptable for the state to take away someone's life, e.g. if a police officer acts justifiably in selfdefence.

Article 3: Prohibition of torture

A person has the absolute right not to be tortured or subjected to treatment or punishment which is inhuman or degrading.

Article 4: Prohibition of slavery and forced labour

A person has the absolute right not to be treated as a slave or to be required to perform forced or compulsory labour.

Article 5: Right to liberty and security

A person has the right not to be deprived of their liberty – 'arrested or detained' – except in limited cases specified in the article (e.g. where they are suspected or convicted of committing a crime) and provided there is a proper legal basis in UK law.

Article 6: Right to a fair trial

A person has the right to a fair and public hearing within a reasonable period of time. This applies both to criminal charges against them and to cases concerning their civil rights and obligations. Hearings must be carried out by an independent and impartial tribunal established by law. It is possible to exclude the public from the hearing (though not from the judgment) if it is necessary to protect things like national security or public order. If it is a criminal charge, the person is presumed innocent until proven guilty according to law and has certain guaranteed rights to defend themselves.

Article 7: No punishment without law

A person normally has the right not to be found guilty of an offence arising out of actions which at the time they committed them were not criminal. They are also protected against later increases in the maximum possible sentence for an offence.

Apart from the right to hold particular beliefs, the rights in Articles 8 to 11 may be limited where that is necessary to achieve an important objective. The precise objectives for which limitations are permitted are set out in each article, but they include things like protecting public health or safety, preventing crime and protecting the rights of others.

Article 8: Right to respect for private and family life

A person has the right to respect for their private and family life, their home and their correspondence. This right can be restricted only in specified circumstances.

Article 9: Freedom of thought, conscience and religion

A person is free to hold a broad range of views, beliefs and thoughts, and to follow a religious faith. The right to manifest those beliefs may be limited only in specified circumstances.

Article 10: Freedom of expression

A person has the right to hold opinions and express their views on their own or in a group. This applies even if those views are unpopular or disturbing. This right can be restricted only in specified circumstances.

Article 11: Freedom of assembly and association

A person has the right to assemble with other people in a peaceful way. They also have the right to associate with other people, which includes the right to form a trade union. These rights may be restricted only in specified circumstances.

Article 12: Right to marry

Men and women have the right to marry and start a family. National law will still govern how and at what age this can take place.

(Article 13 is not included in the Human Rights Act.)

Article 14: Prohibition of discrimination

In the application of the Convention rights, a person has the right not to be treated differently because of their race,

continued on page 9

Human rights flowchart

religion, sex, political views or any other personal status, unless this can be justified objectively. Everyone must have equal access to Convention rights, whatever their status.

Article 1 of Protocol 1: Protection of property

(A 'protocol' is a later addition to the Convention.)

A person has the right to the peaceful enjoyment of their possessions. Public authorities cannot usually interfere with things people own or the way they use them, except in specified limited circumstances.

Article 2 of Protocol 1: Right to education

A person has the right not to be denied access to the educational system.

Article 3 of Protocol 1: Right to free elections

Elections for members of the legislative body (e.g. Parliament) must be free and fair and take place by secret ballot. Some qualifications may be imposed on who is eligible to vote (e.g. a minimum age).

Article 1 of Protocol 13: Abolition of the death penalty

These provisions abolish the death penalty.

Human rights in practice

What does the Human Rights Act mean for public authorities?

The Human Rights Act has the following implications for the work of public authorities:

• It makes it unlawful for public authorities (these include central and local government, the police and the courts) to act in a way that is incompatible with a Convention right. • Anyone who feels that a public authority has acted incompatibly with their Convention rights can raise this before an appropriate UK court or tribunal.

What does the Human Rights Act mean for you as a public official?

All public authorities in the UK have an obligation to respect the Convention rights. That means that you must understand those rights and take them into account in your daytoday work. That is the case whether you are delivering a service directly to the public or devising new policies or procedures.

Points to remember

The rights of an individual should never be allowed to obscure public safety. • If you are unsure, or a matter is particularly complex, consider seeking legal advice. •

Balancing one person's rights against those of the community

The fact that a policy or decision restricts a Convention right does not necessarily mean that it will be incompatible with the ECHR. It is a fundamental responsibility of the state – arising from Article 2 of the Convention itself – to take appropriate steps to protect the safety of its citizens. In particular, if a restriction of a qualified right has a legitimate aim, such as public safety, and the restriction itself does not go any further than necessary to protect this aim, then it is likely that it will be compatible with the Convention. The Convention recognises that there are situations where a state must be allowed to decide what is in the best interests of its citizens, and enables a state, or public authority acting on behalf of the state, to restrict the rights of individuals accordingly.

Frequently asked questions

What does the Human Rights Act do?

It makes the human rights contained in the ECHR enforceable in UK law. This means that it is unlawful for a public authority to act in a way that is incompatible with a Convention right. Anyone who feels that one or more of their rights has been breached by a public authority can raise the matter in an appropriate court or tribunal. If they are unhappy with the court's decision and have pursued the issue as far as it can go in the UK, they may take their complaint to the European Court of Human Rights.

Do judges now have more power than elected politicians?

The simple answer is no. Judges must interpret legislation as far as possible in a way that is compatible with the Convention rights. If this is not possible, courts can strike down incompatible secondary legislation (law made by ministers under powers granted to them in Acts of Parliament), or can make a declaration of incompatibility in relation to primary legislation (Acts of Parliament). They cannot strike down primary legislation.

What is a declaration of incompatibility?

A declaration of incompatibility sends a signal from the courts to Parliament that the UK may be breaching its international obligations under the ECHR. Parliament does not have to change the law: it retains its sovereignty as the UK's lawmaking body.

What difference does the Human Rights Act make?

The principal effect of the Human Rights Act is to enable people to enforce their human rights in the domestic courts. It should mean that people across society are treated with respect for their human rights, promoting values such as dignity, fairness, equality and respect.

Are human rights relevant to every decision I make?

The short answer to this is no. Many everyday decisions taken in the workplace have no human rights implications. However, by understanding human rights properly you are more likely to know when human rights are relevant and when they are not. This should help you to make decisions more confidently, and ensure that your decisions are sound and fair.

What is a public authority? The Human Rights Act says that people carrying out certain functions of a public nature will fall within the public authority definition. The courts are still deciding exactly what this means. The following are definitely public authorities:
• central government • local government • local authorities • police, prison and immigration services• NHS Trusts • courts and tribunals • planning inspectorate • executive agencies • statutory regulatory bodies. This list is not exhaustive. If you are unsure whether or not you work in a public authority you should check with your line manager. However, if you are reading this document, it is likely that you do work for a public authority. In any event, following human rights standards will be good practice, even in matters not strictly covered by the ambit of the Human Rights Act.

Do all new laws have to be compatible with the Human Rights Act? When a minister introduces a Bill to Parliament they are required to confirm in writing that, in their view, the Bill is compatible with Convention rights, or that they are unable to say that it is compatible but that they wish to proceed with the Bill anyway. Therefore it is possible for new legislation to be incompatible. Are all Convention rights guaranteed, whatever the circumstances? Not all Convention rights are formulated in the same way. While some rights are protected absolutely, such as the right to be free from torture, others are limited in certain defined situations, or qualified so as to take account of the rights of others or the interests of wider society. This is explained in greater detail on pages 3 to 4 of this guide. Who can bring a case under the Human Rights Act? Any 'victim' can. It is not necessary to be a UK citizen. Anyone starting proceedings must have been directly affected by an act or omission of a public authority.

Is any other guidance on the Human Rights Act available? For further information about human rights and the Act, we recommend:
- *Human rights: human lives* – a handbook for officials working in public authorities, produced by the Ministry of Justice and available for download on our website at www.justice.gov.uk/about/docs/hr-handbook-public-authorities.pdf
- *A Guide to the Human Rights Act 1998: Third Edition* – produced by the Ministry of Justice and available for download on our website at www.justice.gov.uk/about/docs/act-studyguide.pdf
- If you have any questions about this guidebook or about human rights in general, the Human Rights Division of the Ministry of Justice (MoJ) will be pleased to help. You can contact them on 020 3334 3734, or **humanrights@justice.gsi.gov.uk**. You can also access a range of useful information on MoJ's Human Rights website at www.justice.gov.uk/a-z/humanrights.htm

DCA 45/06 Produced by the Ministry of Justice © Crown copyright October 2006 Printed on paper comprising a minimum of 75% postconsumer waste Alternative format versions are available on request from tel. 020 3334 3734

Chapter 3

Freedom of Expression

Monica Macovei
Human rights handbooks, No. 2

Introduction 5
General considerations on Article 10 6

Protection of freedom of expression – 1st paragraph 8
Freedom to hold opinions 8
Freedom to impart information and ideas 8
Freedom to receive information and ideas 10
Freedom of the press 11
Freedom of radio and television broadcasting 13
What is protected under paragraph 1?
The Court's jurisprudence on specific issues . . 15
The system of restrictions with the exercise of the right to freedom of expression – 2nd paragraph 20
Three requirements for legitimate interference with the exercise of freedom of expression 29
Freedom of expression and national security/territorial integrity/public safety 36
Freedom of expression and prevention of disorder or crime 44
Freedom of expression and morals 47
Freedom of expression and reputation and rights of others. 49
Freedom of expression and the authority and impartiality of the judiciary 57
Protection of journalistic sources and legitimate aims 59
Table of cases 61
Contents

Introduction

The European Convention on Human Rights is the most important form of expression of the attachment of the member states of the Council of Europe to the values of democracy, of peace and justice, and, through them, to the respect of the fundamental rights and freedoms of the individuals living in these societies.1

The European Convention on Human Rights ("the Convention") was signed on 4 November 1950 in Rome. Over the last fifty years the Convention has progressed both by the interpretation given to its texts by the European Court of Human Rights and the European Commission of Human Rights2 and by the work of the Council of Europe. The Council has adopted additional protocols that have broadened the scope of the Convention, resolutions and recommendations that have developed and proposed to the member states standards of behaviour, and imposed sanctions on the states failing to comply with the provisions of the Convention.

Almost all the States Party to the European Convention on Human Rights have integrated the Convention into their national legislation. The Convention is thus part of the internal legal system and is binding on the domestic courts and all public authorities. It further follows that all individuals in the states concerned derive rights and duties from the Convention, so that in the national procedure they may directly invoke its text and case-law, which must be applied by the national courts. Moreover, the national authorities, including the courts, must give priority to the Convention over any national law conflicting with the Convention and its case-law.

The text of the Convention may not be read outside its case-law. The Convention functions under the common law system. The judgments of the European Court of Human Rights ("the Court") explain and interpret the text. They are binding precedents whose legal status is that of mandatory legal norms. Therefore, once the Convention is ratified, the national authorities of all signatory States, including those that practise a civil (continental) law system must consider the Court's judgments as binding law. For this reason this handbook refers extensively to the Court's jurisprudence. In this respect, one must understand that nowadays even the traditionally civil legal systems practise a mixed civil and common law system where the jurisprudence is given equal value to that of the laws enacted by the Parliament.

The interpretation of the Convention's text is dynamic and evolutive, making the Convention a living

1. Introduction to *European Convention on Human Rights – Collected texts*, Council of Europe, 1994.
2. In accordance with Protocol No.11, the European Commission and the European Court on Human Rights joined together in a single body, the European Court of Human Rights.

instrument which must be interpreted in the light of the present day conditions. Accordingly, the Court is (and must be) influenced by the developments and commonly accepted standards in the member states of the Council of Europe.

The overall scheme of the Convention is that the initial and primary responsibility for the protection of the rights set forth in it lies with the Contracting States. The Court is there to monitor states' action, exercising the power of review. The domestic margin of appreciation thus goes hand in hand with the European supervision. The doctrine of the margin of appreciation is applied differently, and the degree of discretion allowed to the states varies according to the context. A state is allowed a considerable discretion in cases of public emergency arising under Article 15 or where there is little common ground between the contracting parties, while the discretion is reduced almost to vanishing point in certain areas, such as the protection of freedom of expression.

This handbook is designed to assist judges at all levels in ensuring that all cases involving freedom of expression are handled in conformity with states' obligations under Article 10 of the Convention as developed by the Court in Strasbourg.

General considerations on Article 10

In the context of effective political democracy and respect for human rights mentioned in the Preamble to the Convention, freedom of expression is not only important in its own right, but also it plays a central part in the protection of other rights under the Convention. Without a broad guarantee of the right to freedom of expression protected by independent and impartial courts, there is no free country, there is no democracy. This general proposition is undeniable.[3]

Freedom of expression is a right in itself as well as a component of other rights protected under the Convention, such as freedom of assembly. At the same time, freedom of expression can conflict with other rights protected by the Convention, such as the right to a fair trial, to respect for private life, to freedom of conscience and religion. When such conflict occurs, the Court strikes a balance in order to establish the pre-eminence of one right over the other. The balance of the conflicting interests, one of which is freedom of expression, takes into account the importance of the other. The Court has repeatedly stated that

Freedom of expression constitutes one of the essential foundations of a democratic society, one of the basic conditions for its progress and for each individual's self-fulfilment.[4]

3. Jochen Abr. Frowein, "Freedom of expression under the European Convention on Human Rights", in Monitor/Inf (97) 3, Council of Europe.

And,

the press plays a pre-eminent role in a State governed by the rule of law.5

The democratic political process and the development of every human being are options for which the protection of freedom of expression is essential. As a matter of principle, the protection given by Article 10 extends to any expression notwithstanding its content, disseminated by any individual, group or type of media. The only content-based restriction applied by the Commission has dealt with the dissemination of ideas promoting racism and the Nazi ideology, and inciting to hatred and racial discrimination. The Commission relied on Article 17 of the Convention and held that freedom of expression may not be used in order to lead to the destruction of the rights and freedoms granted by the Convention.6 Such decisions apply the theory of the paradox of tolerance: an absolute tolerance may lead to the tolerance of the ideas promoting intolerance, and the latter could then destroy the tolerance.

States are compelled to justify any interference in any kind of expression. In order to decide the extent to which a particular form of expression should be protected, the Court examines the type of expression (political, commercial, artistic, etc.), the means by which the expression is disseminated (personal, written media, television, etc.), and its audience (adults, children, the entire public, a particular group). Even the "truth" of the expression has a different significance according to these criteria.

In taking its decisions, the Court in Strasbourg has paid attention to national constitutional practices, including the constitutional practice of the United States, which grants a strong protection to freedom of expression. However, domestic decisions – even those with legal force – have a limited utility for an international body such as the Court, which applies and construes an international treaty. In some cases the Commission and the Court have referred to the International Covenant on Civil and Political Rights or other international documents protecting freedom of expression.

Article 10 of the Convention is structured in two paragraphs.

– The first paragraph defines the freedoms protected.
– The second stipulates the circumstances in which a state may legitimately interfere with the exercise of freedom of expression.

4. Lingens v. Austria, 1986; Sener v. Turkey, 2000; Thoma v. Luxembourg, 2001; Maronek v. Slovakia, 2001; Dichand and Others v. Austria, 2002, etc. A table of cases cited in this study appears on page 61.
5. Castells v. Spain, 1992; Prager and Oberschlick v. Austria, 1995.
6. Kühnen v. the Federal Republic of Germany, 1988; D.I. v. Germany, 1996.

Protection of freedom of expression – 1st paragraph

Article 10, paragraph 1
Everyone has the right to freedom of expression. This right includes the freedom to hold opinions and to receive and impart information and ideas without interference by a public authority and regardless of frontiers. This article shall not prevent States from requiring the licensing of broadcasting, television or cinema enterprises.

Paragraph 1 provides for three components of the right to freedom of expression:
– freedom to hold opinions;
– freedom to impart information and ideas; and
– freedom to receive information and ideas.

These freedoms must be exercised freely, without interference by public authorities[7] and regardless of frontiers.

Freedom to hold opinions

Freedom to hold opinions is a prior condition to the other freedoms guaranteed by Article 10, and it almost enjoys an absolute protection in the sense that the possible restrictions set forth in paragraph 2 are inapplicable. As stated by the Committee of Ministers, "any restrictions to this right will be inconsistent with the nature of a democratic society".[8]

States must not try to indoctrinate their citizens and should not be allowed to operate distinctions between individuals holding one opinion or another. Moreover, the promotion of one-sided information by the State may constitute a serious and unacceptable obstacle to the freedom to hold opinions.

Under the freedom to hold opinions, individuals are also protected against possible negative consequences in cases where particular opinions are attributed to them following previous public expressions.

The freedom to hold opinions includes the negative

freedom of not being compelled to communicate one's own opinions.9

Freedom to impart information and ideas

Freedom to impart information and ideas is of the greatest importance for the political life and the democratic structure of a country. Meaningful free elections are not possible in the absence of this freedom. Moreover, a full

7. Except under the requirements of paragraph 2.
8. Report of the Committee of Ministers, in *Theory and Practice of the European Convention on Human Rights*, Van Dijk and Van Hoof, Kluwer, 1990, p. 413.
9. Vogt v. Germany, 1995.

exercise of the freedom to impart information and ideas allows for a free criticism of the government, which is the main indicator of a free and democratic government. As the Court stated as early as 1976:

The Court's supervisory functions oblige it to pay the utmost attention to the principles characterising a "democratic society". Freedom of expression constitutes one of the essential foundations of such a society, one of the basic conditions for its progress and for the development of every man.10

The freedom to criticise the government was explicitly upheld by the Court in 1986: it is incumbent on the press *to impart information and ideas on political issues just as on those in other areas of public interest. Not only does the press have the task of imparting such information and ideas: the public also has a right to receive them.11*

Obviously, the freedom to **impart** information and ideas is complementary to the freedom to **receive** information and ideas. This is true with respect to printed media as well as to broadcast media. Regarding the latter, the Court has held that states may not intervene between the transmitter and the receiver, as they have the right to get into direct contact with each other according to their will.12

Freedom to impart information and ideas on economic matters (known as *commercial speech*) is also guaranteed under Article 10. However, the Court decided that in economic matters domestic authorities enjoy a broader margin of appreciation.13

Artistic creation and performance as well as its distribution is seen by the Court as a major contribution to the exchange of ideas and opinions, a crucial component of a democratic society. Stating that artistic freedom and the free circulation of art is restricted only in undemocratic societies, the Commission argued:

Through his creative work, the artist expresses not only a personal vision of the world but also his view of the society in which he lives. To that extent art not only helps shape public opinion but is also an expression of it and can confront the public with the major issues of the day.14

Distinction between facts and opinions

Since the freedom discussed refers to imparting both information and ideas, the distinction made by the Court becomes relevant at this early stage. Making a clear distinction between information (facts) and opinions (value judgments), the Court has stated that

the existence of facts can be demonstrated, whereas the truth of value judgments is not susceptible of proof. ... As regards value judgments this requirement is impossible of fulfilment and it

10. Handyside v. the United Kingdom, 1976.
11. Lingens v. Austria, 1986; Sener v. Turkey, 2000; Thoma v. Luxembourg, 2001; Dichand and Others v. Austria, 2002, etc.
12. Groppera Radio AG and Others v. Switzerland, 1990; Casado Coca v. Spain, 1994.
13. Markt Intern Verlag GmbH and Klaus Beermann v. the Federal Republic of Germany, 1989.
14. Otto-Preminger Institut v. Austria, 1994.

infringes freedom of opinion itself, which is a fundamental part of the right secured by Article 10 of the Convention.15

While the opinions are viewpoints or personal assessments of an event or situation and are not susceptible of being proven true or false, the underlying facts on which the opinion is based may be capable of being proven true or false. Equally, in *Dalban*, the Court held:

It would be unacceptable for a journalist to be debarred from expressing critical value judgments unless he or she could prove their truth.16

Consequently, along with information or data that could be verified, opinions, critics or speculations that may not be subjected to the truth proof are also protected under Article 10. Moreover, value judgments, in particular those expressed in the political field, enjoy a special protection as a requirement of the pluralism of opinions, crucial for a democratic society.

The distinction between facts and opinions, and the prohibition of the truth proof with regard to the latter become very important in the domestic legal systems that still require the truth proof for the crime of "insult", which concerns the expression of ideas and opinions. Moreover, even with regards to facts, the Court has recognised the defence of good faith as leaving the media "a breathing space for error". For instance, in *Dalban*17 the Court observed that

there is no proof that the description of events given in the articles was totally untrue and was designed to fuel a defamation campaign against GS …

Basically, the good faith defence comes in exchange for the truth proof. Where a journalist or a publication has a legitimate purpose, the matter is of public concern, and reasonable efforts have been made to verify the facts, the press shall not be liable even if the respective facts prove untrue.

However, a sufficient factual basis must support value judgments. As the Court pointed out

*even where a statement amounts to a value judgment, the proportionality of an interference may depend on whether there exists a sufficient factual basis for the impugned statement, since even a value judgment without any factual basis to support it may be excessive.*18

Freedom to receive information and ideas

The freedom to receive information includes the right to gather information and to seek information through all possible lawful sources. The freedom to receive information also covers international television broadcasts.19

15. Lingens v. Austria, 1986; Jerusalem v. Austria, 2001; Dichand and Others v. Austria, 2002.
16. Dalban v. Romania, 1999.
17. Ibidem.
18. Jerusalem v. Austria, 2001; Dichand and Others v. Austria, 2002.

While the freedom to receive information and opinions relates to the media in that it enables them to impart such information and ideas to the public, the Court also read in this freedom the right of the public to be adequately informed, in particular on matters of public interest.

Freedom of the press

Although Article 10 does not explicitly mention the freedom of the press, the Court has developed extensive case-law providing a body of principles and rules granting the press a special status in the enjoyment of the freedoms contained in Article 10. This is why we think that freedom of the press deserves additional comments under the scope of Article 10. Another argument for a special treatment of freedom of the press is given by national practices: to a large extent, the victims of the infringement of the right to freedom of expression by public authorities are journalists rather than other individuals.

The role of the press as political watchdog was first emphasised by the Court in the *Lingens* case.[20] In newspaper articles the journalist had criticised the then Austrian Federal Chancellor for a particular political move consisting of announcing a coalition with a party led by a person with a Nazi background. The journalist (Mr Lingens) had referred to the Chancellor's behaviour as "immoral", "undignified", demonstrating "the lowest opportunism". Following a private prosecution brought by the Chancellor, the Austrian courts found these statements to be defamatory and imposed a fine on the journalist. While debating the question of guilt, the courts also found that the journalist could not prove the truth of his allegations. With regard to the latter issue, the European Court found the national courts' approach to be wrong, as opinions (value judgments) cannot be demonstrated and are not susceptible of being proven.[21] Looking at the grounds of the journalist's conviction, the Court underlined the importance of freedom of the press in the political debate:

... These principles are of particular importance as far as the press is concerned. While the press must not overstep the bounds set, inter alia, *for the "protection of the reputation of others", it is nevertheless incumbent on it to impart information and ideas on political issues just as on those in other areas of public interest. Not only does the press have the task of imparting such information and ideas: the public also has a right to receive them [...] In this connection, the Court cannot accept the opinion, expressed in the judgment of the Vienna Court of Appeal, to the effect that the task of the press was to impart information, the interpretation of which had to be left primarily to the reader ...*

19. Autronic AG v. Switzerland, 1990.
20. Lingens v. Austria, 1986.
21. See below, page 12.

In the same judgment the Court argued that freedom of the press affords the public one of the best means of discovering and forming an opinion of the ideas and attitudes of political leaders and consequently, the freedom of political debate is at the very core of the concept of a democratic society. This is why the Court affords political debate by the press a very strong protection under Article 10.

Freedom of the press also enjoys a special status where other matters of public concern are at stake. In the *Thorgeirson* case22 the applicant (Mr Thorgeirson) had made allegations in the press of widespread police brutality in Iceland. He referred to police officers as "beasts in uniform" and "individuals reduced to a mental age of a newborn child as a result of strangle-holds that policemen and bouncers learn and use with brutal spontaneity" and described the police force defending itself as "bullying, forgery, unlawful actions, superstitions, rashness and ineptitude". At the domestic level, Mr Thorgeirson was prosecuted and fined for defaming unspecified members of the police. The European Court found that the applicant raised the issue of police brutality in his country and

... it is incumbent on the press to impart information and ideas on matters of public interest.

The Court further stated that

there is no warrant in its case-law to distinguish ... between political discussion and discussion of other matters of public concern.

Finally, the Court characterised the conviction as

capable of discouraging open discussion of matters of public concern.

In *Maronek* the Court viewed the Slovakian housing policy at a period when state-owned apartments were about to be denationalised as a matter of general interest, and afforded the applicant's freedom of expression a stronger protection.23 Other examples can be found in many of the cases against Turkey, where the conflict in south-east Turkey and all the related issues, including the "separatist propaganda" or the question of federalisation, raised in writing or orally, have been matters of public interest.24 Undoubtedly, the Court affords the freedom of the press a strong protection where matters of public interest, other than political, are publicly debated.

Another important issue in the context of the freedom of the press is the publication of rumours and allegations which journalists are not able to prove. As mentioned above,25 the Court has stated that value judgments must not be subject to any proof requirement. In the Thorgeirson case26 the allegations against the police were collected from various sources; basically, the article had mentioned

22. Thorgeir Thorgeirson v. Iceland, 1992.
23. Maronek v. Slovakia, 2001.
24. Sürek and Özdemir v. Turkey, 1999; Sener v. Turkey, 2000; Özgür Gündem v. Turkey, 2000.
25. See above, page 11.
26. See above, page 12.

rumours coming from the public. While the respondent state argued that the applicant's articles lacked an objective and factual basis, since he could not prove the truth of the allegations, the Court found the truth requirement to be an unreasonable, even impossible task, and stated that the press would be able to publish almost nothing if it were required to publish only fully proven facts. Obviously, the Court's considerations have to be placed in the context of public debates on matters of public concern.
Dissemination in the media of statements made by other persons was considered by the Court. In *Jersild* and *Thoma*, the Court stated that
punishment of a journalist for assisting in the dissemination made by another person ... would seriously hamper the contribution of the press to discussion of matters of public interest and should not be envisaged unless there are particularly string reasons for doing so.27
Further, in *Thoma*, where the government reproached the applicant journalist that he did not distance himself from the statements in the quotation, the Court held:
A general requirement for journalists systematically and formally to distance themselves from the content of a quotation that might insult or provoke others or damage their reputation was not reconcilable with the press's role of providing information on current event, opinions and ideas.
Journalistic sources are also protected under Article 10. The Court explained that the protection of the journalistic sources is one of the basic conditions of the press freedom. In the Goodwin case28 the Court argued that
without such protection, sources may be deterred from assisting the press in informing the public on matters of public interest. As a result, the vital public watchdog role of the press may be undermined and the ability of the press to provide accurate and reliable information may be adversely affected.

Freedom of radio and television broadcasting

According to the last sentence of paragraph 1, the right to receive and impart information and ideas "shall not prevent States from requiring the licensing of broadcasting, television or cinema enterprises." This provision was included at an advanced stage of the preparatory work on the Convention, being determined by technical reasons: the limited number of available frequencies and the fact that, at that time, most European states had a monopoly of broadcasting and television. However, the progress in broadcasting techniques has made these reasons disappear. In *Informationsverein Lentia*29 the Court held that following

27. Jersild v. Denmark, 1994; Thoma v. Luxembourg, 2001.
28. Goodwin v. the United Kingdom, 1996.
29. Informationsverein Lentia and Others v. Austria, 1993.

the technical progress in the last decades, the justification of these restrictions cannot be made by reference to the number of available frequencies and channels.

Satellite transmissions and cable television have resulted in a virtually unlimited number of available frequencies. In this context, the State's right to license the media companies received a new sense and purpose, namely the guarantee of liberty and pluralism of information in order to fulfil public demand.30

The Court held that the power of the domestic authorities to regulate the licensing system may not be exercised for other than technical purposes and not in a way which interferes with freedom of expression contrary to the requirements of the second paragraph of Article 10. In the Groppera case31 the Court held:

... *the purpose of the third sentence of Article 10 (1) of the Convention is to make it clear that states are permitted to control by a licensing system the way in which broadcasting is organised in their territories, particularly in its technical aspects. It does not, however, provide that licensing measures shall not otherwise be subject to the requirements of Article 10 (2), for that would lead to a result contrary to the object and purpose of Article 10 taken as a whole.*

In *Autronic AG*32 the Court held that devices for receiving broadcasting information, such as satellite dishes, do not fall under the restriction provided for in the last sentence of the first paragraph. In *Tele 1 Privatfernsehgesellschaft MBH*, the Court found Austria in violation of Article 10 in view of the lack of any legal basis to granting licenses to set up and operate a television transmitter to any station other than the Austrian Broadcasting Corporation.[33]

The public monopolies within the audiovisual media were seen by the Court as contrary to Article 10, primarily because they cannot provide a plurality of sources of information. Such a monopoly is not necessary in a democratic society, and it could only be justified by pressing social needs. However, in modern societies, the multiplication of methods of broadcast communication and the growth of transfrontier television make it impossible to justify the existence of monopolies. On the contrary, the diversity of the public's requirement cannot be covered by only one broadcasting company.[34]

Commercial advertising by the audiovisual media is also protected by Article 10, even though the domestic authorities enjoy a wide margin of appreciation as regards the necessity of restraining it.[35] In principle, advertising

30. Observer and Guardian v. the United Kingdom, 1995; Informationsverein Lentia and Others v. Austria, 1993.
31. Groppera Radio AG and Others v. Switzerland, 1990.
32. Autronic AG v.Switzerland, 1990.
33. Tele 1 Privatfernsehgesellschaft MBH v. Austria, 2001
34. Informationaverein Lentia and Others v. Austria, 1993.
35. Markt Intern Verlag GmbH and Klaus Beermann v. the Federal Republic of Germany, 1989.

should be prepared with responsibility towards society, and the moral values forming the basis of any democracy should be given particular attention. Any advertising aimed at children should avoid information which could harm their interests, and should respect their physical, mental and moral development.

What is protected under paragraph 1? The Court's jurisprudence on specific issues

The "expression" protected under Article 10 is not limited to words, written or spoken, but it extends to pictures,[36] images[37] and actions intended to express an idea or to present information. In some circumstances dress might also fall under Article 10.[38]

Moreover, Article 10 protects not only the substance of the information and ideas but also the form in which they are expressed.[39] Therefore, printed documents,[40] radio broadcasts,41 paintings,42 films43 or electronic information systems are also protected under this article. It follows that the means for the production and communication, transmission or distribution of information and ideas are covered by Article 10, and the Court must be aware of the rapid developments of such means in many areas.

Freedom of expression includes the negative freedom not to speak. The Commission invoked this type of right in *K. v. Austria*, protecting the applicant against self-incrimination in connection with criminal proceedings.

It is characteristic for Article 10 to protect expression which carries a risk of damaging or actually damages the interests of others. Usually, the opinions shared by the majority or by large groups do not run the risk of interference by the states. This is why the protection afforded by Article 10 also covers information and opinions expressed by small groups or one individual even where such expression shocks the majority.

The tolerance of individual points of view is an important component of the democratic political system.

36. Müller and Others v. Switzerland, 1988.
37. Chorherr v. Austria, 1993.
38. Stevens v. the United Kingdom, 1986.
39. Oberschlick v. Austria, 1991; Thoma v. Luxembourg, 2001; Dichand and Others v. Austria, 2002; Nikula v. Finland, 2002.
40. Handyside v. the United Kingdom, 1976.
41. Groppera Radio AG and Others v. Switzerland, 1990.
42. Müller and Others v. Switzerland, 1988.
43. Otto-Preminger Institut v. Austria, 1994.

Denouncing the tyranny of the majority, John Stuart Mill stated:

*if all mankind minus one were of one opinion, mankind would be no more justified in silencing that one person than he, if he had the power, would be justified in silencing mankind.*44

In this respect, the Court has stated that Article 10 protects not only

*the information or ideas that are favourably received or regarded as inoffensive or as a matter of indifference, but also those that offend, shock or disturb; such are the demands of that pluralism, tolerance and broad-mindedness without which there is no democratic society.*45

Opinions expressed in strong or exaggerated language are also protected; the extent of protection depends on the context and the aim of the criticism. In matters of public controversy or public interest, during political debate, in electoral campaigns or where the criticism is levelled at Government, politicians or public authorities, strong words and harsh criticism may be expected and will be tolerated to a greater degree by the Court. In *Thorgeirson*,[46] for instance, the Court found that although the articles contained very strong terms – the police officers were described as "beasts in uniform", "individuals reduced to a mental age of a new-born child as a result of strangle-holds that policemen and bouncers learn and use with brutal spontaneity" and the references to the police force were "bullying, forgery, unlawful actions, superstitions, rashness and ineptitude" – the language could not be viewed as excessive, having in view the aim of urging reform of police. Equally, in the *Jersild* case,[47] the fact that an interview containing racist statements was carried in a serious news programme was significant since the programme was designed to inform a serious audience about events in the community or from abroad. In *Dalban*, where a journalist accused a politician of corruption and of mismanagement of state's assets, the Court held that *journalistic freedom also covers possible recourse to a degree of exaggeration, or even provocation.*[48]

In *Arslan*, the applicant criticised the action of the Turkish authorities in the south-east of the country using a wording described by the Court as of an "undeniable virulence" which "confers a certain amount of vehemence to this criticism". The Court decided however that the applicant's conviction for criticising the government was disproportionate and not necessary in a democratic society.[49]

44. *On Liberty* (1859), Penguin Classics, 1985, p. 76.
45. Handyside v. the United Kingdom, 1976; Sunday Times v. the United Kingdom, 1979; Lingens v. Austria, 1986; Oberschlick v. Austria, 1991; Thorgeir Thorgeirson v. Iceland, 1992; Jersild v. Denmark, 1994; Goodwin v. the United Kingdom, 1996; De Haes and Gijsels v. Belgium, 1997; Dalban v. Romania, 1999; Arslan v. Turkey, 1999; Thoma v. Luxembourg, 2001; Jerusalem v. Austria, 2001; Maronek v. Slovakia, 2001; Dichand and Others v. Austria, 2002.
46. Thorgeir Thorgeirson v. Iceland, 1992.
47. Jersild v. Denmark, 1994.
48. Dalban v. Romania, 1999. Similarly in Prager and Oberschlick v. Austria, 1995; Dichand and Others v. Austria, 2002.
49. Arslan v. Turkey, 1999.

The use of violent terms is given more protection when it comes as a reply to provocation. In *Lopes Gomes da Silva*, the journalist criticised the political beliefs of Mr Resende, a candidate for the municipality, and called him "grotesque", "buffoonish" and "coarse". The criticism followed statements of Mr Resende where he had referred to a number of public figures in a very incisive manner, including by attacking their physical features (for instance, he called a former prime minister of France a "baldheaded Jew"). The Court held that the journalist's conviction violated Article 10, and found that

*the opinions expressed by Mr Resende and reproduced alongside the impugned editorial are themselves worded incisively, provocatively and at the very least polemically. It is not unreasonable to conclude that the style of the applicant's article was influenced by that of Mr Resende.*50

In *Oberschlick (No. 2)* the journalist referred to Mr Haider (leader of the Austrian Freedom Party and Governor) as "an idiot" ("...he is not a Nazi ... he is, however, an idiot"), following Haider's statement that in the second world war the German soldiers fought for peace and freedom. The Court found that Mr Haider's speech was itself provocative, and therefore the word "idiot" did not seem disproportionate to the indignation knowingly aroused by Mr Haider.51

Incitement to violence falls outside the protection conferred by Article 10 where an intentional and direct wording incites violence and where there is a real possibility that the violence may occur. In *Sürek (No. 3)*, while describing the Kurds' national liberation struggle as a "war directed against the forces of the Republic of Turkey" the article asserted that "we want to wage a total liberation struggle". In the Court's view,

the impugned article associated itself with the PKK and expressed a call for the use of armed forces as a means to achieve the national independence of Kurdistan.

The Court further noted that the article was published in the context of serious disturbances between the security forces and the members of the PKK involving heavy loss of life and the imposition of emergency rule in a large part of south-east Turkey. In such a context

the content of the article must be seen as capable of inciting to further violence in the region. Indeed the message which is communicated to the reader is that recourse to violence is a necessary and justified measure of self-defence in the face of the aggressor.

Following this assessment, the Court found that the conviction of the applicant was not contrary to Article 10.52 By contrast, in *Sürek (No. 4)*, where the impugned articles described Turkey as "the real terrorist" and as "the enemy" the Court found that the

50. Lopes Gomes da Silva v. Portugal, 2000.
51. Oberschlick v. Austria (No. 2), 1997.
52. Sürek v. Turkey (No. 3), 1999.

*hard criticism of the Turkish authorities ... is more a reflection of the hardened attitude of one side to the conflict, rather than a call to violence. ... On the whole, the content of the articles cannot be construed as being capable of inciting to further violence. The Court also argued that the public has the right to be informed of a different perspective on the situation in the south-east Turkey, irrespective of how unpalatable that perspective may be for them.*53

The Court concluded that the conviction and sentencing of the applicant were contrary to Article 10.

Equally, in *Karataş*, the Court found that

*even though some of the passages from the poems seem very aggressive in tone and to call for the use of violence ... the fact that they were artistic in nature and of limited impact made them less a call to an uprising than an expression of deep distress in the face of a difficult political situation.*54

Speech promoting Nazi ideology, denying the Holocaust and inciting to hatred and racial discrimination falls outside the protection of Article 10.

In *Kühnen* the applicant was leading an organisation which tried to bring back into the political scene the National Socialist Party, prohibited in Germany. He wrote and disseminated publications where he encouraged the fight for a socialist and independent Greater Germany, stating that his organisation was "against capitalism, communism, Zionism, estrangement by means of masses of foreign workers, destruction of the environment" and in favour of "German unity, social justice, racial pride, community of the people and camaraderie". In another publication, he stated "whoever serves this aim can act, whoever obstructs will be fought against and eventually eliminated".

Relying on Article 10, Mr Kühnen complained against

his conviction by the German courts. The Commission declared the complaint inadmissible, referring to Article 17 of the Convention which prohibits any activity "aimed at the destruction of any of the rights and freedoms set forth herein". The Commission observed that freedom of expression may not be used for the destruction of the rights and freedoms set forth in the Convention. It considered that the applicant's proposals, which advocated national socialism aimed at impairing the basic order of freedom and democracy, ran counter to one of the basic values expressed in the Preamble to the Convention: the fundamental freedoms enshrined in the Convention "are best maintained ... by an effective political democracy". In addition, the Commission found that the applicant's policy clearly contained elements of racial and religious discrimination. Consequently, the Commission decided that the applicant was seeking to use freedom of information set forth in Article 10 as a basis for activities which are contrary to the text and spirit of the Convention, and

53. Sürek v. Turkey (No. 4), 1999.
54. Karataş v. Turkey, 1999.

which, if admitted, would contribute to the destruction of the rights and freedoms set forth in the Convention.55 The denial of the Holocaust56 as a subject of public discourse was also denied the protection of Article 10. In *D.I. v. Germany* the applicant, an historian, was fined for having made statements at a public meetings where he had denied the existence of the gas chambers in Auschwitz, stating that these gas chambers were fakes built up in the early post-war days and that the German tax-payers paid about 16 billion German marks for fakes. The Commission found the complaint inadmissible, noting that the applicant's statements were contrary to the principles of peace and justice expressed in the Preamble to the Convention, and that they have advocated racial and religious discrimination.57

The right to vote is not protected under Article 10. The right to vote is considered a component of States' duty to hold "free elections at reasonable intervals by secret ballot, under conditions which will ensure the free expression of the opinion of the people in the choice of the legislature."58

The Strasbourg institutions were not receptive to the

idea of including the access to information under
Article 10's protection. For instance, in *Leander*59 the applicant
sought confidential information from official files
belonging to the government. He believed that he was
denied a job on account of information in the files, and
wanted to challenge that information. The Court decided
that the applicant enjoyed no protection under Article 10.
While access to information was found to fall outside
Article 10's protection, the Court decided that other provisions
of the Convention may protect such a right in certain
circumstances. In *Gaskin*60 the Court found an Article 8 violation
where the applicant was denied access to information
concerning his private life, in particular the period
when he had been in public child care. The Court argued
its findings by the importance of such information to the
private life of the applicant.
However, the Court stated that
this finding is reached without expressing any opinion on
whether general right of access to personal data and information
may be derived from Article 8 of the Convention.
55. Kühnen v. the Federal Republic of Germany, 1988.
56. The Holocaust is defined as "the state-sponsored, systematic persecution and
annihilation of European Jewry by Nazi Germany and its collaborators between
1933 and 1945. Jews were the primary victims – 6 million were murdered; Gypsies, the
handicapped, and Poles were also targeted for destruction or decimation
for racial, ethnic, or national reasons. Millions more, including homosexuals, Jehovah's
Witnesses, Soviet prisoners of war, and political dissidents
also suffered grievous oppression and death under Nazi tyranny."
http://www.ushmm.org/education/foreducators/guidelines/.
57. D.I. v. Germany, 1996. Similar decisions in Honsik v. Austria, 1995 and Ochensberger
v. Austria, 1994.
58. Article 3 of the Protocol to the Convention.
59. Leander v. Sweden, 1987.
60. Gaskin v. the United Kingdom, 1989.

Elsewhere, the Commission has said that states may
not obstruct by positive action the access to information
which is available and to the general sources of information.
61
In addition, Resolution 428 (1970) of the Parliamentary
Assembly of the Council of Europe reads that the right to
the freedom of expression "includes the right to seek,
receive, impart, make public or distribute information of
public interest" and that the media has the duty to disseminate

general and complete information on matters of public
interest. In addition, public authorities must make accessible,
in reasonable limits, information of public interest.

The system of restrictions with the exercise of the right to freedom of
expression – 2nd paragraph

Article 10 paragraph 2
The exercise of these freedoms, since it carries with it duties and
responsibilities, may be subject to such formalities, conditions,
restrictions or penalties as are prescribed by law and are necessary
in a democratic society, in the interests of national security,
territorial integrity or public safety, for the prevention of
disorder or crime, for the protection of health or morals, for the
protection of the reputation or rights of others, for preventing
the disclosure of information received in confidence or for maintaining
the authority and impartiality of the judiciary.

"The exercise of these freedoms ... may be subject to ..."

Any restriction, condition, limitation or any form of
interference with freedom of expression may only be
applied to a particular exercise of this freedom. The content
of the right to freedom of expression may never be
touched. In this respect, Article 17 reads that
nothing in this Convention may be interpreted as implying for
any State, group or person any right to engage in any activity
or perform any act aimed at the destruction of any of the rights
and freedoms set forth herein or at their limitation to a greater
extent than is provided for in the Convention.
Obviously, a limitation on the content of one right is
similar to the destruction of the said right.
Equally, the national authorities are not required to
interfere with the exercise of freedom of expression every
time one of the grounds enumerated by paragraph 2 is at
stake, as this would lead to a limitation of the content of
this right. For instance, damaging one's reputation or
honour must not be seen as criminal and/or requiring civil
redress in all cases. Similarly, public expression putting at
61. Z. v. Austria, 1988.

risk the authority of the judiciary must not be punished
each time such a criticism occurs. In other words, the
public authorities have only the possibility and not the
obligation to order and/or enforce a restrictive or punitive
measure to the exercise of the right to freedom of expression.
A different approach would lead to a hierarchy of

rights and values or interests, placing freedom of expression at the bottom of the list after, for instance, the right to dignity and honour, morals or public order. Moreover, such a hierarchy would contravene all international treaties which provide for the equality of rights and do not allow permanent limitations on the exercise of one right, since this would be similar to denial of that right.

"The exercise of these freedoms, since it carries with it duties and responsibilities …"

The idea according to which the exercise of freedom of expression carries with it duties and responsibilities is unique in the Convention, and it cannot be found in any of the other provisions regulating rights and freedoms. This text was not interpreted as a separate circumstance automatically limiting the freedom of expression of individuals belonging to certain professional categories that may carry with it "duties and responsibilities". The Court's judgments reflect various views on the "duties and responsibilities" of some civil servants when exercising their freedom of expression. In addition, the jurisprudence has developed from a rather conservative approach giving states stronger powers to a more liberal approach where states enjoy less discretion.

For instance, in *Engel and Others*62 a ban on the publication and distribution by soldiers of a paper criticising certain senior officers was found by the Court as a justified interference with freedom of expression; however, the Court also held that

there was no question of depriving them of their freedom of expression but only of punishing the abusive exercise of that freedom on their part.

In *Hadjianastassiou*63 an officer was convicted for having disclosed information classified as secret. He disclosed information on a given weapon and corresponding technical knowledge capable of causing considerable damage to national security. The Court decided that the conviction was an interference with the officer's freedom of expression which was, however, justified under paragraph 2:

It is … necessary to take into account the special conditions attaching to military life and the specific "duties" and "responsibilities" incumbent on the members of the armed forces …

The applicant, as an officer at the KETA in charge of an experimental missile programme, was bound by an obligation of discretion in relation to anything concerning the performance of

his duties.
62. Engel and Others v. the Netherlands, 1976.
63. Hadjianastassiou v. Greece, 1992.

Almost twenty years after the judgment in *Engel and Others*, in a similar case, the Court changed its view and issued an opposite ruling. In *Vereinigung Demokratischer Soldaten Österreichs und Gubi*64 the authorities prohibited the distribution to servicemen of a private periodical critical of the military administration. The Austrian Government argued that the applicants' periodical threatened the country's system of defence and the effectiveness of the army. The Court did not agree to the government's submissions and held that most of the items in the periodical

... set out complaints, put forward proposals for reforms or encourage the readers to institute legal complaints of appeals proceedings. However, despite the often polemical tenor, it does not appear that they overstepped the bounds of what is permissible in the context of a mere discussion of ideas, which must be tolerated in the army of a democratic State just as it must be in the society that such an army serves.

In *Rommelfanger*65 the Commission said that states had the positive duty to ensure that the exercise of freedom of expression by a civil servant is not subject to restrictions which would affect the substance of this right. Even where the existence of a category of civil servants with special "duties and responsibilities" is accepted, the restrictions applied on their right to freedom of expression must be examined on the same criteria as the restriction applied to others' freedom of expression.

In the *Vogt* case66 the Court held that the way a duty of discretion was imposed on a civil servant was in breach of Article 10. In 1987 Mrs Vogt was fired from the school where she had taught for about twelve years because she was an activist in the German Communist Party, and she refused to dissociate herself from that party. The duty of discretion was introduced after the experience of the Weimar Republic, and it had been justified by the need to prohibit public employees from taking part in political activities contrary to constitutional provisions. Mrs Vogt's superiors decided that she failed to comply with the duty owed by every civil servant to uphold the free democratic system within the meaning of the Constitution and sacked her. The Court held that

Although it is legitimate for a State to impose on civil servants, on account of their status, a duty of discretion, civil servants are individuals and, as such, qualify for the protection of Article 10 ...

Further on, the Court stated that it understood the arguments recalling the history of Germany; however, taking into the absolute nature of the duty of discretion, its general applicability to all civil servants and the absence of a distinction among the private and professional domains, the German authorities had violated both freedom of expression and freedom of assembly.

64. Vereinigung Demokratischer Soldaten Österreichs und Gubi v. Austria, 1994.
65. Rommelfanger v. the Federal Republic of Germany, 1989.
66. Vogt v. Germany, 1995.

The "duties and responsibilities" of judges were considered by the Court in the *Wille* case,67 where the applicant, a high-ranking judge, received a letter from the Prince of Liechtenstein criticising the applicant's statement during an academic lecture on a constitutional issue and announcing his intention not to appoint the applicant to a public post following that statement. At the beginning of its assessment, the Court noted that it

must bear in mind that, whenever the right to freedom of expression of persons in such a position is at issue, the "duties and responsibilities" referred to in Article 10 § 2 assume a special significance since it can be expected of public officials serving in the judiciary that they should show restraint in exercising their freedom of expression in all cases where the authority and impartiality of the judiciary are likely to be called in question.

The Court further noted that although the constitutional issue raised by the applicant had political implications, this element alone should not prevent the applicant from discussing this matter. In finding a violation of Article 10, the Court observed that on a previous occasion the Liechtenstein Government had held a similar view to that of the applicant, and that the opinion expressed by the applicant was shared by a considerable number of people in the country and therefore was not an untenable proposition.

It follows that any national laws or other regulations imposing absolute and unlimited fidelity or confidentiality restrictions on particular categories of civil servants, such as those employed by the intelligence services, army, etc., or the members of the judiciary, would violate Article 10. Such restrictions may be adopted by the member states only where they do not have an overall character but are limited to particular categories of information whose secrecy must be examined periodically, to specific categories of civil servants or only to some individuals belonging to such categories, and are temporary. Where it is argued that the fidelity or confidentiality duty is justified by the interest of defending "national security", member states must define this latter concept in a strict and narrow way, avoiding the inclusion of areas which fall outside the real scope of national security. Equally, states must prove the existence of a real danger against the protected interest, such as national security, and must also take into account the interest of the public in being given certain information. If all these are ignored, such limitations on the freedom of expression have an absolute nature and are inconsistent with Article 10, paragraph 2.

Under the "duties and responsibilities" approach, the Court also argued that the fact that a person belongs to a particular category is a basis for limiting rather than increasing the public authorities' powers to restrict the exercise of that person's rights. Editors and journalists would fall into this category. In the case of the *Observer and Guardian*68 the national courts issued an injunction prohibiting the publication of specific articles on the ground that

67. Wille v. Liechtenstein, 1999.

they would endanger national security. The Court referred to "the duty of the press to impart information and ideas on matters of public concern", adding that the right of the public to receive such information corresponds to the duty of the press to impart such information. Consequently, by having granted the right and the duty to impart information and ideas, the press gained a greater freedom, reducing the state's possibilities of limiting its interventions. Elsewhere, the Court has stated that by reason of the "duties and responsibilities" inherent in the exercise of freedom of expression, the protection of journalists under Article 10 is subject to the proviso that they *are acting in good faith in order to provide accurate and reliable information in accordance with the ethics of journalism.*69 In *Sener* the Court stressed that the "duties and

responsibilities" of media professionals
assume special significance in situations of conflict and tension.
70

Further, the Court held:
Particular caution is called for when consideration is being given to the publication of views which contain incitement to violence against the State lest the media become a vehicle for the dissemination of hate speech and the promotion of violence.
71

Nevertheless, the Court also stressed that
At the same time, where such views cannot be so categorised, Contracting States cannot, with reference to the protection of territorial integrity or national security or the prevention of crime or disorder, restrict the right of the public to be informed of them by bringing the weight of the criminal law to bear on the media. 72

In the instant case, the Court noted that the review published by the applicant – the owner and editor of a weekly review – contained a sharp criticism of the government's policy and of the action of their security forces with regard to the Kurds in south-east Turkey and that certain phrases seemed aggressive in tone. However, the Court found that the article did not glorify violence and did not incite to revenge or armed resistance, and therefore the criminal conviction of the applicant infringed Article 10. The applicant did not overstep the limits of his duties and responsibilities in conflict and tensions, but he offered the public a different perspective on the situation in south-east Turkey, irrespective of how unpalatable that perspective may be for the public.

"Formalities, conditions, restrictions or penalties"

The range of possible interference (formalities, conditions, restrictions or penalties) with the exercise of the

68. Observer and Guardian v. the United Kingdom, 1991.
69. Fressoz and Roire v. France, 1999; Bergens Tidende and Others v. Norway, 2000.
70. Sener v. Turkey, 2000.
71. Ibidem.
72. Ibidem.

right to freedom of expression is very wide, and there are no pre-established limits. The Court examines and decides in each particular case whether an interference exists, looking at the restrictive impact over the exercise of the right to freedom of expression of the specific measure adopted by the national authorities. Such interference could be: criminal convictions73 (with fine or imprisonment), obligations to pay civil damages,74 prohibition of publication75 or of publishing one's picture in the newspaper, 76 confiscation of publications or of any other means through which an opinion is being expressed or an information transmitted,77 refusal to grant a broadcasting license,78 prohibition on exercising the profession of journalist, the order of a court or other authority to reveal journalistic sources and/or the imposition of a penalty for not doing so,79 the announcement by a head of state that a civil servant will not be appointed to a public post following a public statement by the civil servant,80 etc.

Among the different forms of interference, censorship prior to publication is seen by the Court as the most dangerous as it stops the transmission of information and ideas to those who want to receive them. This is why measures undertaken prior to publication, such as the licensing of journalists, the examination of an article by an official before its publication or the prohibition of publication are subjected by the Court to a very strict control. Even if such limitations are temporary they can reduce consistently the value of the information. Confronted with prohibitions on publishing certain articles in a newspaper, the Court held:

Article 10 of the Convention does not in terms prohibit the imposition of prior restraints on publication, as such. ... On the other hand, the dangers inherent in prior restraints are such that they call for the most careful scrutiny on the part of the Court. This is especially so as far as the press is concerned, for news is a perishable commodity and to delay its publication, even for a short period, may well deprive it of all its value and interest.

The prior authorisation of publication, typical for dictatorships, has never been accepted in the democratic societies, and it is in general incompatible with Article 10. The refusal to register the title of a periodical is a distinct form of censorship prior to publication. As the Court stated, such a measure "is tantamount to a refusal to publish it." In *Gaweda* the applicant was refused by the domestic courts the right to register two publications on the

73. Barfod v. Denmark, 1989; Lingens v. Austria, 1986; Dalban v. Romania, 1999.
74. Müller and Others v. Switzerland, 1988.

75. Sunday Times (No. 2) v. the United Kingdom, 1991; Observer and Guardian v. the United Kingdom, 1991.
76. News Verlags GmbH & CoKG v. Austria, 2000.
77. Handyside v. the United Kingdom, 1976; Müller and Others v. Switzerland, 1988.
78. Autronic AG v. Switzerland, 1990.
79. Goodwin v. the United Kingdom, 1996.
80. Wille v. Liechtenstein, 1999.

ground that their titles "would be in conflict with reality". The Court found a violation of Article 10 on the basis that the law regulating the registration of periodicals was not sufficiently clear and foreseeable. In this context, the Court held:

the relevant law must provide a clear indication of the circumstances where such restraints are permissible, and, a fortiori, when the consequences of the restraint, as in the present case, are to block completely publication of a periodical. This is so because of the potential threat that such prior restraints, by their very nature, pose to the freedom of expression guaranteed by Article 10.81

Among the variety of post-expression interference with the freedom of expression, criminal conviction and sentence would probably be the most dangerous for this freedom. In the case of *Castells*, the applicant (a member of the parliamentary opposition) was sentenced to a term in prison for offending the Spanish Government, which he accused in a newspaper of being "criminal" and of hiding the perpetrators of crimes against people in the Basque Country. On this factual background, the Court held that

the dominant position which the government occupies makes it necessary for it to display restraint in resorting to criminal proceedings, particularly where other means are available for replying to the unjustified attacks and criticisms of its adversaries in the media.82

In the case of *Okçuoğlu*, where the applicant was convicted to 1 year and 8 months' imprisonment plus a fine on the charge of "separatist propaganda", the Court held that it was

struck by the severity of the penalty imposed on the applicant ... and the persistence of the prosecution's efforts to secure his conviction.

Further on, the Court held that

the nature and severity of the penalties imposed are also factors to be taken into account when assessing the proportionality of

the interference
and found that the conviction and the sentencing of the applicant were contrary to Article 10.83
Even where the criminal penalties consisted in relatively small fines, the Court argued against such penalties as they could play the role of an implicit censorship. In more cases where journalists were fined the Court held:

"...although the penalty imposed on the author did not strictly speaking prevent him from expressing himself, it nonetheless amounted to a kind of censure, which would be likely to discourage him from making criticism of that kind again in future [...]. In the context of the political debate such a sentence would be likely to deter journalists from contributing to public discussion of issues affecting the life of the community. By the same token, a sanction such as this is liable to hamper

81. Gaweda v. Poland, 2002.
82. Castells v. Spain, 1992.
83. Okçuoğlu v. Turkey, 1999.

the press in performing its tasks as purveyor of information and public watchdog.84

In addition, fines and trial expenses may constitute an interference with the right to freedom of expression where their amount raises the question of the financial survival of the person that is ordered to pay it.85

Civil damages granted for the damages caused to others' dignity or honour may constitute a distinctive interference with the exercise of freedom of expression, regardless of a criminal conviction. In the case of *Tolstoy Miloslavsky* the applicant was found by the national courts (based on the jury system) to have written a defamatory article, and was asked (together with the distributor of the article) to pay the victim civil damages amounting to 1500000 pounds sterling.86 Finding that the amount of the civil damages was in itself an infringement of Article 10, the European Court held:

... it does not mean that the jury was free to make any award it saw fit since, under the Convention, an award of damages for defamation must bear a reasonable relationship of proportionality to the injury to reputation suffered. The jury had been directed not to punish the applicant but only to award an amount that would compensate the non-pecuniary damage to Lord Aldington [the victim].

In addition, the Court found that

the scope of the judicial control ... at the time of the applicant's case did not offer adequate and effective safeguards against a disproportionately large award.
Consequently,
having regard to the size of the award in the applicant's case in conjunction with the lack of adequate and effective safeguards at the relevant time against a disproportionately large award, the Court finds that there has been a violation of the applicant's right under Article 10 of the Convention.

Confiscation or seizure of the means through which information and ideas are disseminated is another possible interference. The time at which such measures are ordered or enforced, respectively prior to or after dissemination, is of no importance. Thus, the Court decided that the temporary confiscation of the paintings considered as obscene by the national courts constituted an interference with the painter's freedom of expression.[87] Equally, the seizure of a film seen by the domestic authorities as containing some obscene scenes was defined by the Court as an interference with the freedom of expression.[88] Seizure of books considered as including some obscene fragments received a similar treatment by the Court.[89]

84. Lingens v. Austria, 1986; Barthold v. the Federal Republic of Germany, 1985.
85. Open Door and Dublin Well Woman v. Ireland, 1992.
86. Tolstoy Miloslavsky v. the United Kingdom, 1995.
87. Müller v. Switzerland, 1986.
88. Otto-Preminger Institut v. Austria, 1994.
89. Handyside v. the United Kingdom, 1976.

Prohibition of advertising is considered by the Court, under particular circumstances, as an interference with the freedom of expression. In the *Barthold* case the applicant was the veterinary surgeon of last resort for the owners of a sick cat because he alone maintained an emergency service in Hamburg. He was interviewed by a journalist who then wrote an article about this lacuna affecting animal welfare in the region. Barthold's fellow veterinarians initiated an action against him under the unfair competition law alleging that he had instigated or tolerated publicity on his own behalf. The Court held that this case was about public discussion of a matter of concern rather than commercial advertising, and found the applicant's conviction unjustified:

[Barthold's conviction] risks discouraging members of the liberal

professions from contributing to public debate on topics affecting the life of the community if even there is the slightest likelihood of their utterances being treated as entailing, to some degree, an advertising effect. By the same token, application of a criterion such as this is liable to hamper the press in the performance of its tasks of purveyor of information and public watchdog.[90]

Certainly, a newspaper item could be tantamount to advertising. Items which are based on public relations profiles would rather be seen as commercial expression. For instance, in the case of *Casado Coca*, the distribution of advertising material by a barrister which had resulted in disciplinary proceedings against him was seen by the Court as commercial expression.[91] Although protected by Article 10, commercial expression is subject to different standards of control than other expressions. For instance, in the case of *Markt Intern*,[92] the Court upheld an injunction against a trade magazine prohibiting it from publishing information about an enterprise operating in its market. Arguing that this was an interference with the exercise of the commercial expression, the Court allowed the national authorities a wider margin of appreciation and found the injunction to be compatible with the requirements of paragraph 2 of Article 10:

… even the publication of items which are true and describe real events may under certain circumstances be prohibited: the obligation to respect privacy of others or the duty to respect the confidentiality of certain commercial information are examples.

However, some dissenting opinions argued that there was no ground for extending the state's margin of appreciation:

Only in the rarest cases can censorship or prohibition of publications be accepted […] This is particularly true in relation to commercial advertising or questions of economic or commercial policy […] The protection of the interests of users and consumers in the face of dominant positions depend on the freedom to publish even the harshest criticism of products […].[93]

90. Barthold v. Germany, 1985.
91. Casado Coca v. Spain, 1994.
92. Markt Intern Verlag GmbH and Klaus Beermann v. the Federal Republic of Germany, 1989.

Independently of a decision based on paragraph 2, commercial expression may be protected under Article 10, and therefore its prohibition or sanction constitutes an

interference with freedom of expression.
An order to reveal journalistic sources and documents as well as the punishment imposed for having refused to do so is seen by the Court as an interference with the exercise of the freedom of expression. In the *Goodwin* case the Court noticed that such measures were indisputably interfering with the freedom of the press, and decided in the favour of the journalist.94

The search of newspaper or broadcasting premises is another form of interference with the freedom of the press. Whether justified or not by a legal warrant, such a search would not only endanger the confidentiality of the journalistic sources, but it would place at risk the entire media and it would function as a censorship for all journalists in the country.

Three requirements for legitimate interference with the exercise of freedom of expression

According to paragraph 2, domestic authorities in any of the Contracting States may interfere with the exercise of freedom of expression where three cumulative conditions are fulfilled:

- the interference (meaning "formality", "condition", "restriction" or "penalty") is prescribed by law;
- the interference is aimed at protecting one or more of the following interests or values: national security; territorial integrity; public safety; prevention of disorder or crime; protection of health; morals; reputation or rights of others; preventing the disclosure of information received in confidence, and; maintaining the authority and impartiality of the judiciary;
- the interference is necessary in a democratic society.

The primary role of Article 10 is to protect everyone's freedom of expression. Therefore, the Court has established rules of strict interpretation of the possible restrictions provided for in paragraph 2. In the *Sunday Times* case95 the Court held:

Strict interpretation means that no other criteria than those mentioned in the exception clause itself may be at the basis of any restrictions, and these criteria, in turn, must be understood in such a way that the language is not extended beyond its ordinary meaning. In the case of exceptional clauses ... the principle of strict interpretation meets certain difficulties because of the broad meaning of the clause itself. It nevertheless imposes a number of clearly defined obligations on the authorities

....
93. Judge Pettiti, dissenting opinion.
94. Goodwin v. the United Kingdom, 1996.
95. Sunday Times v. the United Kingdom, 1979.

Basically, the Court established a legal standard that in any borderline case, the freedom of the individual must be favourably weighted against the State's claim of overriding interest.96
Where the Court finds that all three requirements are fulfilled, the State's interference will be considered legitimate. The burden to prove that all three requirements are fulfilled stays with the State. The Court examines the three conditions in the order provided above. Once the Court finds that the State fails to prove one of the three requirements, it will not give the case further examination and will decide that the respective interference was unjustified, and therefore freedom of expression violated.
"State's interference" must be seen as any form of interference coming from any authority exercising public power and duties or being in the public service, such as courts, prosecutors' offices, police, any law-enforcement body, intelligence services, central or local councils, government departments, army decision-making bodies,
public professional structures. Far from being exhaustive, the above enumeration tries only to picture the possible national authorities whose actions would be capable of limiting the exercise of freedom of expression. It makes no difference for the Court which particular authority interferes with this right; the national government shall be considered as respondent party in all cases brought before the Court in Strasbourg.
The national courts must follow these three requirements when examining and deciding cases in any way involving freedom of expression. The primary aim of the Convention system is that the domestic courts enforce the text of the Convention as developed by the Court's jurisprudence. The European Court must only be the last resort. This is why the national courts are the first and most important instance to ensure the free exercise of freedom of expression and to make certain that eventual restrictions follow the requirements set up in paragraph 2 as explained and developed by the Court.
"The exercise of these freedoms may be subject to ...

restrictions or penalties as are prescribed by law"
According to this requirement, any interference with
the exercise of freedom of expression must have a basis in
the national law. As a rule, this would mean a written and
public law adopted by the Parliament. A national Parliament
must decide whether or not such a restriction should
be possible. For example, in a case regarding a journalist
convicted for defamation, the crime of defamation must
be provided for in the national law. Or, where prohibition
of publication or seizure of the means by which an expression
is disseminated –such as books, newspapers or cameras
– are ordered or enforced, such measures have to rely
on national legal provision. Equally, where a newspaper's
premises are searched or a broadcasting station is taken

96. A. Rzeplinski, "Restrictions on the expression of opinions or disclosure of information on domestic or foreign policy of the state", Budapest 1997, *CoE Monitor* (97) 3.

off air and closed, legal provisions in the national law must
underlie such measures.
The Court has accepted in some very few cases that
common-law rules or principles of international law did
constitute a legal basis for the interference with the freedom
of expression. For instance, in *Sunday Times*, the Court
found that the British common-law rules on contempt of
court were sufficiently precise as to fall under the requirement
"provided by law".97 Also, in *Groppera Radio AG and
Others*98 and *Autronic* AG,99 the Court allowed the state to
rely on domestically applicable rules of public international
law to satisfy this requirement. Although one should
not exclude that rules of common law or customary law
may restrict freedom of expression, this should rather be a
rare exception. Freedom of expression is such an important
value that its restriction should always receive the
democratic legitimacy which is only given by the parliamentary
debates and vote.
This requirement also refers to the quality of the law
even where adopted by the Parliament. The Court has constantly
stated that a law has to be public, accessible, predictable
and foreseeable. As stated in *Sunday Times*,100
*Firstly, the law has to be adequately accessible: the citizen must
be able to have an indication that is adequate in the circumstances
of the legal rules applicable to a given case. Secondly, a
norm cannot be regarded as a "law" unless it is formulated*

with sufficient precision to enable the citizen to regulate his conduct: he must be able –if need be with appropriate advice – to foresee, to a degree that is reasonable in the circumstances, the consequences which a given action may entail. Those consequences need not be foreseeable with absolute certainty: experience shows this to be unattainable. Again, whilst certainty is highly desirable, it may bring in its train excessive rigidity and the law must be able to keep pace with changing circumstances. Accordingly, many laws are inevitably couched in terms which, to a greater or lesser extent, are vague and whose interpretation and application are questions of practice.

Whereas in *Sunday Times* the Court found that the common-law rules fulfilled the "law" requirements, bearing in mind also the legal advice received by the newspaper applicant, in *Rotaru*101 the Court found that the domestic law was not "law" because it was not

formulated with sufficient precision to enable any individual – if need with appropriate advice – to regulate his conduct.

In *Petra*102 the Court decided that

the domestic provisions applicable to monitoring of prisoners' correspondence ... leave the national authorities too much latitude

97. However, following the Court's judgment, formal legislation was adopted in this area.
98. Groppera Radio AG and Others v. Switzerland, 1990.
99. Autronic AG v. Switzerland, 1990.
100. Sunday Times v. the United Kingdom, 1979.
101. Rotaru v. Romania, 2000.
102. Petra v.Romania,1998.

and that the confidential implementing regulations did not satisfy the requirement of accessibility ... and that Romanian law did not indicate with reasonable clarity the scope and manner of exercise of the discretion conferred on public authorities."

Although the *Rotaru* and *Petra* judgments examined and decided violations of Article 8 (the right to privacy), the Court takes the same standards when looking at national laws with respect to freedom of expression. The most recent and important case under Article 10 on the quality of law is probably *Gaweda v. Poland*, where the courts refused the applicant the registration of two periodicals arguing that their titles were "in conflict with reality". The two titles were *The Social and Political Monthly – A European Moral Tribune* and *Germany – a Thousand-year-old*

Enemy of Poland. With respect to the first publication, the domestic courts refused registration considering that the proposed title "would suggest a European institution had been established in Kety, which was clearly not true". The registration of the second publication was denied under the argument that the title "would be in conflict with reality in that it unduly concentrated on negative aspects of the Polish-German relations and thus gave an unbalanced picture of the facts". The Court noted that the domestic courts

have inferred from the notion of "in conflict with reality" ... a power to refuse registration where they consider that a title does not satisfy the test of truth, i.e. that the proposed titles of the periodicals convey an essentially false picture.

The requirement that a title of a magazine embody truthful information

is, firstly, inappropriate from the standpoint of freedom of the press. A title of a periodical is not a statement as such, since its function essentially is to identify the given periodical on the press market for its actual and prospective readers. Secondly, such interpretation would require a legislative provision which clearly authorised the courts to do so. In short, the interpretation given by the courts induced new criteria, which could not be foreseen on the basis of the text specifying situations in which the registration of a title can be refused.

Further, the Court acknowledged that the judicial character of the registration is a valuable safeguard of freedom of the press, but it held that the decisions of the courts must also conform to the principles of Article 10. The Court found that the law, which gave the courts the power to deny registration, among others, if the registration would be "in conflict with reality" were "not formulated with sufficient precision to enable the applicant to regulate his conduct."[103]

The Court interpreted the features of the legal basis of a restriction where measures of secret surveillance were taken against individuals. Thus, in Malone,[104] the Court held that the phrase "prescribed by law"

103. Gaweda v. Poland, 2002.
104. Malone v. the United Kingdom, 1984.

does not merely refer back to domestic law, which is expressly mentioned in the preamble to the Convention ... The phrase thus implies ... that there must be a measure of legal protection in domestic law against arbitrary interferences by public authorities with the rights safeguarded ... Especially where a power of the executive is exercised in secret, the risks of arbitrariness are evident.

In the same judgment, and also in the *Leander*[105] judgment, the Court said that even in areas affecting national security or fighting organised crime where the foreseeable character of the law can be weaker (for the effectiveness of the investigations, for instance), the wording of the law must be nevertheless sufficiently clear as to give individuals an adequate indication of the legal conduct and the consequences of acting unlawfully. In addition, in the latter judgment, the Court said that

in assessing whether the criterion of foreseeability is satisfied, account may also be taken of instructions or administrative practices which do not have the status of substantive law, in so far those concerned are made sufficiently aware of their contents.

The Court held further that

where the implementation of the law consists of secret measures, not open to scrutiny by the individuals concerned or by the public at large, the law itself, as opposed to the accompanying administrative practice, must indicate the scope to the legitimate aim of the measure in question, to give individual adequate protection against arbitrary interference.

Therefore, the national courts must examine the quality of laws, other norms, practices or jurisprudence setting up a restriction on the exercise of freedom of expression. They must first look at the publicity and accessibility requirements, which would usually be fulfilled if the law in question is published. Unpublished internal regulations or other norms will definitely not fulfil these requirements if the individual concerned was not aware of their existence and/or content. Assessing the predictability and the foreseeable character of legal provisions or case-law seems to be more sophisticated. Courts must examine whether the respective provision is drafted in sufficiently clear and precise terms, through well-defined notions, which allow the correlation of the actions to the requirements of the law and define clearly the area of the prohibited conduct and the consequences of breaking the respective provision. The legal norms empowering public authorities to order and adopt secret measures against individuals, such as secret surveillance, must be very strictly scrutinised by courts as the most dangerous interference with the individual

rights.
Where national courts face contradictory legislation, such as between laws or other regulations passed by local authorities and the federal laws and/or the Constitution, judges must apply the legal provisions which best ensure the unrestricted enjoyment of freedom of expression.
105. Leander v. Sweden, 1987.

Moreover, all pieces of national law must be interpreted and applied in accordance with the Court's jurisprudence and principles and, where clear contradictions exist, European law should prevail.

"The exercise of these freedoms ... may be subject to such ... restrictions ... [that] ...are necessary ... in the interest of national security, territorial integrity or public safety, for the prevention of disorder or crime, for the protection of health or morals, for the protection of reputation or rights of others, for preventing the disclosure of information received in confidence, or for maintaining the authority and impartiality of the judiciary."

The list of the possible grounds for restricting the freedom of expression is exhaustive. Domestic authorities may not legitimately rely on any other ground falling outside the list provided for in paragraph 2. Therefore, where called to enforce a legal provision which in any way would interfere with the freedom of expression, the national courts must identify the value or interest protected by the respective provision and check if that interest or value is one of those enumerated in paragraph 2. Only if the answer is affirmative may the courts apply that provision to the individual concerned.

For instance, a criminal action or a civil suit filed against a journalist accused of damaging one's reputation or honour will have the legitimate aim of protecting "the reputation or rights of others". Or, the seizure of an obscene book could have the legitimate aim of protecting the "morals". Or, an injunction against a newspaper publishing classified information could be justified by the interest of "national security". However, the courts must ensure that the interest to be protected is real, and not a mere and uncertain possibility.

Problems may arise in cases of insult or defamation of high officials (including the president of the country, ministers, members of parliament, etc.) or civil servants (including police officers, prosecutors and law enforcement officers, and all public employees).

While the aim of convicting a person who has insulted or defamed a person belonging to any of the two categories might be justified by the need to protect "the reputation or rights of others", a higher penalty – provided by law – than the one provided for insulting or defaming an ordinary person will not be justified. Higher penalties for defaming high officials and civil servants go contrary to the principle of equality before the law. Moreover, such higher penalties would implicitly protect more than the rights of the individuals performing such functions. They would protect abstract notions, such as "state authority" or "state prestige" which are not found in the paragraph 2 list.

Moreover, values such as "image/honour of the country or government", "image/honour of the nation", "state or other official symbols", "image/authority of public authorities" (other than courts) are not provided by paragraph 2, and therefore they are not legitimate aims for restricting freedom of expression. This is why the national courts must not sanction any criticism – expressed through words, gestures, images or in any other way – of such abstract notions, as they fall outside the scope of the area protected under paragraph 2. The explanation of this can be found in the functioning rules of a democratic society, where the criticism of those (individuals and institutions) exercising power is a fundamental right and duty of media, ordinary individuals and society at large. For instance, the destruction of or an "insulting" act against a state symbol would express one's disagreement and criticism with some political decisions, activity of public authorities, public policies in particular areas, or anything else in connection with the exercise of power. Such disagreement and criticism must be free as it is the only way to debate in public the wrongs and find the possible redress. In addition, such general and abstract notions, such as "state authority" would usually cover and hide some private and rather unlawful interests of those in power, or at least their interest to stay in power at all cost.

Where the domestic courts are satisfied that a legitimate aim underlies an interference with freedom of expression, they must then look into the third requirement of paragraph 2, as the Court does, and decide whether such interference is "necessary in a democratic society", following the Court's highly developed principles.

"The exercise of these freedoms ... may be subject to such ... restrictions ... [that] ...are necessary in a democratic society..."

In order to take a decision under this third requirement, the national courts must apply the principle of proportionality, answering the question: "Was the aim proportional with the means used to reach that aim?" In this equation, the "aim" is one or more of the values and interests provided by paragraph 2, for whose protection states may interfere with freedom of expression. The "means" is the interference itself. Therefore, the "aim" is that specific interest invoked by the state, such as "national security", "order", "morals", "rights of others", etc. The "means" is the particular measure adopted or enforced against an individual exercising his/her right of expression. For instance, a "means" could be: a criminal conviction for insult or defamation; an order to pay civil damages; an injunction against publication; the prohibition of the journalistic profession; the search of the a newspaper's premises; the seizure of the means by which an opinion was expressed; etc.

The decision on proportionality is based on the principles governing a democratic society. In order to prove that an interference was "necessary in a democratic society" the domestic courts, as well as the European Court, must be satisfied that a "pressing social need", requiring that particular limitation on the exercise of freedom of expression, did exist. In *Observer and Guardian v. the United Kingdom*106 the Court stated that "the adjective 'necessary', within the meaning of Article 10, paragraph 2, implies the existence of a 'pressing social need'".

The first to assess the existence of a pressing social need are the national authorities which, when doing so, are required to follow the Court's jurisprudence. However, the domestic margin of appreciation goes hand in hand

with a European supervision, embracing both the law and the decisions applying the law, including the decisions issued by independent courts. In this respect, the Court held that "The Contracting States have a margin of appreciation in assessing whether such a need exists, but it goes hand in hand with a European supervision, embracing both the legislation and the decisions applying it, even those given by an independent court."107 The Court is therefore empowered to give the final ruling on whether a "restriction" is reconcilable with the freedom of expression as protected by Article 10. The message to the national courts is that they should follow the Court's jurisprudence from the very first hearing in a freedom of expression case. As the European standards such as the Court's jurisprudence offer freedom of expression a higher protection that the national law and case-law, all judges in good faith cannot do anything but apply the higher European standards. The Court's reasoning in finding the answer to the question "was the restriction necessary in a democratic society?" or "was the aim proportional to the mean?" will be further examined taking into account each of the legitimate "aims" enumerated in paragraph 2. Obviously, the "mean" will in all cases be the same: the interference with freedom of expression.

Freedom of expression and national security/territorial integrity/public safety

One case where the ground of "national security" was raised to restrict freedom of expression is *Observer and Guardian*.108 In 1996, the two newspapers announced the intention of publishing extracts from *Spycatcher*, a book by Peter Wright, a retired intelligence agent. At the time of the announcement, the book was not yet published. Mr Wright's book included an account of alleged unlawful activities by the British intelligence service and its agents. He asserted that MI5 bugged all diplomatic conferences in London throughout the 1950s and 1960s as well as the Zimbabwe independence negotiations in 1979; MI5 bugged diplomats from France, Germany, Greece and Indonesia, as well as Mr Khrushchev's hotel suit during his visit to Britain in the 1950s; that MI5 burgled and bugged Soviet consulates abroad; that MI5 plotted unsuccessfully to assassinate President Nasser of Egypt at the time of the Suez crisis; that MI5 plotted against Harold Wilson during his premiership from 1974 to 1976; and that MI5 diverted its resources to investigate left-wing political groups in Britain.

The General Attorney asked the courts to issue a permanent injunction against the newspapers preventing

106. Observer and Guardian v. the United Kingdom, 1995.

107. Lingens v. Austria, 1986; Janowski v. Poland, 1999; Tammer v. Estonia, 2001, etc.
108. Idem: Sunday Times v. the United Kingdom (No. 2), 1991.

them from publishing extracts from the book. In July 1986 the courts granted a temporary injunction to prohibit publication for the duration of the judicial proceedings regarding the permanent injunction.
In July 1987 the book was published in the United States, and copies of the books were circulating in the United Kingdom as well. Despite this, the temporary injunctions against the newspapers were maintained until October 1988, when the House of Lords refused to grant the permanent injunctions requested by the Attorney General.
The publishers of the *Observer* and the *Guardian* complained to the Strasbourg organs against the temporary injunctions. The British Government argued that at the time the temporary injunctions were ordered, the information to which Peter Wright had had access was confidential. Had this information been published the British intelligence service, its agents and third parties would have suffered huge damages following the identification of agents; relationships with allied countries, organisations and people would have also been damaged; they all would have ceased to trust the British intelligence service. In addition, the government advanced the argument that there was a risk that other current or former agents would follow Mr Wright's example. For the post-publication period, the government relied on the need to assure allied states of the effective protection of information by the British intelligence service. In the government's opinion, the only way to give such assurance was to make clear that officers who threatened to breach their life-long duty of confidentiality could be effectively prevented from doing so by legal action, and that such action would be taken. With regard to the prior restraints on publication, the Court stated that

... the dangers inherent in prior restrictions are such that they call for the most careful scrutiny on the part of the Court. This is especially so as far as the press is concerned, for news is a perishable commodity and to delay its publication, even for a short period, may well deprive it of all its value and interest.

The Court further found that the temporary injunctions were justified prior to the publication of the book but not after this moment. When the book was published in the United States, the information lost its confidential character, and therefore the interest in maintaining the confidentiality of the information in *Spycatcher* and keeping it away from the public eye no longer existed. Under the circumstances, there was not "sufficient" need to maintain the injunctions.

In a partly dissenting opinion Judge Pettiti has stated that the temporary injunctions were not justified even before the publication of the book outside the United Kingdom:

where the press is concerned a delay in relation to items of current affairs deprives a journalist's article of a large part of its interest.

The judge said further that

one gets the impression that the extreme severity of the ... injunction and of the course adopted by the Attorney General was less a question of the duty of the confidentiality than the fear of disclosure of certain irregularities carried out by the security service in the pursuit of political rather than intelligence aims.

In Mr Pettiti's opinion this constituted a violation of the freedom to receive information because

to deprive the public of information on the functioning of State organs is to violate a fundamental democratic right.

Judge De Meyer, also partly dissenting, expressed his agreement with Judge Pettiti and added:

the press must be left free to publish news, whatever the source, without censorship, injunctions or prior restraint: in a free and democratic society there can be no room for restrictions of that kind, and particularly not if there are resorted to, as they were in the present case, for "governmental suppression of embarrassing information" or ideas.

In *Vereniging Weekblad Bluf!*[109] the Court has also examined, based on different facts, the conflict between "national security" and freedom of expression. The applicant, an association based in Amsterdam, was publishing a weekly magazine called *Bluf!*, designed in principle for left-wing readers. In 1987, *Bluf!* obtained a periodic report of the Dutch internal secret service. The report, dated 1981, was marked "confidential" and contained information of interest for the Dutch secret service. The report referred to the Dutch Communist Party and anti-nuclear movements; it mentioned the Arabic League plan to set up an office in The Hague; and it gave information on the activities of the Polish, Romanian and Czechoslovakian secret services in the Netherlands.

The editor of the magazine announced the publication of the report, together with a comment, as a supplement to the issue of 29 April. The same day, the chief of the Dutch internal secret services sent a letter to the public prosecutor's office, stating that the dissemination of the report would break the criminal law. With regard to the secret character of the information in the report, he observed that

although ... the various contributions taken separately do not (or do not any longer) contain any State secrets, they do – taken together and read in conjunction – amount to information whose confidentiality is necessary in the interests of the State or its allies. This is because the juxtaposition of the facts gives an overview, in the various sectors of interests, of the information available to the security service and of the BVD's activities and methods of operation.

As a result, prior to the printing and distribution of the magazine, *Bluf!*'s premises were searched following an order of the investigating judge. The entire print-run of *Bluf!*'s 29 April issue, including the supplement, was seized. During that night, unknown to the authorities, the staff of *Bluf!* reprinted the issue, and about 2500 copies were distributed the next day on the street, to the inhabitants of Amsterdam. The authorities did not stop the distribution.

109. Vereniging Weekblad Bluf! v. the Netherlands, 1995.

In May 1987 the investigating judge closed the investigation against the staff of *Bluf!* without any criminal charge being brought. In the meantime, the association asked for the return of the confiscated copies, but its application was denied. In March 1988, at the request of the public prosecutor, the Dutch courts decided that all copies of that *Bluf!* issue be withdraw from public circulation. The courts relied on the need to protect the national security and argued that the unsupervised possession of those materials was contrary to the law and to the public interest.

The association complained to the Strasbourg institutions, claiming that the Dutch authorities violated its right under Article 10 of the Convention. The government held that the interference with the applicant's freedom of expression was legitimately grounded by the need to protect "national security", giving the following arguments: individuals or groups posing a threat to national security could have discovered, by reading the report, whether and to what extent the Dutch secret service was aware of their subversive activities; the way in which the information had been presented could have also give them an insight into the secret service's methods and activities; these potential enemies could use the information to the detriment of national security.

Examining whether the interference – the seizure and withdrawal from circulation – was "necessary in a democratic society" for the protection of "national security", the Court held:

It is open to question whether the information in the report was sufficiently sensitive to justify preventing its distribution. The document in question was six years old. ... the head of the security service [had] himself admitted that in 1987 the various items of information, taken separately, were no longer State secrets. Lastly, the report was marked simply "Confidential", which represents a low degree of secrecy. [...] The withdrawal from circulation ... must be considered in the lights of the events as a whole. After the newspaper had been seized, the publishers reprinted a large number of copies and sold them in the streets of Amsterdam, which were very crowded. Consequently, the information in question had already been widely distributed when the journal was withdrawn from circulation. [...] In this latter connection, the Court points out that it has already held that it was unnecessary to prevent the disclosure of certain information seeing that it had already been made public or had ceased to be confidential. [...] the information in question was made accessible to a large number of people, who were able in turn to communicate it to others. Furthermore, the events were commented on by the media. That being so, the protection of the information as a State secret was no longer justified and the withdrawal of issue No. 267 of Bluf! no longer appeared necessary to achieve the legitimate aim pursued. [...] In short, as the measure was not necessary in a democratic society, there has been a breach of Article 10.

The judgments in *Observer and Guardian* and *Bluf!* provide for at least two important principles.

The first principle states that once in the public arena, information on national security may not be prohibited,

withdrawn, or the authors of dissemination punished.
The second principle institutes a prohibition on the states to unconditionally define as classified all information in the area of national security and, consequently, to establish a prior limitation on the access to such information. Certain information may indeed be classified where there are serious reasons to believe that its release into the public arena will pose a threat to national security. Moreover, the classified status of information must be limited in time, and the need for maintaining this status must be periodically verified. The interest of the public in knowing certain information should also be considered in the process of classifying or declassifying information related to the national security.

Therefore, legislation prohibiting in absolute and unconditional terms the dissemination of all information in the area of national security, eliminating the public control over the intelligence services' activities, would constitute a breach of Article 10 as not being "necessary in a democratic society". Where faced with legislation providing for general and unconditional prohibition of dissemination of all information in the area of national security, the national courts must reject such a claim, be it criminal or civil. Courts must allow the press, acting on the benefit of the public, to exercise its freedom to identify the malfunctions, illegalities or other wrongs within the intelligence system. The rules developed by the European Court in the instances where freedom of expression conflicted with the interest of defending the national security are the guidelines to be followed at national level. Even where a domestic legal system does not explicitly provide for the "necessity" test, the proportionality principle, and the public interest argument, the national courts must take account of them in their legal thinking and develop the balancing test which would answer the "necessity" question. Another guideline can be found in Principle 12 of the Johannesburg Principles (1995), which reads that

a state may not categorically deny access to all information related to national security, but must designate in law only those specific and narrow categories of information that it is necessary to withhold in order to protect a legitimate national security interest.

In addition, Principle 15 prohibits the punishment of a person on grounds of *national security for disclosure of information if (1) the disclosure does not actually harm and is not likely to harm a legitimate national security interest, or (2) the public interest in knowing the information outweighs the harm from disclosure.* The 1981 Recommendation of the Committee of Ministers of the Council of Europe on the right to access to information held by the public authorities subjects the limitations on access to information to a three-part test: restrictions must be provided by law or practice, be necessary in a democratic society and be aimed at protecting a legitimate public interest. Any denial of information must be explained and subjected to revision. Information in the area of national security is not an exception to this rule. In *Sürek and Özdemir*110 the applicants were convicted by the national courts to six months' imprisonment and a fine each, on the charge of disseminating separatist propaganda. In addition, the printed copies were seized. The applicants published two interviews with a senior figure in the PKK, who condemned the policies of the Turkish authorities in the south-east, which he described as being aimed at driving the Kurds out of their territory and destroying their resistance. He also claimed that the war on behalf of the Kurdish people will continue "until there is only one single individual left on our side." The applicants also published a joint statement issued by four organisations which, like the PKK, were illegal under Turkish law, which plead in favour of recognising the right of the Kurdish people to self-determination and the withdrawal of the Turkish army from Kurdistan. The Court first referred to the criticism of the government – as practised by the publication – and held that *the limits of permissible criticism are wider with regard to the government than in relation to a private citizen or even a politician.* Further, the Court noted that the fact that the interviews were given by a leading member of a proscribed organisation and that they contained hard criticism of official state policy and communicated a one-sided view of the situation and responsibility for disturbances in the south-east Turkey cannot justify in itself an interference with the applicants' freedom of expression. In the Court's view, *the interviews had a newsworthy content which allowed the public both to have an insight into the psychology of those who*

are the driving force behind the opposition to official policy in south-east Turkey and to assess the stakes involved in the conflict.
The Court further held that
domestic authorities failed to have sufficient regard to the public's right to be informed of a different perspective on the situation in south-east Turkey, irrespective of how unpalatable that perspective may be for them.
Concluding, the Court found that the reasons given by the domestic courts to convict the applicants *although relevant, cannot be sufficient for justifying the interferences with their right to freedom of expression.*
Equally, in *Özgür Gündem*, the Court found that convictions for separatist propaganda, which were justified by the Turkish Government on the grounds of protecting national security and preventing crime and disorder, were contrary to Article 10:
the use of the term "Kurdistan" in a context which implies that it should be, or is, separate from the territory of Turkey, and the claims by persons to exercise authority on behalf of that entity may be highly provocative to the authorities.
110. Sürek and Özdemir v. Turkey, 1999.

After referring to the right of the public to be informed on other views than those of the State and the majority of the population, the Court stated that
*While several of the articles were highly critical of the authorities and attributed on lawful conduct to the security forced, sometimes in colourful and pejorative terms, the Court nonetheless finds that they cannot be reasonably regarded as advocating or inciting the use of violence.*111
By contrast, in Sürek (No. 3), the Court found that the grounds of protecting national security and territorial integrity were proportional with the restriction upon freedom of expression due to the capacity of the article to incite violence in south-east Turkey:
*Indeed, the message which is communicated to the reader is that recourse to violence is a necessary and justified measure of self-defence in the face of the aggressor.*112
The difference from the other cases stays in the capacity of the impugned article to steer violence and in the possibility that such violence occur, both elements being determined by the Court on the basis of the concrete circumstances of each case.
"National security" along with "public safety" and

"rights of others" were seen as overriding the interest of protecting freedom of expression in cases where the expression sanctioned by the domestic authorities was aimed at the destruction of the rights set forth in the Convention. In *Kühnen*[113] the applicant was leading an organisation whose aim was to bring the National Socialist Party (prohibited in Germany) back into the political scene. Mr Kühnen disseminated publications encouraging the fight for a socialist and independent Greater Germany. He wrote that his organisation was in favour of "German unity, social justice, racial pride, community of the people and camaraderie" and against "capitalism, communism, Zionism, estrangement by means of masses of foreign workers, destruction of the environment". He also wrote: "whoever serves this aim can act, whoever obstructs will be fought against and eventually eliminated".

Mr Kühnen was sentenced to prison by the German courts.[114] The European Commission of Human Rights noted that the applicant has advocated national socialism aimed at impairing the basic order of freedom and democracy, and that his speech ran counter to one of the basic values expressed in the Preamble to the Convention: the fundamental freedoms enshrined in the Convention "are best maintained … by an effective political democracy". In addition, the Commission found that the applicant's speech contained elements of racial and religious discrimination. Consequently, the Commission held that the

111. Özgür Gündem v. Turkey, 2000.
112. Sürek v. Turkey (No. 3), 1999.
113. Kühnen v. the Federal Republic of Germany; report 1998.
114. The German Penal Code prohibits the dissemination of propaganda by unconstitutional organisations where such propaganda is directed against the basic order of democracy, freedom and understanding of all people.

applicant was seeking to use the freedom of expression for promoting conduct contrary to the text and spirit of the Convention as well as contrary to Article 17 which prohibits the abuse of rights. Concluding, the Commission found that the interference with the exercise of the applicant's freedom of expression was "necessary in a democratic society".

A similar decision was taken in the case of *D.I. v. Germany*,[115] where the applicant (an historian) denied the existence of the gas chambers in Auschwitz, stating that they were fakes built up in the first post-war days, and that the German tax payers paid about 16 billion DM for fakes. The applicant was fined in the national courts. Before the Commission, the government justified this penalty by the interests of protecting the "national security and territorial integrity", "the reputation and rights of others" and for the "prevention of disorder and crime". Applying the proportionality principle, the Commission held:

the public interests in the prevention of crime and disorder in the German population due to insulting behaviour against Jews, and similar offences, and the requirements of protecting their reputation and rights, outweigh, in a democratic society, the applicant's freedom to impart publications denying the existence of the gassing of Jews under the Nazi regime.

In *Honsik*[116] and *Ochensberger*,[117] where the applicants also denied the existence of the Holocaust and incited racial hatred, the Commission reached similar conclusions. "National security" versus freedom of expression was examined by the Court in relation to military secrets. In the *Hadjianastassiou* case,[118] an officer was convicted to a five-month suspended prison sentence for having disclosed classified military information to a private company in exchange for payment. The information concerned a specific weapon and the corresponding technical knowledge, and in the government's view, the disclosure was capable of causing considerable damage to national security. After holding that military information is not excluded from Article 10's protection, the Court found the conviction to be "necessary in a democratic society" for protecting the "national security" and held:

the disclosure of the State's interest in a given weapon and that of the corresponding technical knowledge, which may give some indication of the state of progress in its manufacture, are capable of causing considerable damage to national security. [...] Nor does the evidence disclose the lack of a reasonable relationship of proportionality between the means employed and the legitimate aim pursued.

115. D.I. v. Germany, 1996.
116. Honsik v. Austria, 1995.
117. Ochensberger v. Austria, 1994.
118. Hadjianastassiou v. Greece, 1992.

The *Hadjianastassiou* judgment sends two important messages to the national courts. Firstly, that not all the military information is swept away from the public arena. Secondly, the Court held once again that it is for the national courts to establish in each particular case whether the respective information did pose a real and serious danger to the national security. Such an assessment based on the proportionality principle is the answer to the question whether or not an expression making public military information should or should not be prohibited or sanctioned.

Freedom of expression and prevention of disorder or crime

The national authorities have restricted freedom of expression under the "prevention of disorder" ground in the case of *Incal*.119

Mr Incal, a Turkish national, member of the People's Labour Party (dissolved in 1993 by the Constitutional Court), had distributed leaflets containing virulent remarks about the Turkish Government's policy and called on the population of Kurdish origin to band together to raise certain political demands. The leaflets called people to fight against the "driving the Kurds out" campaign launched by the Turkish security police and local governments, and called this campaign "a part of the special war being conducted in the country at present against the Kurdish people". The leaflet also described the state's action as a "state terror against Turkish and Kurdish proletarians". However, the leaflets did not call for violence or hatred. The Turkish security police considered that the leaflets could be regarded as separatist propaganda. Mr Incal was convicted by the national courts to six months in prison on the charge of incitement to commit an offence. He was also prohibited from entering the civil service and taking part in a number of activities within political organisations, associations and trade unions.

Before the European Court, the Turkish Government argued that the applicant's conviction was necessary in order to prevent disorder, since the language of the leaflets was aggressive, provocative and likely to incite people of Kurdish origin to believe that they were victims of a "special war" and therefore justified in setting up selfdefence committees. The government also argued that "it was apparent from the wording of the leaflets ... that they were intended to foment an insurrection by one ethnic group against the State authorities" and that "the interest in combating and crushing terrorism takes precedence in a democratic society."

The Court did not share the government's views, and referred to the requirement that "actions or omissions of the government" be "subject to the close scrutiny not only

119. Incal v. Turkey, 1998.

of the legislative and judicial authorities but also of public opinion." In order to assess whether the conviction and sentencing of the applicant were "necessary in a democratic society" the Court stressed that

while precious to all, freedom of expression is particularly important for political parties and their active members.

The Court held that it could not identify

anything which would warrant the conclusion that Mr Incal was in any way responsible for the problems of terrorism in Turkey [...] In conclusion, Mr Incal's conviction was disproportionate to the aim pursued, and therefore unnecessary in a democratic society.

In addition to the breach of Article 10, the Court also found a breach of the right to a fair trial (Article 6) since one of the judges on the bench was a military judge. Prevention of disorder or crime, as well as the interest of protecting national security, were argued by the Austrian Government in the case of *Saszmann*.120 The applicant was given a three-month suspended prison sentence for having incited the members of the army, through the press, to disobedience and violation of the military laws. The Commission decided that the applicant's conviction was justified for the maintaining of order in the Austrian federal army and protection of national security:

... the incitement to disregard military laws constituted unconstitutional pressure aiming at the abolition of laws which had been passed in a constitutional manner. Such unconstitutional pressure could not be tolerated in a democratic society.

The Court reached a different conclusion in the case of *Vereinigung Demokratischer Soldaten Österreichs und Gubi*,121 where the Austrian courts prohibited the distribution of a periodical publication among the soldiers in military barracks, which proposed reforms and encouraged the soldiers to take legal actions against the authorities. The Austrian Government argued that the applicants' periodical threatened the country's system of defence, the effectiveness of the army and could lead to disorder and crime.

The Court did not agree with the government's submissions

and held that most of the items in the periodical

... set out complaints, put forward proposals for reforms or encourage[d] the readers to institute legal complaints of appeals proceedings. However, despite their often polemical tenor, it does not appear that they overstepped the bounds of what is permissible in the context of a mere discussion of ideas, which must be tolerated in the army of a democratic State just as it must be in the society that such an army serves.

Therefore, the Court found an Article 10 violation.

"Prevention of disorder or crime" was balanced against political criticism of the government by its political adversaries. In *Castells*122 the Court argued for a strong protection of the freedom of expression on behalf of the political opposition. Mr Castells was senator in the Span-

120. Saszmann v. Austria, 1997.
121. Vereinigung Demokratischer Soldaten Österreichs und Gubi v. Austria, 1994.
122. Castells v. Spain, 1992.

ish Parliament representing a political organisation favourable to the independence of the Basque Country. In 1979, he wrote an article entitled "Outrageous impunity", which was published in a national daily newspaper. Mr Castells accused the government of failure to investigate the murders in the Basque Country and stated: "the perpetrators of these crimes act, continue to work and remain in posts of responsibility, with total impunity. No warrant has been issued for their arrest." He also accused the government of complicity in those crimes:

the right wing, who are in power, have all the means at their disposal (police, courts and prisons) to seek out and punish the perpetrators of so many crimes. But don't worry, the right will not seek itself out. [...] Those responsible for public order and criminal prosecutions are the same today as they were before.

Referring to the extremist groups guilty of these crimes, he wrote:

they have substantial files which are kept up to date. They have a considerable supply of weapons and of money. They have unlimited material and resources and operate with complete impunity ... it can be said they are guaranteed legal immunity in advance.

Mr Castells further stated:

behind these acts there can only be the government, the party of government and their personnel. We know that they are increasingly going to use as a political instrument the ruthless

hunting down of Basque dissidents and their physical elimination
... But for the sake of the next victim from our people,
those responsible must be identified right away with maximum
publicity.

Mr Castells was charged with offending the government,
convicted, and sentenced to one year in prison,
which he never served.

Before the Court, the Spanish authorities argued that
Mr Castells' conviction served to prevent "disorder and
crime". Examining whether the interference was "necessary
in a democratic society", the Court held:

While freedom of expression is important for everybody, it is
especially so for an elected representative of the people. He represents
his electorate, draws attention to their preoccupations
and defends their interests. Accordingly, interference with the
freedom of expression of an opposition Member of Parliament,
like the applicant, calls for the closest scrutiny on the part of
the Court.

The Court then observed that

Mr Castells did not express his opinion from the senate floor, as
he might have done without fear of sanctions, but chose to do
so in a periodical. That does not mean, however, that he lost his
right to criticise the government.

Further, the Court referred to the criticism of the government:

The limits of permissible criticism are wider with regard to the
government than in relation to a private citizen, or even a politician.
In a democratic society the actions or omissions of the
government must be subject to the close scrutiny not only of the
legislative and judicial authorities but also of the press and
public opinion. Furthermore, the dominant position which the
government occupies makes it necessary for it to display
restraint in resorting to criminal proceedings, particularly
when other means are available for replying to the unjustified
attacks and criticisms of its adversaries or the media.

The Court found a violation of Article 10. In addition,
a concurring opinion held that

there are no grounds for affording better protection to the institutions
than to individuals, or to the government than the
opposition.

Similar, in accordance with the lessons derived from
the previous judgments, the national courts must understand
that even if in principle the incitement to legal disobedience
is punishable, judges must not automatically

apply a prohibition provided by law. Judges must weigh the conflicting interests and apply the proportionality principle while deciding whether punishing a particular exercise of the freedom of expression is "necessary in a democratic society". Moreover, as shown by the *Castells* judgment, national courts must refrain from punishing criticism of the state authorities. Such criticism, even harsh, is part of the political pluralism and plurality of opinions.

Freedom of expression and morals

The conflict between "morals" and freedom of expression brings new interpretations to the principle of proportionality. In principle, in such cases, the Court leaves the national authorities a wider margin of appreciation justified by the specificity of the "morals" in each member state or even in the different regions within the same country.

In *Müller and Others*[123] the national authorities' interference with freedom of expression was considered by the Court as reasonable and "necessary in a democratic society" for the protection of "morals". In 1981, during an exhibition of contemporary art, Mr Müller painted and exhibited three large paintings showing acts of sodomy, bestiality, masturbation and homosexuality. The exhibition was accessible to the general public, free of charge, without any age restriction. The Swiss courts fined Mr Müller and the organisers of the exhibition and seized the paintings, which were handed for preservation to an art museum. However, they were returned in 1988. In Strasbourg, Mr Müller and the organisers of the exhibition claimed that both the conviction and the seizure had violated their right to freedom of expression.

The Court referred to the lack of a uniform concept of morals within the territory of the Contracting Parties. The Court held that the national courts were in a better position than the international judge to decide on issues of

123. Müller and Others v. Switzerland, 1988.

"morals", having in view the former's direct contact with the reality in their countries. The Court further stated that *the paintings in question depict in a crude manner sexual relations, particularly between men and animals ... the general public had free access to them, as the organisers had not imposed any admission charge or any age-limit. Indeed, the paintings were displayed in an exhibition which was unrestrictedly*

open to – and sought to attract – the public at large.
The Court also held that the arguments of the
national judges, who found that the images were "liable
grossly to offend the sense of sexual propriety of ordinary
sensitivity" by the "emphasis on sexuality in some of its
crudest forms" were not unreasonable. The unlimited
access of children played an essential role in the *Müller*
judgment, as it played in the *Handyside* case,124 where the
applicant had published and distributed to pupils a book
seen as obscene by the British authorities.
Another type of conflict between "morals" and freedom
of expression was examined by the Court in the case
of *Open Door and Dublin Well Woman*.125 Open Door Counselling
Ltd and the Dublin Well Woman Centre were non-governmental
and non-profit organisations in Ireland, where
abortion was prohibited. The two organisations offered
advice to pregnant women, and the Dublin Well Woman
Centre provided a large series of services in the area of
family planning, pregnancy, health, sterilisation, etc. It also
offered to pregnant women information on the possibilities
of abortion outside Ireland, such as the addresses of
some clinics in the United Kingdom. Both organisations
restricted themselves to providing advice; the decision on
abortion was left to the women. In 1983 the Dublin Well
Woman Centre published a brochure criticising two recent
constitutional amendments. The first amendment gave to
anyone the right to file applications with the courts requiring
the prohibition on imparting information on abortions
outside Ireland. The second constitutional amendment
gave anyone the right to request court injunctions against
pregnant women who intended to leave the country.
In 1986, following an application filed by the Irish
Society for the Protection of Unborn Children, the Irish
courts decided that the activity of imparting information
on abortion was in violation of the Constitution and some
provisions of the criminal law. The courts issued a permanent
prohibition against the Dublin Well Woman Centre
and Open Door on giving advice or help the pregnant
women on abortion outside Ireland. The two organisations
complained in Strasbourg claiming that their right to
impart and receive information was violated. Four individual
women joined them, two as direct victims of the prohibition
and two as virtual victims.
Discussing the "morals" as a legitimate aim, the Court

argued that the protection of the unborn children relies on profound moral values of the Irish people, and held that although the margin of appreciation of the national authori-

124. Handyside v. the United Kingdom, 1976.
125. Open Door and Dublin Well Woman v. Ireland, 1992.

ties is wider with respect to "morals", it is not unlimited: the national authorities do not have "an unfettered and an unreviewable" discretion. Further on, the Court examined whether the interference answered a "pressing social need" and whether it was proportionate to the legitimate aim pursued. The Court was struck by the absolute nature of the injunctions issued by the Irish courts, which imposed a perpetual and general prohibition "regardless of age or state of health or their reason of seeking counselling on the termination of pregnancy". The Court held that such a restriction was too large and disproportionate. Arguing the disproportionate nature of the interference, the Court noted the existence of other sources of obtaining information (magazines, telephone books, people living abroad), all proving that the need of a restriction imposed on the applicants was not a pressing one.

Here again, the national courts are taught that general and/or perpetual prohibitions on freedom of expression, even in areas as sensitive as morals, are unacceptable. National courts are given guidelines for applying the proportionality principle: the target group of the expression is important, being relevant if children and youth are also addressed; measures to limit the access to the respective form of expression is relevant, as proving the care for reducing the "immoral" impact; a real damage to "morals" should be identified, to avoid arbitrariness.

Freedom of expression and reputation and rights of others

Protection of "reputation and rights of others" is by far the "legitimate aim" most frequently used by the national authorities for restricting freedom of expression. Rather often, it has been invoked to protect politicians and civil servants against criticism. This is why, under this item, the Court has developed a large jurisprudence, demonstrating the high protection afforded to freedom of expression, in particular to the press. The media's privileged place derives from the Court's view of the central role of political expression in a democratic society both with respect to the electoral process and to daily matters of public interest. With regard to the language, the Court has accepted severe and harsh criticism as well as coloured expressions as the latter have the advantage of drawing attention to the issues under debate.

In *Lingens*[126] – a landmark case – the Court balanced freedom of the press against the right to reputation of a high public official. In October 1975, following general elections in Austria, Mr Lingens published two articles criticising the Federal Chancellor, Mr Bruno Kreiski, who had won the elections. The criticism focused on the political move of the Chancellor, who had announced a coalition with a party lead by a person with a Nazi background, and on the Chancellor's systematic efforts to sustain politically

126. Lingens v. Austria, 1986.

the former Nazi. The Chancellor's behaviour was characterised as "immoral", "undignified", demonstrating "the basest opportunism". Following a private prosecution brought by the Chancellor, the Austrian courts found these statements insulting and sentenced the journalist to a fine. The national courts also found that the journalist could not prove the truth of his allegation of "basest opportunism".

Before the European Court, the Austrian Government claimed that the applicant's conviction was aimed at protecting the reputation of the Chancellor.

Looking into the requirement of the necessity of the interference "in a democratic society", the Court developed some very important principles. Politicians must display wider tolerance to media criticism:

Freedom of the press affords the public one of the best means of discovering and forming an opinion of the ideas and attitudes of political leaders. More generally, freedom of political debate is at the very core of the concept of a democratic society which prevails throughout the Convention. The limits of acceptable criticism are accordingly wider as regards a politician as such than as regards a private individual. Unlike the latter, the former inevitably and knowingly lays himself open to close scrutiny of his every word and deed by both journalists and the public at large, and he must consequently display a greater degree of tolerance.

The Court did not exclude the protection of politicians' reputation but held that

in such cases the requirements of such protection have to be weighed in relation to the interests of open discussion of political issues.

The political context of the contested articles was of relevance:

The impugned expressions are therefore to be seen against the background of a post-election political controversy; ... in this struggle each used the weapons at his disposal; and these were in no way unusual in the hard-fought tussles of politics.

The impact of the applicant's conviction upon the freedom of the press in general was another element which the Court found relevant:

As the government pointed out, the disputed articles had at the time already been widely disseminated, so that although the penalty imposed on the author did not strictly speaking prevent him from expressing himself, it nonetheless amounted to a kind of censure, which would be likely to discourage him from making criticisms of that kind again in future; ... In the context of political debate such a sentence would be likely to deter journalists from contributing to public discussion of issues affecting the life of the community. By the same token, a sanction such as this is liable to hamper the press in performing its task as purveyor of information and public watchdog.

The Austrian courts' approach with regard to the truth proof defence was found by the Court to be wrong. The Court emphasised the distinction between "facts" and "value judgments", holding that the truth of the "value judgments" is an impossible task. The applicant's opinions about the Chancellor's political conduct were a mere expression of the right to hold and impart opinions rather than the right to impart information. While the existence of facts can be demonstrated, the truth of the valuejudgments is not susceptible of proof. The requirement of proving the truth of value judgments infringes the heart of the freedom of opinion. The Court also observed that the facts on which Mr Lingens had founded his valuejudgments were undisputed, and he was in good faith.

The principles developed by the Court in the area of political criticism and the distinction between facts and opinions were reaffirmed in many further judgments.127 Thus, in *Dalban*, the Court held that

it would be unacceptable for a journalist to be debarred from expressing critical value judgments unless he or she could prove their truth.

In addition, in *Schwabe*, the Court referred to the language:
in a short contribution to a discussion on the behaviour of politicians and their political morals, not every word can be weighed to exclude any possibility of misunderstanding
In *Oberschlick (No. 2)*, the use of the word "idiot" to describe the behaviour of a politician was found admissible. 128 And, in *Lopes Gomes da Silva*, where a candidate to the local elections was called "grotesque", "buffoonish" and "coarse", the Court found that although incisive, the wording was not exaggerated and it came in response to a provocative speech by the candidate. The Court also stated that
political invective often spills over into the personal sphere, such are the hazards of politics and the free debate of ideas, which are the guarantees of a democratic society.129
In *Oberschlick, Dalban, Dichand* and many other judgments the Court held that:
journalistic freedom also covers possible recourse to a degree of exaggeration, or even provocation.130
However, even press freedom is not absolute. In *Tammer* the Court found in favour of private life. The impugned remarks were related to aspects of Ms Laanaru's private life which she described in her memoirs written in her private capacity. Ms Laanaru had been assistant to the Minister of the Interior (her husband, who had previously been prime minister). The impugned remarks regarded her role as a mother and in breaking up her husband's previous family. Finding against a violation of Article 10, the Court argued that
despite her continued involvement in the political party the Court does not find it established that the use of the impugned terms in relation to Ms Laanaru's private life was justified by considerations of public concern or that they bore on a matter of general importance.131

127. Oberschlick v. Austria, 1991; Schwabe v. Austria, 1992; Dalban v. Romania, 1999, etc.
128. Oberschlick v. Austria (No. 2), 1997.
129. Lopes Gomes da Silva v. Portugal, 2000.
130. For more on the "language" see above, page 17.

Following the Court's principles, any internal law protecting by special or higher penalties politicians and in general all high officials (such as the president, the prime minister, ministers, members of the Parliament, etc.)

against insult or defamation, in particular by the press, would be incompatible with Article 10. Where such provisions exist and are invoked by the politicians, the national courts must abstain from enforcing them. In exchange, the general legal provisions on insult and defamation could be relied on.

Moreover, where the honour and reputation of politicians conflict with the freedom of the press, the national courts must carefully apply the proportionality principle and decide whether the conviction of a journalist is a necessary measure in a democratic society, looking at the guidelines provided by the Court in cases such as *Lingens*. Similarly, where the national law provides for the truth proof defence in cases of insulting expressions, the domestic courts must abstain from requesting such evidence, following the Court's distinction between facts and opinions. Moreover, the good faith defence must be accepted in cases of defamation, which essentially concerns facts. If at the time of publication the journalist had sufficient reasons to believe that a particular piece of information was true, he/she should not be sanctioned. The news is a *perishable commodity and to delay its publication, even for a short period, may well deprive it of all its value and interest.*[132] This is why a journalist should only be required to make a reasonable check and to assume in good faith the accuracy of the news. Another argument in this respect concerns the absence of intent, on the part of the journalist, to defame the alleged victim. As long as the journalist believed the information be true, such intent is lacking and therefore the journalist's conduct may not be sanctioned under provisions prohibiting intentional defamation; intentional defamation is what all criminal laws provide for.

The national courts must also refrain from applying criminal sentences, in particular imprisonment. Such sentences endanger the very core of the freedom of expression and function as censorship for the entire media, hampering the press in its role of public watchdog.

All the above guidelines provided by the European Court to the national courts apply equally to the criticism of civil servants or to any other criticism intended to bring into the public debate matters of interest for the large public or communities.

In Thorgeirson[133] the Court upheld the freedom of the press in the context of criticism aimed at civil servants. The applicant (a writer) published in a daily newspaper two articles on police brutality. The first article took the form of

[131.] Tammer v. Estonia, 2001.
[132.] Sunday Times (No. 2) v. the United Kingdom, 1991.
[133.] Thorgeir Thorgeirson v. Iceland, 1992.

a letter addressed to the Minister of Justice who was called on to institute a commission

to investigate the rumours, gradually becoming public opinion, that there is more and more brutality within the Reykjavík police force and being hushed up in an unnatural manner.

Except for a journalist who had been victim of police brutality, the applicant did not indicate names of other victims. Describing the police officers and their behaviour, Mr Thorgeirson used, among others, the following expressions: "wild beasts in uniform that creep around, silently or not, in the jungle of our town's night-life"; "individuals reduced to a mental age of a new-born child as a result of strangle-holds that policemen and bouncers learn and use with brutal spontaneity instead of handling people with prudence and care"; and "allowing brutes and sadists to act out their perversions". Following a television programme where the police denied the allegations of brutality, the applicant published a second article, stating that "[police] behaviour was so typical of what is gradually becoming the public image of our police force defending itself: bullying, forgery, unlawful actions, superstitions, rashness and ineptitude". The applicant was sentenced to a fine for defamation of unspecified members of the police.

Before the European Court, the government argued that the conviction was aimed at protecting the "reputation ... of others", namely of the police officers, and, in addition, that the limits of acceptable criticism are wider only with regard to political speech. The Court, however, observed

that there is no warrant in its case-law for distinguishing, in the manner suggested by the government, between political discussion and discussion of other matters of public concern.

With regard to the language, the Court stated that

both articles were framed in particularly strong terms. However, having regard to their purpose and the impact which they were designed to have, the Court is of the opinion that the language used cannot be regarded as excessive.

The Court concluded that

the conviction and sentence were capable of discouraging open discussion of matters of public concern

and that the reasons advanced by the government did not proved the proportionality of the interference to the legitimate aim pursued. The applicant's conviction was therefore not "necessary in a democratic society".

In *Thoma*, a journalist was ordered to pay civil damages for having stated that all the Water and Forestry Commission officials but one were corruptible. The Court found a violation of Article 10, taking into account the wide debate on this topic and the general interest raised by it. Referring to the criticism of civil servants, the Court held:

Civil servants acting in official capacity are, like politicians, subject to wider limits of acceptable criticism than private individuals. However, it cannot be said that civil servants knowingly lay themselves open to close scrutiny of their every word and deed to the extent politicians do and should therefore be treated on equal footing with the latter when it comes to criticism of their conduct.[134]

"Rights of others", namely religious freedom versus freedom of expression, were examined by the Court in *Otto-Preminger Institut*.[135] The applicant, an association based in Innsbruck, announced a series of six showings accessible to the general public of the movie *Council in Heaven*, directed by Werner Schroeter. The announcement carried a statement to the effect that, in accordance with the law, persons under the age of seventeen were prohibited from seeing the film. The film portrayed the God of the Jewish religion, Christian religion and Islamic religion as an apparently senile old man prostrating himself before the Devil with whom he exchanged a deep kiss, calling Devil his friend. Other scenes showed the Virgin Mary listening to an obscene story and a degree of erotic tension between the Virgin Mary and the Devil. The adult Jesus Christ was portrayed as a low-grade mental defective. The Virgin Mary and Jesus Christ were shown in the film applauding the Devil.

Prior to the first showing, at the request of the Innsbruck diocese of the Roman Catholic Church, the public prosecutor instituted criminal proceedings against the director of the Otto-Preminger Institut under the charge of "disparaging religious doctrines". After seeing the film, a domestic court granted its seizure. Consequently, the public showings did not take place. The criminal proceedings were discontinued, and the case was pursued only to the effect of the seizure. The Otto-Preminger Institut complained to the European Commission, arguing that its right under Article 10 was violated by the seizure of the film. The Commission shared this view.

Before the Court, the government argued that the seizure of the film was aimed at "protection of rights of others", in particular of right to respect for religious feelings, and at the "prevention of disorder". The right to respect for religious feelings is part of the right to thought, conscience and religion provided for in Article 9 of the Convention. Looking at the legitimacy of this aim, the Court held:

Those who choose to exercise the freedom to manifest their religion, irrespective of whether they do so as members of a religious majority or a minority, cannot reasonably expect to be exempt from all criticism. They must tolerate and accept the denial by others of their religious beliefs and even the propagation by others of doctrines hostile to their faith. However, the manner in which religious beliefs and doctrines are opposed or denied is a matter which may engage the responsibility of the State, notably its responsibility to ensure the peaceful enjoyment of the right guaranteed under Article 9 to the holders of those beliefs and doctrines. Indeed, in extreme cases the effect of particular methods of opposing or denying religious beliefs can be such as to inhibit those who hold such beliefs from exercising

134. Thoma v. Luxembourg, 2001.
135. Otto-Preminger Institut v. Austria, 1994.

their freedom to hold and express them [...] The respect for the religious feelings of believers as guaranteed in Article 9 can legitimately be thought to have been violated by provocative portrayals of objects of religious veneration; and such portrayals can be regarded as malicious violation of the spirit of tolerance, which must also be a feature of democratic society. The Convention is to be read as a whole and therefore the interpretation and application of Article 10 in the present case must be in harmony with the logic of the Convention.

Further, the Court referred to the duty of avoiding

expressions that are gratuitously offensive to others ... such do not contribute to any form of public debate capable of furthering the progress in human affairs.

Defending its position, the government stressed the role of religion in the everyday life of the people of Tyrol, where the proportion of the Roman Catholic believers was 87%.

Balancing the two conflicting values, the Court held that it could not:

disregard the fact that the Roman Catholic religion is the religion of the overwhelming majority of Tyroleans. In seizing the film, the Austrian authorities acted to ensure religious peace in that region and to prevent that some people should feel the object of attacks on their religious beliefs in an unwarranted and offensive manner. It is in the first place for the national authorities, who are better placed than the international judge, to assess the need for such a measure in the light of the situation obtaining locally at a given time. In all the circumstances of the present case, the Court does not consider that the Austrian authorities can be regarded as having overstepped their margin of appreciation in this respect.

Consequently, the seizure of the film did not violate Article 10.

It is interesting to note that three dissenting judges argued in favour of a violation of Article 10:

it should not be open to the authorities of the State to decide whether a particular statement is capable of "contributing to any form of public debate capable of furthering progress in human affairs"; such a decision cannot but be tainted by the authorities' idea of "progress". [...] The need for repressive action amounting to complete prevention of the exercise of freedom of expression can only be accepted if the behaviour concerned reaches so high a level of abuse, and comes so close to a denial of the freedom of religion of others, as to forfeit for itself the right to be tolerated by society. [...] the film was to have been shown to a paying audience in an "art cinema" which catered for a relatively small public with a taste for experimental films. It is therefore unlikely that the audience would have included persons not specifically interested in the film. This audience, moreover, had sufficient opportunity of being warned beforehand about the nature of the film. [...] It does appear that there was little likelihood in the instant case of anyone being confronted with objectionable material unwittingly. We therefore conclude that the applicant association acted responsibly *in such a way as to limit, as far as it could reasonably have been expected to, the possible harmful effects of showing the film.*

The need to protect "rights of others" versus freedom of imparting and receiving information was also examined by the Court in the context of some racist statements broadcast on television with the mere purpose of informing the public about the carriers of the racist speech.
In the case of *Jersild*136 the applicant was a television journalist who was convicted by the national courts for aiding and abetting the dissemination of racist statements. He took the initiative of preparing a programme where three members of a youth group sharing racist views were invited and interviewed. The journalist knew in advance that racist statements were likely to be made during the interviews and had encouraged such remarks. Editing the interviews, the journalist included the offensive assertions. The interviews were presented during a serious television programme intended for a well-informed audience, dealing with a wide range of social and political issues, including xenophobia and immigration. The audience could hear statements such as: "It's good being a racist. We believe Denmark is for the Danes"; "People should be allowed to keep slaves"; "Just take a picture of a gorilla ... and then look at a nigger, it's the same structure body and everything ... flat forehead"; "A nigger is not a human being, it's an animal, that goes for all the other foreign workers as well, Turks, Yugoslavs and whatever they are called", etc. The young men were also asked questions about their place of live and work and their criminal record.
The main reason why the national courts found the journalist guilty was the lack of a final statement by which, in the courts' opinion, he should have explicitly criticised the racist views expressed during the interviews.
Before the European Court, the government justified the conviction by the need to protect the rights of those insulted by the racist statements. The Court emphasised the vital importance of combating racial discrimination, stressing that the matter broadcast by the applicant was of high public concern. Looking at how the programme was prepared and presented, the Court found that *it could not objectively have appeared to have as its purpose the*

*propagation of racist views and ideas. On the contrary, it
clearly sought – by means of an interview – to expose, analyse
and explain this particular group of youth, limited and frustrated
by their social situation, with criminal record and violent
attitudes.*
Criticising the national courts' approach on how the
journalist should have counterbalanced the racist statements,
the Court held that
*the methods of objective and balanced reporting may vary considerably,
depending among other things on the media in question.
It is not for this Court, nor for the national courts for that
matter, to substitute their own views for those of the press as to
what technique of reporting should be adopted by journalists.*
Discussing news reporting based on interviews,
whether edited or not, the Court held that the punishment

136. Jersild v. Denmark, 1994.

of a journalist for assisting in the dissemination of statements
made by another person in an interview
*would seriously hamper the contribution of the press to discussion
of matters of public interest and should not be envisaged
unless there are particularly strong reasons for doing so.*
The Court found a violation of Article 10.

Freedom of expression and the authority and impartiality of the judiciary

The Court's jurisprudence under this heading shows
that although the judiciary enjoys a special protection, it
does not function in a vacuum, and questions about the
administration of justice may be part of the public debate.
In the *Sunday Times* case 137 the government justified
injunctions against publication of a newspaper article by
the interest of protecting the impartiality of the judiciary
and preserving the trust of the public in the judicial
authorities. Following the use of the sedative "thalidomide"
between 1959 and 1962 many children were born
with severe malformations. The drug was produced and
sold by Distillers Company Ltd, which withdraw it from the
market in 1961. Parents sued the company, asking for civil
damages; negotiations between the parties continued for
many years. The parties' transactions had to be approved
by the courts. All newspapers, including *The Sunday Times*,
covered the issue extensively. In 1971 the parties started
negotiations to set up a charity fund for the children with
malformations. In September 1972 *The Sunday Times* published
an article entitled "Our thalidomide children: a

cause for national shame", criticising the company for the reduced amount of money paid to the victims and for the small amount which the company intended to put into the charity fund. *The Sunday Times* announced that it would describe, in a future article, the circumstances of the tragedy. At the request of the company, the Attorney General asked the court to issue an injunction against the newspaper, arguing that the publication of the announced article would obstruct justice. The injunction was granted and *The Sunday Times* refrained from publication.

Before the European Court, *The Sunday Times* claimed a violation of Article 10. The government justified the injunction by the need to maintain the "authority and impartiality of the judiciary", since thalidomide cases were still pending before the courts. The Court stated that

There is general recognition of the fact that the courts cannot operate in a vacuum. Whilst they are the forum for the settlement of disputes, this does not mean that there can be no prior discussion of disputes elsewhere, be it in specialised journals, in the general press or amongst the public at large. Furthermore, whilst the mass media must not overstep the bounds imposed in

137. Sunday Times v. the United Kingdom, 1979.

the interests of the proper administration of justice, it is incumbent on them to impart information and ideas concerning matters that come before the courts just as in other areas of public interest. Not only do the media have the task of imparting such information and ideas: the public also has a right to receive them.

In the particular circumstances of the case, the Court observed that the "thalidomide disaster" was a matter of undisputed public concern. In addition, the families involved in the tragedy as well as the public at large had the right to be informed on all the facts of this matter. The Court concluded that the injunction ordered against the newspaper "did not correspond to a social need sufficiently pressing to outweigh the public interest in freedom of expression within the meaning of the Convention."

In the case of *De Haes and Gijsels*[138] the applicants, two journalists, reported in a newspaper on a case pending before the courts. In five articles they criticised in virulent terms the judges of a Court of Appeal who had decided, in a divorce case, that the two children of the divorced family would live with their father. The father, a well-known notary, had previously been accused by his former wife and her parents of sexual abuse of the two children. At the time of the divorce, the investigation against the notary was closed without indictment.

Three judges and a prosecutor sued the two journalists and the newspaper, asking civil damages for defamatory statements. The civil courts found that the two journalists had cast strong doubts on the impartiality of the judges by writing that they had intentionally ruled wrongly due to their close political relationship with the notary. The journalists were obliged to pay civil damages (a symbolic amount) and to publish the judgment in six newspapers at their own expense.

The Court recognised that members of the judiciary must enjoy public trust and therefore they must be protected against destructive attacks lacking any factual basis. Moreover, since they have a duty of discretion, judges cannot respond in public to various attacks, as, for instance, politicians are able to do. The Court then considered the articles and noted that many details were given, including experts opinions, proving that the journalists had carried out serious research before informing the public on this case. The articles were part of a large public debate on incest and on how the judiciary dealt with it. Giving due importance to the right of the public to be informed on an issue of public interest, the Court decided that the national courts' decision was not "necessary in a democratic society", and that therefore Article 10 had been violated.

In principle, the defamation of a judge by the press takes place as part of a debate on the malfunction of the judicial system or in the context of doubting the independence or impartiality of judges. Such issues are always important for the public and must not be left outside the public debate, in particular in a country experiencing the

138. De Haes and Gijsels v. Belgium, 1997.

transition to an independent and effective judiciary. This is why the national courts must weigh the values and interests involved in case where judges or other judicial actors are criticised. Courts must balance the honour of the judge in question against the freedom of the press to report on matters of public interest, and decide the priority in a democratic society.

Certainly, where the criticism is primarily aimed at insulting or defaming the members of the judiciary without contributing to the public debate on the administration of justice, the protection afforded to freedom of expression may be narrower. Another relevant issue under this head is the possibility of publicly contesting a final judicial decision.

Protection of journalistic sources and legitimate aims

A particular component of freedom of expression is the protection of journalistic sources, which may conflict with any of the legitimate aims referred to in paragraph 2. The *Goodwin* judgment[139] is significant for the balance between the interests of justice and rights of others on the one hand, and the desire to protect sources on the other hand.

Mr Goodwin, a journalist with *The Engineer*, received from a "source", by telephone, information on the Tetra Ltd company. The source stated that the company was on the way to obtaining a large credit when it had major financial problems. The information was not asked for and no payment was made. In the course of preparing an article on this subject, the journalist telephoned the company and asked for comments. Following this conversation, the company asked the court for an injunction on the publication of Mr Goodwin's article, arguing that its economic and financial interests would be seriously hampered if the information were to become public. The injunction was granted, and the company sent a copy to all major newspapers. Further, the company asked the court to request the journalist to reveal the name of his source. It was argued that this would help the company to identify the dishonest employer and initiate proceedings against him. The journalist repeatedly denied the court's request and did not reveal the source. He was fined on the charge of "obstruction of justice".

Before the European Court, the applicant claimed that the court order requesting him to reveal the source, as well as the fine for not doing so had both infringed his right to freedom of expression. Recalling that "freedom of expression constitutes one of the essential foundations of a democratic society and that the safeguards to be afforded to the press are of particular importance", the Court further held that the

139. Goodwin v. the United Kingdom, 1996.

protection of journalistic sources is one of the basic conditions for press freedom, as is reflected in the laws and the professional codes of conduct in a number of Contracting States and is affirmed in several international instruments on journalistic freedoms [...] Without such protection, sources may be deterred from assisting the press in informing the public on matters of public interest. As a result the vital public-watchdog role of the press may be undermined and the ability of the press to provide accurate and reliable information may be adversely affected. Having in view the importance of journalistic sources for press freedom in a democratic society and the potentially chilling effect of a disclosure order, the Court found that both the order requiring the applicant to reveal his source and the fine imposed upon him for having refused to do so gave rise to a violation of his right to freedom of expression.

Following the *Goodwin* judgment, on 8 March 2000 the Committee of Ministers of the Council of Europe adopted Recommendation No. R (2000) 7 on the right of journalists not to disclose their sources of information.

In countries where the legal protection of journalists' sources is not enacted, the courts must afford it as part of

www.ingramcontent.com/pod-product-compliance
Lightning Source LLC
Chambersburg PA
CBHW020729180526
45163CB00001B/160